EVERYDAY VIOLENCE
IN THE LIVES OF YOUTH

EVERYDAY VIOLENCE
IN THE LIVES OF YOUTH
SPEAKING OUT AND PUSHING BACK

Edited by
Helene Berman, Catherine Richardson/Kinewesquao,
Kate Elliott and Eugenia Canas

Fernwood Publishing
Halifax & Winnipeg

Editing and design: Brenda Conroy
Cover design: John van der Woude
Printed and bound in Canada

Published by Fernwood Publishing
32 Oceanvista Lane, Black Point, Nova Scotia, B0J 1B0
and 748 Broadway Avenue, Winnipeg, Manitoba, R3G 0X3
www.fernwoodpublishing.ca

Fernwood Publishing Company Limited gratefully acknowledges the financial support of the Government of Canada, the Canada Council for the Arts, the Manitoba Department of Culture, Heritage and Tourism under the Manitoba Publishers Marketing Assistance Program and the Province of Manitoba, through the Book Publishing Tax Credit, for our publishing program. We are pleased to work in partnership with the Province of Nova Scotia to develop and promote our creative industries for the benefit of all Nova Scotians.

Library and Archives Canada Cataloguing in Publication

Title: Everyday violence in the lives of youth : speaking
out and pushing back / edited by Helene
Berman, Catherine Richardson/Kinewesquao, Kate Elliott and Eugenia Canas.
Names: Berman, Helene, 1950- editor. | Richardson,
Catherine Lynn, 1962- editor. | Elliott, Kate,
1987- editor. | Canas, Eugenia, 1973- editor.
Description: Includes bibliographical references and index.
Identifiers: Canadiana (print) 20200185764 | Canadiana
(ebook) 20200185802 | ISBN 9781773631035
(softcover) | ISBN 9781773631042 (EPUB) | ISBN 9781773631059 (Kindle)
Subjects: LCSH: Youth and violence,—Canada. | LCSH: Arts,—Therapeutic use.
Classification: LCC HQ799.2.V56 E94 2020 | DDC 303.60835,—dc23

Contents

We dedicate this book to the youth who took part in this project and to young people everywhere who speak out and push back to end all forms of structural violence.

Acknowledgements

We would like to begin by acknowledging that this study and hence, the writing of this book has taken place on many different Indigenous lands, in Canada. Some of these territories are unceded lands, where no treaty facilitated the changing of the political landscape from Indigenous into a colonial-settler society. Western University, where the study began due to the inspiration and activity of Dr. Helene Berman, is located on the territory of the Anishinaabek, Haudenosaunee, Lūnaapéewak and Attawandaron Peoples. We would like to acknowledge the ancestors who were the traditional caretakers of the land, as well as all our ancestors, as authors, who have also survived in a direct line from the time of the first ancestor on Mother Earth. In addition to the many First Nations, we also acknowledge the Métis and the Inuit Peoples who also live in various communities in Canada and whose young ones have also shared their knowledge in this study.

We would also like to raise our hands to the many individuals and organizations who contributed to this work, in both direct and indirect ways. To all who have recognized that the violence we experience in our everyday lives profoundly shapes our physical and emotional health, even when that violence cannot be seen, we thank you.

We are grateful to the Canadian Institutes for Health Research, Institute for Gender and Health, for a Team Grant, Promoting Health through Collaborative Engagement with Youth in Canada: Overcoming, Resisting and Preventing Structural Violence, which enabled us to conduct the research on which this book is based. We also thank the staff at Fernwood, most notably Candida Hadley, Beverley Rach and Brenda Conroy, for their meticulous, thoughtful and enthusiastic comments throughout. To our funders and our editors, we are particularly appreciative of the support provided for work that pushes boundaries and extends prevailing conceptualizations of research, health and violence.

We extend tremendous appreciation to our national coordinator, Maria Callaghan, whose dedication to every aspect of this project was invaluable. Her patience, thoughtful input, friendship and utmost degree of professionalism ensured that we remained on track and achieved our stated goals and objectives.

The research described in this book could not have been successful without the wholehearted participation of so many youth. In particular, we thank Alia El-Tayeb, Michelle Brake and Jessica Yee, who, alongside our co-editor Eugenia Canas, assumed leadership on the National Youth Advisory Board (NYAB) at various times. We also acknowledge the contributions of all the young people who participated as advisors in the NYAB: Amanda Ghazale Aziz, Breann Maxwell, Curtis J. Kechego, Dobijoki (Emanuela) Bringi, Gina Uppal, Jayson Tower, Julia Tadman, co-editor Kate Elliott, Mina Harker, Keara Yim and Santiago Vargas. Despite our initial plan for a two-year term in the NYAB, many of these young people remained involved with this project throughout the five years. We are thankful for their commitment and the continuing inspiration they provided us.

As well, we acknowledge Janie Dolan-Cake for her assistance in drafting the Indigenous research report and Zeina Allouche-Ismael for facilitating our final meeting and conference.

We thank the many members of the academic community from Halifax to Victoria, and many places in between, who came from diverse disciplinary backgrounds to engage in a research endeavour that required working in partnership with youth and community partners. In many respects, this project asked us to step outside of our comfort zones, to give up — or at the very least, to share — power in a novel research initiative. We say a warm thank you to Dominique Damant, Marnina Gonick, Myrna Dawson, Stephen Gaetz, Simon Lapierre, Amanda Grzyb and Joan Samuels-Dennis, whose contributions, large and small, are greatly appreciated. We also are grateful to our lead knowledge user, Maria Luisa Contursi from Mindyourmind

Post-doctoral fellows reflect the future cohort of researchers, and we are inspired by, and grateful to, Catherine Flynn, Kristy Buccieri and co-author in this book Rita Henderson. We also extend our appreciation to doctoral student Nada Nessan for her contributions. Your wonderful insights, questions and contributions only served to strengthen our work.

It takes a community to prepare a collaborative publication, including all the various ideas, forms of creativity, energy and commitment. To you all, we, the co-editors and authors, are grateful.

Author Biographies

Co-Editors

HELENE BERMAN, RN, PhD, is a distinguished university professor emerita at the University of Western Ontario and a fellow in the Canadian Academy of Health Sciences. Her program of research, funded by grants from the Canadian Institutes of Health Research (CIHR), Social Sciences and Humanities Research Council (SSHRC) and Status of Women Canada, has focused on the subtle and explicit forms of violence in the lives of girls and young women. In recent years, she has extended that work to include boys and young men. With a lengthy history of community-based research, Dr. Berman played a lead role in the establishment of the Centre for Research on Health Equity and Social Inclusion and serves as the Centre's founding academic director.

CATHERINE RICHARDSON/KINEWESQUAO is a Métis counsellor specializing in violence prevention and recovery. She lives on the territory of the Kanien'kehá:ka Nation and is an associate professor in the School of Social Work at the University of Montreal. Dr. Richardson is a co-founder of the Centre for Response-Based Practice. Her recent research projects relate to violence prevention with Indigenous youth, women and families. She is the author of *Belonging Métis* and co-editor of *Calling Our Families Home: Métis Experiences with Child Welfare* and *Failure to Protect: Moving Beyond Gendered Responses*. Her work has influenced the development of dignity-driven practice in the Child and Family Services of New South Wales, Australia. She is involved in Indigenous community projects and was twice a delegate to the UN Permanent Forum on Indigenous Issues. She is co-authoring a forthcoming book related to Métis social policy.

KATE ELLIOTT, BSN, MPH, MD, is a member of the Métis Nation of Greater Victoria. She has a passion for Indigenous youth engagement and traditional beadwork. Elliott possesses an undergraduate degree in nursing and a master's in public health and social policy from the University of Victoria.

Elliott is completing her residency in Indigenous Family Medicine at the University of British Columbia.

EUGENIA CANAS, PhD, uses participatory and ethnographic approaches to understand how youth perspectives affect the delivery of health services. She is a founding member of the Centre for Research on Health Equity and Social Inclusion (CRHESI), which is dedicated to knowledge generation and translation through partnerships between academia and community organizations. Canas served as National Youth Advisory Board co-coordinator in the Voices against Violence project from 2011 to 2017 and is a post-doctoral associate with the Faculty of Information and Media Studies at the University of Western Ontario.

Contributing Authors

LYNDA M. ASHBOURNE, PhD, is an associate professor in the Department of Family Relations and Applied Nutrition at the University of Guelph. She is a registered psychotherapist and couple and family therapist. She conducts research examining how broader social systems and events (cultural influences, marginalization, war) influence relationships and meaning-making in interaction with others.

MICHELLE BRAKE is a young geographer from Halifax looking to change the world with maps. She was a member of the National Youth Advisory Board for the Voices against Violence Project and served as a National Youth Coordinator. She views this work as one avenue to strive for long-term, broad-based, meaningful structural change throughout society. Her technical background and experiences with the project have pushed her to explore the ways that maps can be used as a method for storytelling.

JENNIFER FALLIS has worked for a number of child and family service organizations in Winnipeg, most recently as a policy analyst with Manitoba's General Child and Family Services Authority. She works with Manitoba Economic Development and Training on initiatives related to improving education and employment outcomes for youth transitioning from CFS care. In addition to her MSW from the University of Manitoba, Jennifer holds a BA in sociology from the University of Winnipeg.

MINA HARKER is a writer/artist and trans girl living in Calgary.

RITA HENDERSON, PhD, is an assistant professor and models-of-care scientist in the Departments of Family Medicine and Community Health Sciences at the University of Calgary's Cumming School of Medicine. Her interests in health inequities range from population health to clinical intervention research and the integration of these. She earned a PhD addressing social impacts of multi-generational trauma, which she carries into her current work.

YASMIN JIWANI is a full professor in the Department of Communication Studies and a Concordia University research chair on intersectionality, violence and resistance. Her research focuses on a critical interrogation of the ways that racist-sexism is conceptualized and ideologically utilized in popular discourse. The particular sites she has examined include media reportage of violence against Indigenous and racialized immigrant women, representations of Indigenous and Muslim youth in the popular press, and discourses of resistance by marginalized groups in film and other popular media. Her recent project is centred on cyber-memorials and virtual graveyards as reflections of the vernacular. She is the author of *Discourses of Denial: Race, Gender and Violence* and co-editor of *Girlhood: Redefining the Limits* and *Faces of Violence in the Lives of Girls*.

HOLLY JOHNSON is an associate professor in the Department of Criminology at the University of Ottawa. Her research examines criminal justice and social responses to gender-based and structural violence through innovative methodologies.

JESSICA JUSTRABO is the Bridges Out of Poverty coordinator at Goodwill Industries and manages their Circles initiative. She has worked and volunteered for more than ten years in areas of poverty, mental health and justice. Jessica serves as the community co-lead for the poverty focus of a SSHRC-funded study exploring mobilizing narratives for policy and social change.

KENDRA NIXON, PhD is an associate professor in the Faculty of Social Work at the University of Manitoba and is the director of RESOLVE, a tri-prairie research network on gender-based violence. Kendra's research interests include intimate partner violence, children's exposure to violence, mothering within the context of violence, child maltreatment, family violence and sexual exploitation. She has conducted research within a variety of institutional settings, including child welfare, the police, the civil and criminal courts, and correctional facilities.

ABE OUDSHOORN, RN, PhD is an assistant professor in the Arthur Labatt Family School of Nursing at Western University. He worked as a nurse with people experiencing homelessness, and his research focuses on health, homelessness prevention, mental health and poverty. Dr. Oudshoorn is chair of the London Homeless Coalition.

CATHRYN RODRIGUES earned a bachelor's of health sciences from the University of Calgary. She works as a research assistant for the Hotchkiss Brain Institute and on projects involving health promotion, community capacity building, structural violence and homelessness.

JENNA ROSE SANDS is a Cree Ojibwe artist who is turning her emotional exhaustion over the current state of Indigenous affairs into informative zines that educate and question widespread prejudice regarding Indigenous Peoples. Focusing each zine on the experiences and stories of Indigenous people who have endured a multitude of atrocities committed by the Canadian government, Sands pairs words with dynamic mixed media to produce powerful and visually engaging works. Sands is trying to change language and ideas one zine at a time: <www.atrocitiesagainstindigenouscanadians.com>.

ANSHINI SHAH is a student at St. George's University, in Grenada, West Indies. She earned her BA in international relations from the University of Calgary. She is interested in using her social science background to assess the influence of colonialism on the health of vulnerable populations.

WILFREDA E. THURSTON is a professor emerita in the Department of Community Health Sciences, University of Calgary. She worked in the social service sector, including government services, a women's centre and a shelter for women. Feminist analysis and advocacy for women's health and gender equality in medicine and society generally have shaped her career. Her research has included the role of the public health sector in prevention of violence against girls and women, especially those marginalized by racialization.

RACHEL WARD is an MD/MSc student in the Department of Community Health Sciences, Cumming School of Medicine, University of Calgary. Rachel's research interests include medical education and exploring how systemic and institutional structures influence the health and well-being of individuals and populations. She hopes to apply a health inequities lens when entering medical practice and aims to help create health-care systems that are safer for patients and trainees.

ALEX WERIER is completing a master's degree in anthropology at Simon Fraser University. Her thesis examines gender, voice and sound, focusing on the ways in which trans women understand, use or alter their voices.

PART I

Why Y-Par? And What Is It?

I

Re-Thinking Violence, Re-Thinking Health and Re-Thinking Research

Helene Berman, Catherine Richardson/Kinewesquao, Kate Elliott, Eugenia Canas

Over the past two decades, Canadian researchers have contributed substantially to an enriched understanding of the range and complexities of young people's experiences of violence. While this body of work has been instrumental in the development of a multitude of anti-violence programs for youth, it also has notable limitations. First, the vast majority of this work focuses on various forms of *interpersonal* violence, including intimate partner violence, sexual harassment, sexualized assault, dating violence and, more recently, cyber-violence, but has little to say about *structural* violence. Second, much of the research in the area of violence among young people lacks a contextual analysis, including intersectional considerations of gender, race and social class within a colonial society on stolen Indigenous land. This tendency is particularly evident in the area of bullying, which is often approached in a decontextualized manner — de-gendered, de-classed and de-raced. Finally, the existing research tends to focus on the effects or impacts of violence and bullying, but omits the rich and nuanced responses and resistance of the youth. These responses and resistance point to the "resilience" or "strong-spiritedness" of youth and the knowledge, intelligence, capacity, skills, acumen and experience youth possess that can help them negotiate difficult situations. However, although youth are responsive, strategic and adaptable across contexts, they also require "positive social responses" during and after experiencing violence in order to feel like they matter, like there is a place and purpose for them in society and on the planet (Richardson and Wade 2008). The high rates of suicide amongst marginalized youth may demonstrate that resilience is not so simple, and we believe this is an important sign that we must address racialized violence and hate (Reynolds 2016) to create societies which are inclusive, compassionate and responsive to youth needs. Youth research should assist in youth self-empowerment, providing opportunities for increased input, feedback, awareness and pride in their ability to act, even when victory may seem impossible.

This book is the culmination of a five-year research initiative, conducted in five Canadian provinces, that explored the issue of structural violence as it impacts youth in our/their everyday lives. At the heart of this project, groups with different populations of youth used arts-based methods to address varied aspects of structural violence. Consistent with our belief that young people need to be at the table when discussing issues of importance to them, we used a youth-centred participatory action research (Y-PAR) methodology. We established the National Youth Advisory Board (NYAB), and we hired two national youth coordinators to work with this board. The governance structure was designed to privilege the voices of the youth through all components and stages of the project. Throughout this book, we describe our processes in detail and share what we learned, what worked well, what worked not-so-well and the challenges we faced.

Ignoring the Violence Embedded in Structures and Systems

Many of the anti-violence programs in Canadian schools are framed around the notion of bullying and emphasize the importance of respect, which is positioned as the opposite of bullying. They include prescriptions about how to foster respect for self and others and strategies that young people can use to avoid and resist bullying. Inherent in this conceptualization is the idea that the problem lies within the individual — the bully or the victim — reflecting a personal character flaw. As we have learned in earlier research (Berman and Jiwani 2014), much of what gets labeled as "bullying" can and should more aptly be described as racism, homophobia, classism, ableism or sexism. When we mislabel the problem, our ability to address it is limited. Youth, particularly young women and LGBTQ2S+individuals, challenge this conceptualization of bullying within the Me Too movement and speak out against sexualized harassment and rape and the structures that condone this form of violence. Similarly, young Indigenous activists name structural violence and demand social change within Indigenous rights movements, such as Idle No More and Standing Rock. Both of these movements make explicit the links between structural violence and the health outcomes for those harmed by that violence. We have begun to recognize that violence is not only a social problem, but that it also has significant adverse consequences for health.

This book extends current knowledge by exploring the complex dimensions of structural violence, the "everyday violence" to which many young people in Canada are routinely subjected and which gives rise to multiple manifestations of interpersonal violence as well as economic and health-related problems. We offer multiple perspectives and possibilities for youth that move beyond a psychiatric lens, which prioritizes individualistic rather than social understandings and solutions. Vancouver therapist Vikki Reynolds demonstrates an alternative perspective for youth in her article "The Problem's Oppression Not Depression" (2013, published in *Stay Solid! A Radical Handbook for Youth*). Reynolds notes that structural violence is subtle and insidious and that the long-term impacts are perhaps more harmful than those associated with more overt forms of violence. Moreover, because the violence is embedded in the system and there is no identifiable perpetrator, structural and systemic forms of violence may be harder to name and to address. Reynolds tries to address this by naming a perpetrator: "Hate." According to Reynolds, "Hate" means state neglect, exclusion, acts of violence, humiliation and degradation. Without this identifiable perpetrator it can be difficult to solicit assistance from family, friends and professionals, as the violence is so often invisible and there are no clear pathways for resolution or justice. As well, when children learn that impunity exists for certain forms of societal violence, they get the message that it is somehow acceptable. This is how violence may be perpetuated across generations. As our research shows, however, creating a safe space in which youth can critically examine and articulate the many ways that structural violence shapes everyday life can serve as a health promotion strategy and a means of empowerment.

Toward a Definition of Everyday Violence

The notion of "everyday violence" evokes images that are difficult to reconcile with prevailing, though often idealized, conceptualizations of children and youth. Historically, childhood has been depicted as a time of innocence, and adolescence as a time for trying out adult roles, for experimenting and taking risks, but doing so within relatively safe parameters. The reality, however, is quite different. Recent global events, including mass shootings in schools, remind us that many young people in North America and elsewhere live amid danger and indeed are not safe. Such horrific acts typically give way to a collective sense of horror, shame and guilt and are accompanied, at least in the short term, by pleas for action on the part of governments, until the media turn their attention elsewhere. Scholars such as Thomas McGaith (2018) identify this form of violence on the part of disenfranchised men as a byproduct of capitalism. In an economic worldview based on competition and "survival of the fittest" in the business world, values such as sharing, compassion and understanding are not foregrounded. Some young men were taught that their feelings do not matter as much as their accomplishments. Wally Gordon (1997) makes links between violence and capitalism because of the inequalities that are bred and necessary for profit generation, such as maintaining a large pool of unemployed workers from which business can draw at low wage levels. Thus, society becomes highly competitive, rather than cooperative, particularly when the left (e.g., labour unions, social justice organizations) is attacked by government. Further, these inequalities play out in areas of race and racism, with many of the U.S. school shooters being white men with racist (and often sexist) ideologies, seeing themselves as the victims. Organizations such as the National Rifle Association in the U.S. perpetuate racism by making guns accessible for race-based crimes (Riley 2018). The "shooter" at Ecole Polytechnique in Montreal blamed young women engineering students for taking up the space that should have been provided to him, as a white male. He murdered fourteen women, shooting also at the men who tried to protect them. Although not limited to capitalist societies, structural violence is enhanced by the state's goal of keeping society stratified and maintaining differences between the wealthy and those living in poverty.

In addition to these highly public forms of violence, including racial and gender-based hatred, other acts of violence occur on a daily basis and are so pervasive and unrelenting that they go largely unnoticed. These acts warrant consideration and analysis. While some of these accounts can be described as interpersonal violence, it is the structure or system that emboldens some at the expense of others. The macro-politics influence micro-interaction. For example, the fact that perpetrators who harm Indigenous women in Canada are likely to get away with it does not deter men from attacking them. The low rates of sentencing in Canadian cases of rape and sexualized violence also offer relative impunity to perpetrators, with less than 1 percent serving time (Johnson 2012). In the United States, gender-based violence against women and girls has increased since Trump became president (Levin 2017; Huang and Low 2017). The public sexism of the president gives permission for other males to enact these same forms of violence, even in elementary schools.

The understanding of everyday violence that informs our work is derived from the ideas of John Galtung (1990), who coined the phrase "structural violence" in 1969. According to Galtung, structural violence directs our attention to the root causes of violence at the systemic level. In essence, structural violence is enacted when a group or structure monopolizes resources and penalizes others for both lacking those resources and trying to access those resources. Built into the structure of a society, structural violence "shows up as unequal power and, consequently, as unequal life chances" (Galtung: 171). When violence is successfully obfuscated, it appears to be an inseparable part of the society or the culture. A popular meme circulating on social media illustrates this issue of structural violence: "Just because you are white doesn't mean you don't have problems — it just means you don't have problems that stem from racial oppression." Such ideas try to promote understanding about what it means to live amid violence and discrimination on a daily basis and be subjected to the violence of the system.

The Pervasiveness of Cultural Violence

Structural violence is thus a process by which some groups are denied access to resources, and this inequality is maintained by what Galtung refers to as "cultural violence," which is enacted through language, religion and ideology. Structural violence can manifest in physical violence, but it also manifests indirectly in ways that are less visible. As anthropologist Nancy Scheper-Hughes (2004: 13) observed, structural violence is "violence that is permissible, even encouraged." It refers to the often-invisible patterns of inequality that reproduce social relations of exclusion and marginalization through ideologies, stigmas and discourses attendant to gender, race, class and other markers of social identity. Structural violence "normalizes," for example, poverty, sexual harassment, racism and colonialism, erasing their social and political origins so that they become taken-for-granted as natural and inevitable consequences of individual characteristics or choices. In essence, structural violence fuels inequality between social groups, and this is initiated and maintained through the acts of government and institutions (James et al. 2003).

Other scholars describe structural violence in terms of "systems of oppression" (Boute 1998; Hill Collins 2009) or as violations of human rights (Ho 2007). Despite its pervasive existence and harm towards young people, structural violence is a relatively understudied phenomenon. It has been suggested that structural violence differs from other types of interpersonal violence in three major respects: 1) power relations are less visible and exist in various forms, infused in existing social hierarchies; 2) it functions at the macro level to shape individual behaviours; and 3) its problematic effects are pervasive and enduring, not just appearing sporadically in response to discrete violent acts (Montesanti and Thurston 2015). While structural forms of violence are often normalized — expressed in subtle and invisible ways — their negative consequences are highly visible, creating identity categories of marginalization and inequity that are evident in many aspects of everyday life among youth in Canada. For example, if the state propagates the notion that people must work to receive money, there is less likelihood that the population will expect higher rates of social welfare or a guaranteed annual income. Government rhetoric often casts people who don't work and who receive state money as lazy and a drain on society. Capitalist systems benefit from the notion that people must work, even for minimum wage. Some would say this is a form of economic structural violence.

Our conceptualization of everyday violence is derived from these ideas and is understood as a process that creates and maintains inequalities within different social groups. Rather than focusing on dichotomized notions of victims and perpetrators, which locate the problem of violence within individuals who are deemed good or bad, violent or non-violent, our attention to structural violence directs us to examine the *everydayness* of violence from the vantage point of complex political, social, historic and economic processes. In other words, it is not that human beings are inherently violent but rather that certain contexts and social formations, in effect, produce violence. From this perspective, the imposition of gendered, racialized and/or class-based social hierarchies, the curtailment of life chances, legacies of colonialism and the normalization of dominant discourses that often reflect the perspectives of the perpetrators, are also recognized as forms of violence. Although these forms of violence are often invisible, they are no less deleterious in their effects. Through structural violence, persons are socially and culturally marginalized in ways that deny them the opportunity for physical and emotional well-being and for full participation in society.

Conceptualizing Health

In the context of our research, "health" is defined holistically and is congruent with the World Health Organization's (2005) definition of health as a resource for everyday living. It is situated within a "social determinants of health" framework. Consistent with Indigenous notions of health, we understand that health is much broader than the health of the individual, but rather that it encompasses the entire community. Understanding how gender, race and class intersect and are expressed in disparate chances for health and well-being among Canada's youth is a considerable challenge. More than the absence of disease, health is a positive process of reaching one's potential and is experienced and understood differently across and within cultural groups. As set out in the Ottawa Charter for Health Promotion, an international agreement signed in 1986, peace, shelter, education, food, income, stable ecosystem, sustainable resources, social justice and equity are the prerequisites for health. Our research is premised on the view that, to prevent interpersonal violence, it is essential to ameliorate structural inequities and the social conditions, such as racism, gender inequality and poverty, that can foster violence (Thurston 1998; Thurston, Cory and Scott 1998). Youth resistance to violence was taken up theoretically and explored in the research because resistance to violence and oppression are considered both a symptom of health and health inducing (Wade 1997: 23). By not merely focusing on impacts and effects of violence, it becomes possible to get at youth agency, activity, thought-processes and spirited responses, all of which remain concealed when attention is paid exclusively to symptoms and other manifestations of illness.

Influenced in part by the tenets of critical social theory, our conceptualization of health encompasses an analysis of the manner by which dominant social, political and economic structures and policies contribute to, or limit, health and illness. For example, the complex vulnerabilities of Indigenous youth stem from a legacy of oppression and colonization and the multigenerational effects of social isolation, racism, entrenched poverty and historical trauma (Chandler and Lalonde 2009). The ways in which health is experienced by individuals and families are shaped by history, significant others, politics, social structures, gender, race and class. Understandings of health must, therefore, include making connections and achieving syntheses that go beyond the perception and knowledge of the individual (Commission on the Social Determinants of Health 2008).

One of the central premises of our research was that engagement with youth to challenge, overcome and resist structural violence is a health promotion strategy. We define health promotion as a process whereby individuals gain increased control over their health and the determinants of health (World Health Organization 2005). This process includes developing a critical awareness of one's social reality, participating in one's empowerment, social or civic engagement, and participating in the community. In the specific context of youth health promotion, key components include enhanced self-esteem, self-efficacy and civic engagement (Flicker et al. 2008). We demonstrate throughout this book that there is a direct relationship between youth health promotion and the participatory action research approaches that we employed to empower youth to overcome, resist and prevent structural violence in their lives. In the words of one youth participant, "Really, I think that structural violence has had … really, it's torn people down and it makes us feel powerless and of course it's going to have a negative impact on individual health, our families' health, our community health across the nation."

Although studies have consistently shown health to be determined by multiple factors, most research and interventions focusing on the links between health and violence rely on definitions of abuse and maltreatment at the level of individuals. Although still limited, there is some research evidence which shows that the health burdens associated with structural violence are substantial; much less, however, is known about how this process occurs, how structural violence shapes the everyday lives of youth, how they resist it and how it affects their health. Where our work departs from established trends is our focus on the development of a comprehensive, integrated and multi-faceted analysis of structural violence, an analysis that has been achieved in collaboration with youth and knowledge users from across Canada. Through processes of socialization, youth who are marked as being different by virtue of their skin colour, religious/cultural differences or sexual orientation are marginalized. It is the violence of this process of marginalization, often referred to as "othering," that needs to be further scrutinized. In this book, we clarify how this is accomplished and who benefits. We identify and discuss the policy implications and burdens that accrue from living in marginal spaces. Through youth voices, we demonstrate how gender, race, class and sexual orientation come together to increase vulnerability to different forms of violence.

Articulated within the contemporary Canadian landscape, issues of gender, structural violence and health assume a heightened significance and are directly implicated in questions of identity and belonging, experiences of exclusion, stigma and discrimination, policies of multiculturalism and immigration, and the contemporary climate of heightened surveillance and criminalization. In short, within the "matrix of domination" (Hill Collins 2009) of racism, sexism and classism, how do young people fare, how are their lives impacted and how can they participate in the development of strategies to overcome, resist and prevent structural violence? These questions form the point of departure for this anthology.

Doing Research in Partnership with Youth

At the start of the project, we hired two national youth coordinatrs, who established the National Youth Advisory Board (NYAB), comprising ten youth, thereby ensuring a youth voice from the outset. The NYAB developed the terms of reference, which laid out the principles that would govern the NYAB and the scope of its activities. Representatives from the NYAB participated actively on the Steering Committee for the overall project team, which met monthly via teleconference.

Over the course of the research, we conducted thirty research groups in five provinces across Canada, with each group composed of youth who have been described as marginalized, vulnerable and silenced. The groups included newcomer populations, LGBTQ2S+ youth, Indigenous youth, homeless and unhoused youth and youth involved with the justice system. While the groups explored different angles and perspectives on structural violence, we acknowledged the intersecting social locations and how particular locations made certain groups targets for structural violence while limiting the possibilities of their resistance. Groups typically included twelve youth. The youth decided which form of the arts they would employ to bring their message forward. Methods included photo novella, collage, zine creation, video creation and spoken word, as well as painting and drawing. The groups provided the youth with opportunities to discuss their everyday lives and interactions with different systems, including education, justice, health and the Department of Indian Affairs. The arts-based approach, in addition to sharing in circle for discussing and debriefing, has been used successfully with populations who may not be best served by words (Parsons and Boydell 2012; Yassi et al. 2016). The chosen methodology was derived from our assumption that art can be used to create increased psychological and cultural safety when processes are explored mindfully and respectfully.

The groups found that they could articulate their ideas and confront complex emotions and topics at their own pace. They could document their ideas and experiences visually and use these visuals to view the personal implications of social problems, hone collective analyses and find pathways for addressing oppressive social structures (Hartman et al. 2011). As well, researchers have noted that the arts can provide access to rich description, highlighting lived experience and meaning, and attend to contextual factors. This helps increase a shared critical awareness of how oppressive life experience relates to the quality of their health and well-being. Art provided a rich medium for exploring the "small acts of living" that help to preserve dignity in the face of social harm and humiliation (Wade 1997).

Addressing Everyday Violence: What We Did and How We Did It

Catherine Richardson and Allan Wade (2008) write that whenever people are mistreated, they resist in some way. Resistance and these "small acts," although seldom able to stop the violence due to inherent differences in power, serve as dignity-preserving protest (Wade 1997; Goffman 1963). Resistance can be described as:

> Any mental or behavioural act through which a person attempts to expose, withstand, repel, stop, prevent, abstain from, strive against, impede, refuse to comply with or oppose any form of violence or oppression (including any type of disrespect), or the conditions that make such acts possible, may be understood as a form of resistance. (Wade 1997: 25)

Resistance is just one of many responses to violence and not all responses can be categorized as resistance. The creation of art can be considered an act of resistance when it performs any of the above functions, including signalling opposition to the violence.

The research we conducted is best defined as an arts-based implementation of youth-centred participatory action research (Y-PAR), funded through a Canadian Institutes of Health Research Team Grant. The formal title, Promoting Health through Collaborative Engagement with Youth: Overcoming, Resisting, and Preventing Structural Violence, was later modified when youth expressed their view that this title was cumbersome and did not fully reflect the essence of the project. Thus, the working title became Voices against Violence: Youth Stories Create Change. Prior research with girls and young women conducted by members of our team (Berman and Jiwani 2014) gave us the opportunity to consider the notion of youth as peer mentors and co-researchers, to learn about the many potential challenges inherent in such partnerships and to contemplate ways of overcoming these within a research context. Here we extend our work to include boys and young men, reflecting our belief that if we are serious about ending violence, we must also engage this group in the effort.

The everyday violence we address throughout this book is the result of social and structural inequities and is manifest in myriad ways, including racism, sexism, classism and homophobia. Unlike highly visible forms of violence such as intimate partner violence, civil war and genocide, everyday violence is more insidious. Through the telling of our stories and our best efforts at youth-centred PAR, it is our hope that readers will gain insights into how we can establish meaningful partnerships with youth — learning from both our successes and our mistakes. The book is divided into three sections. In Part 1, Why Y-PAR? And What Is It?, we provide the background to our research and present the research methodology and methods. In addition to the current chapter, Chapter 2, "Using Y-PAR and the Arts to Address Structural Violence in the Lives of Youth: Methodological Considerations," describes in detail the theoretical and methodological perspectives and approaches that informed this initiative. Chapter 3, "From Protection to Expulsion: A Critical Examination of Aging Out of Care," explores the experiences of the youth who have been wards of the state and who are often placed in numerous foster, group or adoptive homes. Chapter 4, "Symbolic and Discursive Violence in Media Representations Portrayals of Indigenous and Muslim Youth in the Canadian Press" offers insights into the ways that mainstream media shape prevailing discourses about youth in general, and Muslim and Indigenous youth in particular, and in the process, neglect consideration of the structural forms of violence that are so central to their everyday realities.

In Part 2, Voices against Violence: Youth Stories Create Change, Chapters 5–8 describe several of the research groups that we conducted. Chapter 5, "Indigenous Youth and Uses of Art in the Fight for Justice, Equality and Culture in Canada," demonstrates how ethical and respectful research can be conducted with Indigenous youth, including interaction with community and Elders. Here, we highlight the colonial context and the particular challenges faced in relation to the Indian Act, structural racism and the privilege of many Canadians to remain oblivious to issues that harm Indigenous youth and communities. Chapter 6, "Structural Violence in the Lives of Youth Experiencing Homelessness," explores youth who face homelessness or are only sporadically and temporarily housed. Living in shelters and on the street poses particular challenges, intertwined with struggles related to mental health. This chapter explores emotional experiences, such as anxiety, depression and PTSD and how they relate to a lack of safety, to uncertainty, to high-risk living and to experiences of historical violence. Chapter 7, "Newcomer Youth Seeking Inclusion and Caring Responses after Arriving in Canada," focuses on experiences shared by the immigrant and refugee youth population. Chapter 8, "Trans Pirates for Justice: Gender and Sexual Minority Youth Resist Structural Violence in Systems of Care," focuses on structural violence and mistreatment directed towards sexual minority and gender-fluid youth. Language and the inaccurate use of pronouns and labelling are taken up as examples of indignity and humiliation that are directed at non-heteronormative youth. It explores painful aspects of state-managed living, such as issues of identity, cultural erasure, impoverization, theft and loss of possessions and mental health issues. Chapter 9, "The Emotional Exhaustion Created by Systemic Violence and How We Respond through Social Movement and Action," offers a personal reflection from a young Indigenous woman and her effort to address structural violence through zines.

The final section of the book is called Speaking Out and Pushing Back:

Learning from Youth. Chapter 10, "Can It Make a Difference? Evaluating y-par as a Health Promotion Strategy," presents various avenues to analyzing research effectiveness and what makes research "valid" in non-positivist terms, such as how it can enhance lives in the community, contribute to greater cultural knowledge and support effective policy development. Chapter 11, our final chapter, "Speaking Truth to Power," offers summary thoughts, examples of findings and research creation and critical reflection and suggestions for others working with this population. We trust that the reader will come away will inspirational stories and sharing from the youth as well as rich information about this methodological approach, which has helped us connect with youth around their crucial life experiences of harm, disconnection, resistance and, we hope, future belonging, inclusion and feelings of being valued. Indigenous cultures believe that children are gifts from the Creator. Though these ones have grown, they continue to carry the gifts, importance and contributions that will nurture our communities and the generations that follow. We cannot forget them.

About the Co-Editors

Our research was conceptualized from the onset as a partnership with youth. We paid careful attention throughout all stages of the project as to how youth would be involved, from the conceptualization of the project, throughout implementation, evaluation and decisions about what to do with the knowledge we generated. Given the central place of youth voices in this work, it is therefore not surprising that among the four co-editors of this edition, two (Elliott and Canas) are young and emerging researchers, respectively, and two (Berman and Richardson) are more senior and well-established researchers. We have all entered this research space in different ways, for different reasons and with different — as well as some shared — hopes and dreams. We offer here brief autobiographical statements in order to situate ourselves in the work and thereby provide meaningful context, culture and history.

Kate Elliott is Cree-Métis with family ties to Selkirk, Manitoba. She has lived much of her life on Vancouver Island, on the traditional land of the Coast and Straight Salish Peoples. She is a member of the Métis Nation of Greater Victoria and was involved with local governance and in charge of a youth program. While she was doing her bachelor of science in nursing at the University of Victoria in 2011 she began to realize the health and social implications of structural violence for Indigenous Peoples. She continued to advocate for Indigenous Peoples in the health professions and received a master of public health and social policy with a specialization in Aboriginal health and is now in medical school. In addition to numerous other volunteer projects, Kate has been highly involved in the Voices against Violence project and served in an elected role as Minister for Youth and Sport for Métis Nation British Columbia. Kate recognized that the Métis in British Columbia are less visible and less acknowledged than they are in the traditional Prairie Provinces. She wanted to change this but has faced a profound ignorance of who the Métis are, in part because of how the "pan-Aboriginal" approach invisibilizes discreet First Nations, Métis and Inuit. Kate is dedicated to fighting racism and exclusion in the health care profession and brought this analysis into the Voices against Violence project, facilitating a Métis research retreat for Métis youth on Canada's west coast.

Helene Berman grew up in a suburban New York Jewish liberal household during the 1950s and 1960s. It was there that she first learned about inequality and social justice, about hatred and prejudice, about labour struggles and civil rights and about the value of collective action. She remembers that the city of New Rochelle, where she lived, was where the first northern busing case took place. (Busing was part of a desegregation movement in the U.S., where African American children were integrated into the mainstream white school system. It was met with racist backlash and violence.) Helene remembers, as a child, playing "protest" during recess and marching in civil rights parades. She attended the University of Wisconsin during the Vietnam War and was involved in anti-war protest and the feminist movement during the era of *Our Bodies Our Selves*, Gloria Steinem and *Ms Magazine*. She carried her activism into her studies and work as a nurse and, as a descendant of Holocaust survivors, became increasingly aware of the persistence of trauma from historical violence. Applying successfully to the Canadian Institutes of Health Research and then coordinating the Voices against Violence project helped to advance the reality that racism and discrimination are indeed issues negatively affecting health. Her commitment to conduct research that is participatory, engaged and activist helps to create spaces within a research context where power differentials and hierarchies can be interrogated, where we can re-think what it means to do research, how we understand health and how we conceptualize violence.

Catherine Richardson/Kinewesquao is a Métis educator, with Cree/ Dene and Gwichin ancestry, and a therapist. She says she became an anti-racism activist in elementary school. She started to speak out when she saw darker skinned children being isolated and picked on by others, segregated in special education classes. She recalls later learning that many of these children were Indigenous and were adoptees or foster children in the child welfare system. Today she identifies proudly as Métis and, after years of learning about Canada's history of colonialism and writing a PhD dissertation on Métis identity, she became truly aware of the massive dispossession for Indigenous Peoples and the deliberate violence on behalf of the government. Since then she has been a practitioner and teacher of response-based practice, advancing therapeutic processes for naming and recovering from violence.

Eugenia Canas came to Canada from El Salvador when she was fourteen years old. She brought with her a love of art and a deep sensibility as to how structures of power and individual agency interact with each other to shape people's lives. Eugenia studied art and literature, visual linguistics and later art therapy to get at these issues. Her experience in coordinating the Voices against Violence National Youth Advisory Board motivated her to pursue doctoral studies. In her community-research and scholarly work since, Eugenia has been committed to illuminating what aspects of our institutions and professional work serve to uphold, or invalidate, the voices of populations who have previously been excluded from shaping our society.

Beyond Boundaries: Working across Difference

Our research team is composed of individuals from highly diverse backgrounds. Collectively, we work in varied settings with different sets of priorities and, at times, competing agendas. We are youth, and we are adults. Some have advanced degrees, others have none. Some are employed within university settings, where engaging in research is an expectation of our professional roles. However, within the academic environment, there is typically a well-understood hierarchy of types of research and a set of values associated with each. Accordingly, the randomized control trial is positioned at the top — the "gold standard" for knowledge generation

— while qualitative research and indeed participatory action research are accorded a lower place. Others on our team work on the front lines, in community organizations where research is valued and appreciated, but not integral to one's employment, and is often done on one's own time.

Throughout this book, we describe the research that has been conducted with different populations of youth across Canada, and the strategies we have used to transcend the boundaries and straddle the multiple divides that we inevitably encountered. We describe how relationships and networks were built in order to facilitate the ongoing research activity. The final chapter offers critical reflections on our process, with the hope that others can benefit from our insights and the many lessons learned along the way.

References

Berman, H., and Y. Jiwani (eds.). 2014. *Faces of Violence in the Lives of Girls.* London, ON: Althouse Press.

Boute, J. 1998. "La violence ordinaire dans les villes sub sahariennes." *Cahiers de l'UCAC,* 3: 39–60.

Chandler, M.J., and C.E. Lalonde. 1998. "Cultural Continuity as a Hedge against Suicide in Canada's First Nations." *Transcultural Psychiatry,* 35, 2: 191–219.

Chandler, M.J., and C.E. Lalonde. 2009. "Cultural Continuity as a Moderator of Suicide Risk among Canada's First Nations." In L.J. Kirmayer and G.G. Valaskakis (eds.), *Healing Traditions: The Mental Health of Aboriginal Peoples of Canada.* Vancouver: UBC Press.

CSDH (Commission on Social Determinants of Health). 2008. *Closing the Gap in a Generation: Health Equity through Action on the Social Determinants of Health. Final Report of the Commission on Social Determinants of Health.* Geneva, World Health Organization.

Flicker, S., O. Maley, A. Ridgley, S. Biscope, C. Lombardo, and H. Skinner. 2008. "Using Technology and Participatory Action Research to Engage Youth in Health Promotion." *Action Research,* 6, 3: 285–303.

Galtung, J. 1990. "Cultural Violence." *Journal of Peace Research,* 27, 3: 291–305.

Goffman, E. 1963. *Stigma.* London: Penguin Books.

Gordon, Wally. 1997. "Capitalism and Violence." *Medicine, Conflict, Survival,* 13, 1: 63–66.

Hartman, L., A. Mandich, L. Magalhaes, and T. Orchard. 2011. "How Do We 'See' Occupations? An Examination of Visual Research Methodologies in the Study of Human Occupation." *Journal of Occupational Science,* 18, 4: 292–305.

Hill Collins, P. 2009. *Black Feminist Thought: Knowledge, Consciousness, and the Politics of Empowerment,* 2nd edition. New York: Routledge.

Ho, Kathleen. 2007. "Structural Violence as a Human Rights Violation." *Essex Human Rights Review,* 4, 2: 1–17.

Huang, J., & Low, C. 2017. "Trumping Norms: Lab Evidence on Aggressive Communication before and after the 2016 US Presidential Election." *American Economic Review,* 107(5), 120-24.

James, S., J. Johnson, C. Raghavan, T. Lemos, M. Barakett, and D. Woolis. 2003. "The Violent Matrix: A Study of Structural, Interpersonal and Intrapersonal Violence Among a Sample of Poor Women." *American Journal of Community Psychology,* 31, 1: 129–141.

Johnson, H. 2012. "Limits of a Criminal Justice Response: Trends in Policing and Court Processing of Sexual Assault." In E. Sheehy (ed.), *Sexual Assault in Canada: Law, Legal Practice and Women's Activism.* Ottawa: University of Ottawa Press.

Levin, B. 2017. "Research Shows Donald Trump Is Making Men More Sexist." *Levin Report, Vanity Fair,* 27 March.

McGath, T. 2018. "You Won't Say It So I Will. Capitalism Is the Underlying Cause of Mass Shootings in the U.S." Retrieved on Mar 5, 2019 from Medium.com <https://medium.com/@tamcgath/you-wont-say-it-so-i-will-capitalism-is-the-underlying-cause-of-mass-shootings-in-the-us-8266508ccdfe?fbclid=IwAR0Rv 57Ua0VkPMZStWgifhFrC4NIMWsE6XDnWKkzkcDDZhBaZ__vZedG3BQ>.

Montesanti, S.R., and W.E. Thurston. 2015. "Mapping the Role of Structural and Interpersonal Violence in the Lives of Women: Implications for Public Health Interventions and Policy." BMC *Women's Health,* 15: 100. DOI: 10.1186/ s12905-015-0256-4.

Parsons J.A., and K.M. Boydell. 2012. "Arts-Based Knowledge Translation: Some Key Considerations for Health Professionals." *Journal of Interprofessional Care,* 26, 3: 170–172.

Reynolds, V. 2013. "The Problem's Oppression Not Depression." In M. Hearn and Purple Thistle Centre (eds.), *Stay Solid! A Radical Handbook for Youth.* Oakland: CA: AK Press.

___. 2016. "Hate Kills: A Social Justice Response to 'Suicide.'" In J. White, J. Marsh, M. Kral, and J. Morris (eds.), *Critical Suicidology: Towards Creative Alternatives.* Vancouver, BC: UBC Press.

Richardson, C., and A. Wade. 2008. "Taking Resistance Seriously: A Response-Based Approach to Social Work in Cases of Violence against Indigenous Women." In S. Strega and J. Carriere (eds.), *Walking This Path Together: Anti-Racist and Anti-Oppressive Child Welfare Practice.* Winnipeg, MB: Fernwood Publishing.

Riley, R. 2018. "What Do Most of America's Mass Shootings Have in Common?" *Detroit Free Press,* 16 Feb.

Scheper-Hughes, N. 2004. Dangerous and Endangered Youth Social Structures and Determinants of Violence. *Annals New York Academy of Science, 1036,* 13–46.

Thurston, W.E. 1998. "Health Promotion from a Feminist Perspective: A Framework for an Effective Health System Response to Woman Abuse." *Resources for Feminist Research,* 26, 3/4: 175–202.

Thurston, W.E., J. Cory, and C.M. Scott. 1998. "Building a Feminist Theoretical Framework for Screening of Wife-Battering: Key Issues to Be Addressed." *Patient Education and Counselling,* 33, 3: 299–304. DOI: 10.1016/S0738-3991(98)00029-9.

Wade, A. 1997. "Small Acts of Living: Everyday Resistance to Violence and Other

Forms of Oppression." *Contemporary Family Therapy*, 19, 1: 23–39.
World Health Organization. 2005.
Yassi, A., J.B. Spiegel, K. Lockhart, L. Fels, E. Boydell, and J. Marcuse. 2016. "Ethics in Community-University-Artist Partnered Research: Tensions, Contradictions and Gaps Identified in an 'Arts for Social Change' Project." *Journal of Academic Ethics*, 14 (7 April): 199–220. DOI: 10.1007/s10805-016-9257-7.

2

Using Y-PAR and the Arts to Address Structural Violence in the Lives of Youth

Methodological Considerations

Eugenia Canas, Helene Berman,
Catherine Richardson/Kinewesquao, Abe Oudshoorn

The research project Voices against Violence: Youth Stories Create Change, which formed the basis for this book set out to investigate structural violence from the perspectives of young people using a youth-centred participatory action research (Y-PAR) approach. We created research groups in six Canadian provinces, with each group comprising a distinct population of youth typically considered "vulnerable" or "marginalized." We ran groups with Indigenous youth, homeless youth, newcomer youth and LGBTQ2S+/sexual minority youth. Each group focused on a different dimension of structural violence, reflecting the realities of their everyday lives. At the same time, we recognized that everyone has multiple and intersecting identities and it is not possible to explore any one dimension of lived experience or structural violence in isolation. Investigations of poverty, for example, would often lead to conversations about racism or homophobia as well.

The goals of this national research project were to: a) create a better understanding of the impacts of different forms of structural violence on the health and well-being of youth; b) raise awareness of the different inequalities and exclusions youth experience; c) identify important social concerns and outline ideas/strategies for change; and d) explore youth-centred participatory action research approaches as a strategy for health promotion. Through its five years, the Voices against Violence project resulted in thirty research groups, involving approximately 360 youth as co-researchers. This approach entailed engaging youth as co-creators of knowledge, drawing upon their status as experts of their own experience.

In applying Y-PAR and striving to remain loyal to its theoretical and conceptual underpinnings, we encountered several challenges and opportunities, which we explore in this chapter. One of the most important components of this project and a mechanism to realize the values of Y-PAR was the National Youth Advisory Board (NYAB). This board, which was created at the outset of the project and stood at the heart of our governance structure, participated in the research and knowledge translation activities for the duration of the grant. In addition to Y-PAR, the project also used art-based approaches to support the research and participatory aims of this project. We describe our perception of the merits and limits to art-based research in this context; our consensus is that the use of diverse art modalities enabled us to create safe and equitable spaces for youth to reflect upon their lives.

Contemplating Youth-Centred Research in an Adult-Centric World

Y-PAR is an empirical methodological approach in which people directly affected by a problem under investigation engage as co-researchers in the research process. This engagement may vary but generally includes collaboration towards action or intervention with respect to a particular problem (Cahill 2007; Rodriguez and Brown 2009). Participatory research strategies that emphasize community partnerships and the inclusion of individuals whom the research knowledge is meant to serve are increasingly used in health and social-sciences research (Minkler and Wallerstein 2011). Such approaches rely on various degrees of participation, from youth-led to youth-centred, and often feature sequential reflection and action, carried out *with* and *by* those most affected by the knowledge rather than *on* them (Cornwall and Jewkes 1995; Flicker and Guta 2008).

Developing Complex Awareness, Voice and Identity

The participatory process in this national initiative was chosen to allow for the development of youths' awareness of structural violence and their complex identities in relation to it. This growth of awareness aligns well with Paulo Freire's concept of critical consciousness raising (1970). Writing from educational and philosophical perspectives, Freire posited that consciousness raising would allow oppressed groups to regain their sense of humanity by knowledgeably acting, using language and self-expression as weapons to name, analyze, deconstruct and challenge unequal conditions. Of primary importance is Freire's assertion that critical awareness of one's situation occurs through acquisition of particular and appropriate forms of language, which in turn contributes to individuals having a voice that may be heard, upon which action may be taken. Freire's conviction that "every human being, no matter how 'submerged in the culture of silence,' is capable of looking critically at the world in a dialogical encounter with others" (33) is increasingly supported by literature and programming on youth health. Matthew Diemer, Luke Rapa, Catalina Park and Justin Perry (2017) elaborated on such work with youth to develop and validate a scale for assessing critical consciousness as it increases through PAR processes. In employing this conceptual frame from PAR, our research team sought to create opportunities, often in the form of art-based activities, for youth to critically reflect on such embedded and invisible elements of their social experience.

Additionally, Y-PAR has been used by various scholars to challenge essentialist readings and characterizations of youth. In that sense, it contributes to a more complex and nuanced understanding of, not only what we know *with youth*, but what we know *about youth*. Leah Levac (2013) conducted a Y-PAR study with young mothers to counter prevailing and neoliberal understandings of young mothers as problems to be solved, as well as to explore and enhance their leadership abilities and collective efficacy. Similarly, in this project, our research team sought to support rich understandings of youths' complex and intersecting social positions, in order to see the nuanced ways that structural violence affects their lives, as well as their potential forms of resistance and resilience.

Creating Spaces for Consciousness Raising

Freire viewed consciousness raising as a form of human development. From his perspective, critical engagement with the structures that shape everyday experience is not merely a pedagogical necessity, but a moral, ethical and human rights issue (Macedo, in Freire 1970: 20). Fortunately, that notion has resonated widely. In the context of necessary change to the institutions and policies that affect youth health, this type of engagement on the part of youth is stated as a basic human right consistent with

Article 12 of the United Nations Convention on the Rights of the Child (1989). Scholars in various areas of youth development support this lens, noting the connection between oppression and healthy development. Jeanne Brooks-Gunn and Greg Duncan (1997) noted that forms of oppression experienced by youth can trigger depression, hopelessness and suicidal tendencies. Shawn Ginwright and Taj James state that "the trauma of persistent oppression coupled with isolation and the inability to confront and change these oppressive conditions has led scholars to believe that the presence of both can be lethal" (2002: 31). Consistent with these perspectives, the objectives of the Voices against Violence project conceptualized understanding, confronting and resisting structural violence as health promotion strategies. All Voices against Violence activities held, at their core, a commitment to involve the youth participants. The youth were engaged throughout all stages of the research process, from the full spectrum of question generation and governance to data-gathering, analysis and knowledge translation. Throughout this project, we strove for adherence to Y-PAR values in the conduct of individual research groups, in the methods employed and in the quality of engagement with the NYAB.

The stated commitment by the adult researchers in this project was to create a space where youth had equitable access to conversations about the systems that impact their health. At pragmatic levels, supportive environments were made possible by concerted investments from the project. Regular face-to-face project meetings, where youth had opportunities to meet alone, without adult team members, allowed them to build trust among themselves and to develop a familiarity with the national research team. These gatherings also afforded youth the opportunity to help shape the agendas for discussion and to play a lead role on some components of the full-team working sessions.

Challenging the Role of Knowers in Y-PAR

One of the epistemological assumptions of Y-PAR is that youth are experts on their own lives, with the potential to be "researchers, not just the researched" (Torre and Fine 2006: 458). Their knowledge of everyday experiences is held on par with other forms of knowing. As such, recent contributions to Y-PAR challenge the processes of traditional academic research, which has conventionally located expertise inside institutions. An argument increasingly put forth in the literature is that to engage in genuinely collaborative research, adult researchers must relinquish the role of sole experts in the creation of knowledge (Rodriguez and Brown 2009). This effort to foreground the voices and experiences of persons previously excluded as knowers or experts resonates with what other scholars in the participatory literature have highlighted as an essential principle (Israel et al. 2010; Stacciarini et al. 2011). Margaret Cargo and Shawna Mercer suggest that participatory research conducted in rigorous adherence to its values results in "the integration of researchers' theoretical and methodological expertise with nonacademic participants' real-world knowledge and experiences into a mutually reinforcing partnership" (2008: 327). Other researchers developing Y-PAR as an approach argue that the knowledge generated in these processes is a "shared critical consciousness" that includes youth and adult perspectives — a type of knowledge that is distinct from solely youth or adult perspectives (Maiter et al. 2013).

A critical emancipatory approach of this nature holds particular challenges when working with populations of youth who have largely been excluded from the knowledge-generation process. It is one thing to treat youth as knowers, per se, acknowledging that their perspectives on their own lives hold authority. It is another challenge entirely to hold up that knowledge on par with academic and scholarly forms of knowing, which have conventionally held power in the research and dissemination process. As we described later, the foundational processes in this research — such as collective definition of the term "policy" and its impacts on the lives of youth, and strategies employed for the development of terms of reference for the NYAB engagement over the life of the project — were created under the leadership of youth. In both cases, these processes ensured that young people defined for themselves the fundamental concepts that informed the project, as well as ways their work together would proceed.

Challenging the Location of Power

In order to realize its social justice and epistemological principles, an internally rigorous Y-PAR process requires continuous attention to power relations among co-researchers. This process is particularly important when the research team is diverse and includes adult academic researchers and community-based or non-adult co-researchers (Cornwall and Jewkes 1995; Minkler and Wallerstein 2011). While adults from community and university contexts may bring their diverse perspectives into conversation and thus negotiate various positions of power as "knowers" in the context, this type of self-assertion may be more difficult for youth. Various scholars have proposed approaches to this negotiation of power, with the aim of creating non-hierarchical structures and spaces where new knowledge can be generated. Helene Berman and Yasmin Jiwani (2014) describe this dimension of participatory process as a necessary values stance and not merely a series of specific techniques.

Other scholars have developed this aspect of Y-PAR implementation by describing the nuances of its processes. In an investigation of Y-PAR and health in the nursing field, Susan Kirk (2007) focused on the process of informed consent and confidentiality when working with children and youth, with a view to understanding how these "standard" research protocols influence power relations between children/youth and adults. Angela Cameron, Pamela Murray, Jasmine MacAdam and Zara Suleman (2014) employed an intersectional analysis in their work with marginalized girls to examine the various dimensions of power and (dis)empowerment experienced every day by newcomer youth, as well as opportunities for resistance. In a collaborative examination of how and why violence happens in the lives of girls in New Brunswick, these researchers explored the action component of Y-PAR in relation to youths' ability to inform youth-affecting policies. In their work, the ability of youth co-researchers to inform policy constituted a shift in the traditional hierarchies of power that shape the lives and experiences of girls and young women.

Enacting Y-PAR Values
The central activity undertaken by our research team was the formation of research groups comprised of different populations of youth. Within each group, efforts were made to acknowledge and address power imbalances. Toward this end, researchers employed self-reflexive practices where they acknowledged their own biases and the implications of power in their roles. Similarly, the youth themselves had opportunities to reflect on their own identities as these were brought into the research. Youth in the NYAB and in the research groups were frequently in positions to lead the discussions, facilitate warm-up and check-in exercises and provide input into the action goals and activities of their group or meeting.

As this project unfolded in six provinces across Canada, an important opportunity to enact Y-PAR values in relation to the distribution of power within the research team presented itself. Midway through the project, several participants expressed discomfort with a survey tool that was part of the project evaluation process. Although approved by the NYAB and included as part of our research protocol, some questions in the survey evoked discomfort for several youth; for others, the process of completing a highly structured, computer-based survey in the context of an arts-informed and highly creative discussion space felt incongruous. Some went so far as to say that the questions felt demeaning and themselves constituted a form of "structural violence." These issues were brought forward at a national team meeting. Despite a full agenda, we all recognized the importance of this issue and the need to provide a space whereby the many perspectives could be shared, heard and acted upon. Through dialogue among the youth-inclusive research team, we collectively determined that we could obtain comparable data through other qualitative methods and ultimately abandoned the survey as originally constructed. This flexibility allowed us to both be responsive to and respectful of our co-researchers while simultaneously meeting the requirements for rigorous research evaluation. This type of flexibility and receptivity to emerging ideas is critical in the context of participatory research approaches, congruent with the tenets that call for the creation of a self-critical community, ongoing self-reflection and the active commitment to create spaces for youth empowerment (Flicker and Guta 2008; Ozanne and Saatcioglu 2008). This negotiation represents a fine balance that researchers designing participatory projects face and resonates with Cahill's characterization of project ownership rooted in true participation, claimed by the youth themselves (Cahill 2007). While we need to articulate our methods sufficiently to satisfy concerns among funders and ethics review boards, we also have an obligation to listen authentically and respond to issues and concerns raised by participants. From our perspective, an ethic of doing no harm means that the youth-centredness of Y-PAR ultimately trumps an inflexible adherence to methods initially set out by the research protocol: if youth perceive the research process to be disempowering or oppressive, the priority must be to change the process and creatively consider alternative ways to achieve the study objectives.

The National Youth Advisory Board:
A Vehicle for Youth Voices to Be Heard and Acted Upon

At the start of the project, we hired two national youth coordinators who established the NYAB, thereby ensuring a youth voice from the outset. Together the group created terms of reference, a living document that captured their vision for the purpose and goals of the NYAB, described its manner of operation and outlined their aspirations for how youth co-researchers and others in the research team would communicate with one another. The terms of reference was revisited on a regular basis, as new members of the NYAB joined and as a mechanism to re-ignite engagement among long-standing members. As well, members of the NYAB participated actively on the steering committee and in other committees within the national project. Three working groups were established, which focused on evaluation, policy and media; each of these groups included youth researchers, academic researchers and knowledge users. As noted previously, youth also participated in the co-creation of a document that described how to talk with young people about policy — what this term means in everyday language, why policy is important and strategies to ensure the presence of youth voices at policy-making tables. Through the various engagement processes and the enactment of deep trust and respect, we were able to foster long-term and continuous communication among youth from across the country and with academic researchers on the team.

One of our earliest conversations with members of the NYAB concerned the formal title of the project, Promoting Health through Collaborative Engagement with Youth: Overcoming, Resisting, and Preventing Structural Violence, which was viewed as cumbersome and overly academic. Subsequently, a more youth-friendly working title, Voices against Violence: Youth Stories Create Change, was adopted. Members of the NYAB were central to the development of the project website and have continued to participate actively in knowledge translation and dissemination activities. In recognition of the significant and sustained role that many of the youth played throughout the project, some transitioned from youth advisory board members to paid positions as research assistants at the university leading the project. NYAB members also created job descriptions and opportunities that advanced the project, were exciting to them and fostered their own learning needs, goals and life plans. These opportunities allowed the youth to tap into their own areas of expertise. Several brought skills in journalism, social media, arts and youth engagement. Through the project's yearly team meetings, youth from the NYAB consistently assumed central roles that helped to shape the discussions and decisions of the national team. To foster cohesion among this group, funding and support were provided for the NYAB to meet as a group prior to national meetings. As active participants, the youth significantly impacted the development and implementation of the project and described increasing capacities as partners in research. Similarly, they developed increasingly prominent roles in the project's knowledge translation strategy, contributing to it in diverse and creative ways and presenting at conferences alongside other researchers in the team. Youth were given priority for conference travel funds — based on the commitment to youth participation and the assumption that many academic team members had access to other funds for this purpose.

The sustained engagement of youth in the NYAB is testament to the effectiveness of engagement efforts in this project. Although we initially asked each young person to commit to a two-year term with the NYAB, several members remained actively involved throughout the duration of this five-year initiative, despite the often busy and changing conditions of their lives.

Art-Based Methods as an Instrument to Examine Structural Violence

The use of art-based approaches was one way to create spaces for populations of youth who have historically been denied opportunities to reflect on the conditions, contradictions and circumstances of their lives. These approaches supported the Y-PAR epistemological shift to the ways participants themselves can interpret, give meaning to and make sense of their experiences and definitions of health (Harrison 2002).

Art also provided an even "playing field" to facilitate discussion. Youth do not typically use the language of "structural violence" or "policies" to describe experiences of social exclusion or other forms of oppression. Thus, PAR aims to use language that is appropriate and accessible, beginning with discussions about their everyday lives and interactions with different systems. The use of art-based approaches meant that everyone in the room was at similar levels of expertise and fluency in sharing their experiences. The ability to draw a stick figure or glue an image to a page was celebrated in all co-researchers, be they long-established academics or youth.

Current Understandings Regarding the Use of Art in a Research Context

The scholarly literature on art-based methods highlights their potential to support populations who may not be best served by verbal or written research methods. Artmaking enables participants to articulate their ideas and face complex emotions and topics at their own pace, in accessible formats (Boydell et al. 2012). Some scholars argue that the growing use of arts-based knowledge creation and dissemination strategies is driving an important shift in our understanding of what counts as evidence, as well as appreciation for the complexity and multidimensionality involved in creating new knowledge in the health sciences, social sciences and humanities (Boydell et al. 2016; Skinner and Masuda 2013). Others note that arts-based methods have the advantage of eliciting information and supporting the expression of precisely those populations that are often excluded from dominant health discourses (Hartman et al. 2011). Tom Barone and Elliot Eisner (2011) describe how powerful symbols can be in calling forth feelings and spaces that often stay hidden. Others suggest that art-based methods can provide new ways for persons to view their problems, which may lead to new ways for approaching solutions (Leavy 2015).

Art-based approaches provided a particularly nuanced lens for the task of understanding the relationship between the conditions of youths' lives and their health. Consistent with what others have noted in the scholarly literature, art-based research generated rich description, highlighted lived experience and enhanced understanding, moving participants to critical awareness of their health-related issues (Boydell et al. 2012; Fraser and al Sayah 2011).

Of particular relevance for our investigation of structural violence is Sheelagh Broderick's observation that arts-based approaches are inherently critical, providing a perspective that naturally "engages with structures that maintain and reproduce systems of inequality in local, regional and global contexts" (2011: 106). Others argue that art-based methods hold the potential to elicit "critical reflection by agents on the extent to which contextual/cultural factors influence and shape their understandings, assumptions and practices, as well as how these factors facilitate or impede change efforts" (Kontos and Poland 2009: 3).

Using Art to Examine Everyday Violence in the Lives of Youth

Across the 30 groups conducted by our research team, the forms of art-based activities used included digital storytelling, Talking Circle with Elders, facilitated socio-dramas, zines, body-mapping, painting and creating murals, painted t-shirts, photovoice, collage and spoken word/poetry. Decisions as to what art medium to use were made by the youth and reflected their interests, capacities and vision within the supportive environment provided by the group facilitators. In essence, youth generated ideas about what they wanted to discuss through the art, as well as the particular forms of artmaking they wanted to use. Wherever necessary and appropriate, support included materials and sometimes capacity, such as in the case of videography. The youth created art products over the course of a single research session or over several sessions, and later described their creations in the context of group discussions. In most groups, field notes were taken to accompany the description. In many instances, interpretation and analysis followed the discussion, with invitations from the facilitators to connect the personal narrative with the sociocultural context, and to invite others in the room to explore the complex dynamics at work.

Providing Opportunities to Share According to One's Comfort Level

Consistent with the findings of others who have used art-based methods, artmaking in this project provided a rich opportunity for young people to concretely explore an aspect of their identity or lives, while fully retaining the ability to share (or not share) however much (or little) they were comfortable with. Art created in this manner, within the safe space of Y-PAR, supported young people in gaining awareness of both individual and collective processes. The art served as the stimulus to initiate discussion, allowing others to make new connections, and provided supportive opportunities for youth to articulate their experiences of inclusion and/or exclusion and its impacts on their health. As Susan Jones, Yoolee Kim and Kristen Skendall (2012) note, in telling and listening to stories, participants begin the process of turning the gaze from self to others and connecting the personal to the cultural and structural. The art can thus become a transitional object that both speaks for the youth and allows the youth the opportunity to return for further critical reflection and growth of awareness.

Images as Data and Reflections as Data

In a methodological review of arts-based methods in the sociology of health and illness, Barbara Harrison (2002) notes that, for many, it is the reflexivity between image and verbalization which produces the data for the investigator. The use of the visual, Harrison proposes, "may be simply a technical means to an end: that is, the generation of verbal data for analysis" (845–846). In one of our research groups, youths' reflections on photographs they had taken through a photovoice process were used as direct statements and accompanied the images when the research was shared at conference presentations and team meetings. In another group, the youth co-researchers decided to create a public wiki to collectively house all the session notes, art products and selected journal entries from the group sessions. Participants further created specific theme pages, where they collectively summarized their views on themes emergent from the research process.

Challenges in Using Art-based Approaches

Given the scope and complexity of this national project, it is not surprising that we encountered several challenges implicit in the use of art-based methods. A principal one was the question of "what constitutes the data" in this project. For various researchers in the project who were unaccustomed to using art-based processes, the drawings and collages created by youth may have been emotionally resonant but presented difficulties in terms of analysis and even description. This reflection on the part of our research team aligns with those of other researchers who have engaged in art-based processes. Anni Raw, Sue Lewis, Andrew Russell and Jane Macnaughton (2012) lament the tension between the evocative, powerful nature of art-based outputs and the challenges of articulating their impact as part of the discourse of health evidence.

In our project, researchers and facilitators alike felt that the art could not be interpreted by anyone except its maker. But, because audio-recording and transcription were not used to document the youths' interpretation of their work, some meaning and knowledge may have been lost through the art-based processes in various groups. Similarly, the creation of such diverse (and dispersed) art products presented some challenges in terms of late-stage knowledge translation opportunities. Though the permission to share the art had been made explicit as part of the project's informed consent and ethics review board application, some group facilitators felt that youth should have a chance to consent to sharing their art every time it was shared or reproduced. This stance translated to difficulties in sharing some of the images created by the youth earlier in the timeline of the project, since it became difficult or impossible to reach them.

Art-Based Approaches in Support of Y-PAR

Challenges notwithstanding, the use of art-based approaches in this inquiry was instrumental in supporting the emancipatory and social-justice orientation of participatory action research. As in other examples of arts-based health research (see, for example, Broderick 2011) the art-based activities in Voices against Violence engaged and empowered young people to articulate their views on health and to speak to policy and program decision-makers.

Within each research group, artmaking allowed youth and adults to engage with each other within a welcoming space, where adult academics' language capacities did not outshine or silence youths' emerging ability to discuss structural violence. Because art is so personal, it did not assimilate youths' experiences into the existing academic discourses on the topic and did not prompt them to employ words or terms that did not come from their own experiences. Similar to findings reported by other scholars on the use of art-based approaches, in this research, art was a means to give voice to populations who previously lacked the language to describe their experiences or points of view (Eisner 2008; Knowles and Cole 2008).

Consistent with the priorities of Y-PAR, the artmaking supported the emergence of youths' critical consciousness by facilitating conversations on topics that may have been otherwise difficult, either individually or in a group. Two groups in the project used body-mapping as a means to explore the impacts of structural violence on youths' physical health. Using life-sized body outlines as platforms for discussion, youth talked about sexual health, food insecurity and the impacts of poverty upon their bodies. These issues may have been too personal to discuss individually, or the youth may have felt too vulnerable to do so without the medium of art as a vehicle through which to share complex ideas and feelings. The body outline on the page provided the necessary distance to discuss hunger, anger, the need to feel clean and the need for touch.

The art-based activities also allowed youth to make connections between personal experiences and the social and structural conditions of their lives. Their explorations of the relationships between everyday experiences of exclusion, belonging and well-being revealed information about social determinants of health as well as possibilities for structural change. As others have described, art in this project served to humanize and legitimize the experiences of youth who have been traditionally marginalized from evidence that informs policy and health-care delivery.

Finally, art-based approaches provided resonant and enduring mechanisms for continuing discussion of issues that matter to youth. In the final stages of this national project, members of the NYAB played a critical role in collecting, curating and sharing images of the art created through the five years of the project. The NYAB held an exhibition of this work at a final meeting of our national team of academic researchers, youth and knowledge users. This process gave policy-makers and leaders within organizations that serve youth the opportunity to experience the diversity of expression and perspectives shared by youth in Voices against Violence and re-ignite discussion of the issues that mattered to these young people. Members of the NYAB subsequently collaborated to create postcards featuring some of the art created, with the aim of sharing these postcards across Canada and beyond.

Conclusion

In striving to enact the values of Y-PAR in this project, many of our activities could not be ascertained in advance. Instead, the concrete activities and questions generated by each of the research groups emerged through the weeks or months they spent together. In the same vein, the finer themes and hands-on methods for analysis and discussion could not be fully designed at the beginning of each group. As such, processes were emergent, unpredictable and distinct across every one of the thirty research groups. The specific focus of each group emerged according to the needs of the youth involved and the contextual interests of both the youth and the organization or research facilitators working together. Nonetheless, all groups aimed to create spaces to discuss the lived experiences of social and structural exclusion or belonging, with an aim of understanding the impacts on the identities and well-being of these youth. The chapters in Part 2 describe specific research groups with these different populations of youth and provide more detailed descriptions of our application of participatory and art-based methods as tools to recognize the multiple, complex and intersecting experiences of these remarkable young people.

References

Barone, T., and E.W. Eisner. 2011. *Arts Based Research*. Thousand Oaks, CA: Sage.

Berman, H., and Y. Jiwani (eds.). 2014. *Faces of Violence in the Lives of Girls*. London, ON: Althouse Press.

Boydell, K.M., B. Gladstone, T. Volpe, B. Allemang, and E. Stasiulis. 2012. "The Production and Dissemination of Knowledge: A Scoping Review of Arts-Based Health Research." *Forum: Qualitative Social Research*, 13, 1: 1–30.

Boydell, K.M., M. Hodgins, B.M. Gladstone, E. Stasiulis, G. Belliveau, H. Cheu, and J. Parsons. 2016. "Arts-Based Health Research and Academic Legitimacy: Transcending Hegemonic Hegemonic Conventions." *Qualitative Research*, 16, 6: 681–700.

Broderick, S. 2011. "Arts Practices in Unreasonable Doubt? Reflections on Understandings of Arts Practices in Healthcare Contexts." *Arts and Health*. 13 June. DOI: 10.1080/17533015.2010.551716.

Brooks-Gunn, J., and G. Duncan. 1997. "The Effects of Poverty on Children." *Future Child*, 7, 2: 55–71.

Cahill, C. 2007. "Repositioning Ethical Commitments: Participatory Action Research as a Relational Praxis of Social Change." *ACME: An International Journal for Critical Geographies*, 6, 3: 360–373.

Cameron, A., P. Murray, J. MacAdam, and Z. Suleman. 2014. "Policy in the Lives of Marginalized Girls: Mapping the Disjunctures." In H. Berman and Y. Jiwani (eds.), *Faces of Violence in the Lives of Girls*. London, ON: Althouse Press.

Cargo, M., and S. Mercer. 2008. "The Value and Challenges of Participatory Research: Strengthening Its Practice." *Annu. Rev. Public Health*, 29: 325–350.

Cornwall, A., and R. Jewkes. 1995. "What Is Participatory Research?" *Social Science and Medicine*, 41, 12: 1667–1676.

Diemer, M., L. Rapa, C. Park and J. Perry. 2017. "Development and Validation of the Critical Consciousness Scale." *Youth and Society*, 49, 4: 461–483.

Drew, S.E., R.E. Duncan, and S.M. Sawyer. 2010. "Visual Storytelling: A Beneficial but Challenging Method for Health Research with Young People." *Qualitative Health Research*, 20, 12: 1677–1688.

Eisner, E. 2008. "Art and Knowledge." In J.G. Knowles and A.L. Cole (eds.), *Handbook of the Arts in Qualitative Research*. Thousand Oaks, CA: Sage.

Flicker, S., and A. Guta. 2008. "Ethical Approaches to Adolescent Participation in Sexual Health Research." *Journal of Adolescent Health*, 42, 1: 3–10.

Fraser, K.D., and F. al Sayah. 2011. "Arts-Based Methods in Health Research: A

Systematic Review of the Literature." *Arts and Health*, 3, 2: 110–145. DOI: 10.1080/17533015.2011.561357.

Freire, P. 1970. *Pedagogy of the Oppressed*. New York. Continuum.

Ginwright, S., and T. James. 2002. "From Assets to Agents of Change: Social Justice, Organizing, and Youth Development." *New Directions for Youth Development*, 96: 27–46.

Harrison, B. 2002. "Seeing Health and Illness Worlds—Using Visual Methodologies in a Sociology of Health and Illness: A Methodological Review." *Sociology of Health and Illness*, 24, 6: 856–872.

Hartman, L.R., A. Mandich, L. Magalhães, and T. Orchard. 2011. "How Do We 'See' Occupations? An Examination of Visual Research Methodologies in the Study of Human Occupation." *Journal of Occupational Science*, 18, 4: 292–305.

Israel, B.A., C.M. Coombe, R.R. Cheezum, A.J. Schulz, R.J. McGranaghan, R. Lichtenstein, and A. Burris. 2010. "Community-Based Participatory Research: A Capacity-Building Approach for Policy Advocacy Aimed at Eliminating Health Disparities." *American Journal of Public Health*, 100, 11: 2094–2102.

Jones, S.R., Y.C. Kim, and K.C. Skendall. 2012. "(Re-) Framing Authenticity: Considering Multiple Social Identities Using Autoethnographic and Intersectional Approaches." *Journal of Higher Education*, 83, 5: 698–724.

Kirk, S. 2007. "Methodological and Ethical Issues in Conducting Qualitative Research with Children and Young People: A Literature Review." *International Journal of Nursing Studies*, 44, 7: 1250–1260. DOI: http://dx.doi.org.proxy1.lib.uwo.ca/10.1016/j.ijnurstu.2006.08.015.

Knowles, J.G., and A.L. Cole. 2008. *Handbook of the Arts in Qualitative Research: Perspectives, Methodologies, Examples, and Issues*. Thousand Oaks, CA: Sage.

Kontos, P., and B. Poland. 2009. "Mapping New Theoretical and Methodological Terrain for Knowledge Translation: Contributions from Critical Realism and the Arts." Implementation Science, 4: 1. DOI: 10.1186/1748-5908-4-1.

Leavy, P. 2015. *Method Meets Art: Arts-Based Research Practice*. Guilford Publications.

Levac, L. 2013. "'Is This for real?'Participatory Research, Intersectionality, and the Development of Leader and Collective Efficacy with Young Mothers." *Action Research*, 11, 4: 423–441.

Maiter, S., A.J. Joseph, N. Shan, and A. Saeid. 2013. "Doing Participatory Qualitative Research: Development of a Shared Critical Consciousness with Racial Minority Research Advisory Group Members." *Qualitative Research*, 13, 2: 198–213.

Minkler, M., and N. Wallerstein (eds.). 2011. *Community-Based Participatory Research for Health: From Process to Outcomes*. John Wiley and Sons.

Ozanne, J.L., and B. Saatcioglu. 2008. "Participatory Action Research." *Journal of Consumer Research*, 35, 3: 423–439.

Raw, A., S. Lewis, A. Russell, and J. Macnaughton. 2012. "A Hole in the Heart: Confronting the Drive for Evidence-Based Impact Research in Arts and Health." *Arts and Health*, 4, 2: 97–108.

Rodríguez, L.F., and T.M. Brown. 2009. "From Voice to Agency: Guiding Principles for Participatory Action Research with Youth." *New Directions for Youth Development*, 123: 19–34.

Skinner, E., and J.R. Masuda. 2013. "Right to a Healthy City? Examining the Relationship Between Urban Space and Health Inequity by Aboriginal Youth Artist-Activists in Winnipeg." *Social Science and Medicine*, 91: 210–218.

Stacciarini, J.M.R., M.M. Shattell, M. Coady, and B. Wiens. 2011. "Community-Based Participatory Research Approach to Address Mental Health in Minority Populations." *Community Mental Health Journal*, 47, 5: 489–497.

Torre, M.E., and M. Fine. 2006. "Participatory Action Research (PAR) by Youth." *Youth Activism: An International Encyclopedia*, 2: 456–462.

UNICEF. 1989. Convention on the Rights of the Child.

3

From Protection to Expulsion

A Critical Examination of Aging Out of Care

Jennifer Fallis and Kendra Nixon

A lot of kids have their parents to go home to. They live with their parents till they're twenty. Twenty-five. If anything bad happens they have their parents to fall back on. If anything bad happens to us, we don't have anybody to fall back on. — *Former youth in care, Manitoba, 2017*

Each year approximately 6,000 Canadian youth "age out" of the child protection system (CPS) because they have reached the legal age of majority (Mann-Feder 2011). Depending on the province or territory this often means the termination of substitute care at age 18 or 19. For many young people, the transition to adulthood is a time of anticipation and excitement. However, for youth in care, this milestone can be a time of great uncertainty and fear, as many have not acquired the competencies and skills necessary to manage adult tasks independently, and few have family support to help them out (Schibler and McEwan-Morris 2006). The loss or alienation of familial relationships, contributing to the loneliness and isolation youth in care may experience, can also be attributed to the structure of child protection and methods of intervention, including sanctioning of continued family involvement and visitation and frequent use of non-familial substitute care arrangements. This, in combination with the often abrupt termination of CPS involvement at the age of majority and inconsistent support offered during this process, makes aging out of care a difficult transition, leaving many youth susceptible to long-term negative outcomes.

Despite intentions of protection, CPS involvement and policy specific to youth transitioning out of care can contribute to youths' vulnerability, putting them at risk of poor outcomes. Being cut off from the CPS system upon reaching the age of majority, many youth have no choice but to care for themselves with limited life skills, inadequate financial resources and few support networks (Tweddle 2007). This is compounded with feelings of loss and isolation when the supportive networks that were once part of their daily life are disconnected during and beyond their transition from care. For this population, expulsion rather than transition better describes the experience of leaving the CPS system (Reid and Dudding 2006).

In addition to interviews and focus groups with youth, the Voices against Violence: Youth Stories Create Change research study set out to undertake critical and historical analyses of relevant policies. Such analyses would help the team to identify ways in which institutions wittingly or unwittingly contribute to the victimization or vulnerability of diverse groups of youth and the different ways in which these policies influence them. This chapter represents an example of one such critical analysis — how Canadian CPS policy perpetrates and perpetuates structural violence against youth who age out of government care.

Adverse Outcomes among Youth Aging Out of Care

Young adults face adverse outcomes following their transition from the CPS system. Research suggests that this group experiences lower levels of academic attainment and increased levels of income assistance reliance; they are more likely to parent at a younger age, experience housing instability and homelessness, and be involved in the criminal justice system; they have fragile support networks and significant mental health concerns; and they are more likely to be victims of violence (Courtney, Dworksy, Brown et al. 2011; Rutman, Hubberstey and Feduniw 2007).

Educational attainment is associated with nearly all markers of health, well-being and social inclusion (Rutman and Hubberstey 2016). Youth aging out of care, however, frequently struggle to complete high school and are less likely to continue on to post-secondary studies (Ontario Office of the Provincial Advocate for Children and Youth 2012). This in turn affects the ability of many young adults to achieve self-sufficiency. Across Canada, academic completion rates differ significantly between youth leaving care and their peers. In Ontario, 44 percent of youth in care are expected to graduate from high school compared to an 81 percent graduation rate for all Ontario students (Ontario Office of the Provincial

Advocate for Children and Youth 2012). Similarly, approximately one-third of Manitoba youth in care graduated from high school in comparison to their peers (not in care) who graduate at a rate of 89 percent (Brownell et al. 2015). Rates for beginning and completing post-secondary studies are far worse. In British Columbia, youth who were never in care were more than twenty times more likely to enroll in post-secondary education than youth who had been in care (Ontario Office of the Provincial Advocate for Children and Youth 2012).

Not surprisingly, a significant number of youth experience income instability when they leave care and often depend on social assistance, essentially transferring from one government department (CPS) to another (income assistance). In their study of former youth in care, Deborah Rutman, Carol Hubberstey and April Feduniw (2007) found that the main source of income for 40 percent of participants was social assistance (with other participants relying on the income of a boyfriend or significant other), compared to 2.5 percent of young adults receiving income assistance within the general population. Once on social assistance, it can be difficult for youth to become self-reliant (Ontario Office of the Provincial Advocate for Children and Youth 2012). Of particular concern is the change in financial support between the two systems. With an already modest allowance for rent and daily living support, youth transitioning from CPS to income assistance often find their support reduced even further, creating challenges in maintaining their current living situation (Schibler and McEwan-Morris 2006). Moreover, the loss of agency support in dealing with issues related to housing (e.g., rental payments, conflict resolution) creates further vulnerability, resulting in many youth losing the housing established for them while in care (McEwan-Morris 2012).

Motherhood poses a further disadvantage for young women exiting from CPS care, as they are more likely to parent at a younger age in comparison to their peers (Courtney et al. 2011). Early childbearing creates additional barriers and exacerbates the experience of poverty for young women, as they are most likely to become the custodial parent. In addition, male youth who leave the foster care system early (e.g., before their 19th birthday) are more likely to become fathers (Oshima et al. 2013). Not only does early childbearing create vulnerability for poverty, this also increases the possibility of intergenerational involvement with the CPS system. In their study of adolescent mothers, Elizabeth Wall-Wieler, Marni Brownell, Deepa Singal, Nathan Nickel and Leslie Roos (2018) found that mothers who were in the care of CPS were more likely to have their children taken into care before the child's second birthday in comparison to adolescent mothers not in care.

Youth leaving care are also over-represented among the Canadian homeless population. In their examination of systemic pathways to youth homelessness, Mark Courtney, Christina Maes Nino and Evelyn Peters (2014) found that the majority of youth (82 percent) surveyed were previously involved with CPS, and participants described inadequate transitions from care and preparation for adulthood being directly related to their homelessness. Notably, over half of these participants (56 percent) experienced homelessness within the first year of leaving care. Youth who exit care at younger ages (e.g., between 16 and 18) are even more likely to be in the homeless population as compared to those youth who exited care at age 18 (Serge et al. 2002). Youth in care are also greatly over-represented among those reported missing (Bennett 2016).

Youth who are involved with CPS demonstrate an increased risk for mental health problems related to histories of neglect or violence within their family and other destabilizing experiences prior to coming into care, being in care or being placed in care as a result of a psychiatric disorder (Alberta Office of the Child and Youth Advocate 2013). The experience of leaving care itself can contribute to negative outcomes related to mental health. Youth may feel forced into independence through the loss of CPS support, which can be internalized as abandonment and they revisit past experiences of trauma and loss (B.C. Representative for Children and Youth 2014). In Rutman, Hubberstey and Feduniw's study of former youth in care (2007), depression was the most frequently reported health concern being experienced by nearly half of participants. The continuum of care between CPS systems and adult mental health service systems is of particular concern for youth leaving care. Many young people leaving care experience the loss of critical supports, including doctors and counsellors and access to covered medication, drastically diminishing their ability to manage their mental illness (Ontario Office of the Provincial Advocate for Children and Youth 2012).

Youth leaving care are also more likely to have problems with alcohol and drug use into their adult years. Sarah Narendorf and J. Curtis

McMillen (2010) found that rates of substance use disorders were higher for this group in comparison to the general population, and leaving care was specifically associated with marked increases in substance use. This increased vulnerability results from the experiences of being involved with CPS, including histories of maltreatment and multiple placements, compounded by leaving care with poor support networks.

Studies suggest that youth leaving care may also be more at risk of violence. Young women, in particular, are more likely to be targets of sexualized violence when transitioning out of care (Rutman, Hubberstey and Feduniw 2007), and are also more likely to report physical violence at the hands of their partner (Courtney, Dworsky, Brown et al. 2011). More young men exiting care may also be the victims of violent crime. Mark Courtney, Amy Dworsky, JoAnn Lee and Melissa Raap (2010) found that young men previously in care were more than twice as likely as young women to report being the victims of violent crime. These young men were also more likely than young women to have been arrested, convicted and incarcerated since leaving care.

Voices of Youth Leaving Care

Research and initiatives across Canada have further documented the firsthand experiences of youth transitioning from the care of CPS (Alberta Office of the Child and Youth Advocate 2013; B.C. Representative for Children and Youth 2014; Schibler and McEwan-Morris 2006). Many youth and young adults surveyed relay a common experience of loss, inconsistent support and an expectation that they would achieve self-sufficiency by the age of majority that in no way reflected their reality.

Ontario's Youth Leaving Care Hearings, organized by youth and held in November 2011, saw two days of public hearings allowing youth to "speak to their parent" regarding the experience of aging out of care and how this transition could be improved. Feedback regarding the experience of aging out of care was summarized: "We are vulnerable, we are isolated, we are left out of our own lives, no one is really there for us, care is unpredictable, and care ends and we struggle" (Our Voice Our Turn 2012). Many young people described the loneliness and abandonment they felt or anticipated feeling once discharged from CPS. As described by one youth:

I already had my family taken away once, and it was probably the hardest thing in my life. I didn't know where else to turn or what I was going to do, and when I turn 21, it's all going to happen again.

The primary recommendation to emerge from these hearings was the need for a fundamental overhaul of the current CPS system to better prepare young people exiting care to succeed. But the youth also noted that any action plan developed to implement changes should include the direct consultation and input of young people in and from care.

Significant barriers and negative outcomes encountered by youth leaving care are not a result of "problem youth," but rather larger systemic issues that prevent the successful transition of youth from the care of CPS systems through adulthood (Reid and Dudding 2006). Youth-aging-out-of-care policy that is predicated on the norms of "mainstream society" (e.g., that youth will be supported by their natural families) can be considered a form of structural violence that youth experience. These policies assume that youth exiting from care have the same support networks and educational/employment opportunities as their peers and fail to realize the realities and barriers that youth encounter (described earlier). These problematic assumptions inhibit the realization of these youths' basic needs and unique circumstances, putting them at further disadvantage (Gil 1999). Specific populations of youth in care are further marginalized and vulnerable to negative outcomes, including Indigenous, LGBTQ2S+ and immigrant and refugee youth.

Indigenous Youth

The over-representation of Indigenous children and youth within CPS is a significant policy challenge for Canada (Tilbury and Thoburn 2011). While Indigenous Peoples comprise approximately 4 percent of the general population in Canada, Indigenous children account for nearly 50 percent of all children and youth in foster care (Aboriginal Children in Care Working Group 2015). Within the Prairie Provinces, the rate of Indigenous children and youth in care is significantly higher. For example, 89 percent of the more than 10,000 children and youth in care in Manitoba identify as Indigenous (Manitoba Families 2017). In addition to funding and jurisdictional issues that have complicated service delivery to families, Indigenous CPS agencies are often working with families with complex needs intertwined with racist and destabilizing colonial policies, intergenerational trauma and suffering related to colonialism (Sinha and Kozlowski 2013). Consequently, the larger needs of families related to health, well-being and caring for children often far outreach the capacity of CPS. Societal apathy and indifference toward the victimization and violence Indigenous children and youth are more likely to experience further permit the continuation of policies and practices that facilitate the over-representation and intergenerational involvement of Indigenous children, youth and families within CPS (Bennett 2016).

The material effects of colonization have been well documented, including the loss of land, language, family harmony, collective wealth and intact community approaches to parenting (McKenzie and Shangreaux 2011). These losses are compounded with the historical mass removal of children through institutional colonial interventions, including the residential school system and the Sixties Scoop, two potent examples of the structural violence perpetuated against Indigenous children and families. Such violence has produced devastating intergenerational trauma and long-term effects within Indigenous families, including violence and substance abuse (McKenzie and Shangreaux 2011). Thousands of Indigenous children and youth experienced violence and suffered severe emotional, physical and sexual abuse within residential schools. Consequently, many learned to understand violence as a means of meeting needs. The further abuse of Indigenous children throughout the Sixties Scoop (mass removal of children from their communities during the 1960s and 1970s and placement in non-Indigenous homes as foster or adopted children) and increased risk of exposure to violence, exploitation and abuse once placed in the care of CPS have also been widely reported (Bennett 2016). Therefore, generations of Indigenous children and youth have been subjected to violence not only in their family home or community, but then again once placed in government care.

The National Child Incidence Study further indicates that most Indigenous children are removed from their homes, and remain in the care of CPS, for reasons of neglect — predominantly tied to poverty, poor housing conditions and colonial-based patterns of material disadvantage and inequality persistent within Indigenous communities (Sinha et al. 2011). Indigenous children are also more likely to come to the attention of CPS authorities than non-Indigenous children, maltreatment is more likely to be substantiated in cases involving Indigenous children, and cases are more likely to stay open for ongoing service. Indigenous youth are also more likely to experience multiple foster care placements and are less likely to return to the care of their families (de Finney and di Tomasso 2015). Indigenous children in care are also more likely to be placed in non-Indigenous settings, where it can be very difficult to learn and develop a sense of cultural identity (Bennett 2016). The permanent removal from family and multiple placements with non-familial caregivers can further disconnect Indigenous youth from community and cultural identity — and in turn a sense of belonging (de Finney and di Tomasso 2015). Canada's CPS system, therefore, can be described as a form of discrimination and structural violence against Indigenous children and youth (Foster 2018). Researchers and Indigenous leaders have identified that CPS has been and continues to be a tool used to further perpetuate the colonization of (and structural violence against) Indigenous Peoples (Bennett 2016).

Recommendations for the CPS system to better respond to the unique needs of Indigenous youth leaving care include providing enhanced transition planning and robust services and supports beyond the age of majority. Positive self-identity, including cultural identity and a sense of belonging, is an important component of successfully transitioning to adulthood. When youth have a strong sense of who they are and where they come from, they are better able to set life goals and determine the type of adult they want to be (B.C. Representative for Children and Youth 2014).

Connections to culture and community, intertwined with time to develop a positive sense of self and identity, are critical components in planning for and successfully transitioning Indigenous youth involved with CPS to emerging adulthood, and there is some evidence to suggest that culturally tailored interventions and approaches can improve outcomes for Indigenous youth (Aboriginal Children in Care Working Group 2015). In a study of Inuit youth transitioning from a CPS care facility, researchers noted that positive transitions for youth, including changes in high risk behaviour, were associated with an ongoing connection to family, community and culture while living in out-of-home care (Fraser et al. 2012). However, the time and flexibility that is required to meet the needs of Indigenous youth, specifically needs related to identity and belonging, may be hindered by aging-out-of-care policy and Eurocentric perspectives regarding adulthood. Elders remind us that accountability to young people (in many Indigenous communities) transcends legal definitions and is based on knowledge and standing in the community, not an age limit or ability to live independently. Moreover, the rigid distinction between "youth" and "adult," rooted in Eurocentric child development theories and imposed on Indigenous Peoples, is problematic for Indigenous youth involved with CPS, specifically regarding expectations of self-sufficiency by the age of majority and being unable to return for support after aging out (de Finney and di Tomasso 2015). Policy and legislation not only restrict time and flexibility needed for youth to address larger and complex issues of cultural identity, but may also contradict cultural beliefs and practices related to the transition to adulthood. CPS aging-out-of-care policy, therefore, can be understood as a form of structural violence that is perpetrated against Indigenous youth and Indigenous culture.

LGBTQ2S+ Youth

The exact number of young people in care who identify as LGBTQ2S+ is not precisely known. The number has been estimated to be between 5 and 10 percent; however, this does not appear to be based on any specific research or data, and, in fact, likely underestimates the true number due to youth who do not disclose or who actively hide their sexual orientation/gender identity (Dworsky 2013). More current research suggests that as many as one in five youth in care struggle with issues related to sexual orientation and/or gender identity (Shpiegel 2016). Although there is limited research in Canadian CPS regarding LGBTQ2S+ youth, recent studies suggest that sexual minority youth leaving care are particularly vulnerable to negative outcomes and likely require more intensive supports during their transition to emerging adulthood (Shpiegel and Simmel 2016).

Youth identifying as LGBTQ2S+ face a number of unique challenges during adolescence, including lack of acceptance, negative or abusive responses from both family and peers, and a reluctance to disclose sexual orientation for fear of how others will respond (Kufeldt and McKenzie 2011). Actual or perceived lack of support during this critical period of development, in addition to abuse or traumatic experiences, elevate the risk of negative outcomes in emerging adulthood. Consequently, LGBTQ2S+ youth are disproportionately represented in rates of academic underachievement, violence, homelessness, substance abuse, depression, emotional distress and suicidal ideation (Flicker et al. 2010; Shpiegel and

Simmel 2016). Upon CPS involvement, identified LGBTQ2S+ youth are at further risk of harassment, discrimination or possibly physical violence perpetrated by care providers, staff or peers (Alberta Office of the Child and Youth Advocate 2017). Victimized because of their sexual orientation or gender identity, and with the risk of continued harassment and violence, many youth may choose the perceived "safety" of the street and subsequently become entrenched in poverty and homelessness (Dworsky 2013).

Appropriate responses to LGBTQ2S+ youth in care can be diminished by uncertainty among CPS professionals regarding how best to respond to them (Kufeldt and McKenzie 2011). Of greater concern, however, are CPS professionals who may label LGBTQ2S+ youth in care as "difficult," resulting in less responsive care for these vulnerable youth (Mallon, Aledort and Ferrera 2002). These same youth may also be discharged from care upon reaching the age of majority due to "non-compliance" or being perceived as unwilling to work collaboratively with their worker or agency. To be discussed further, extensions of care or continued CPS support beyond the age of majority is not a defined right, but rather a service offered at the discretion of a CPS agency or social worker. As a result, when LGBTQ2S+ youth are discharged from care under these circumstances, there has often been minimal planning done to thoroughly address and prevent negative outcomes, including homelessness, exposure to violence and poor physical or mental health (Mallon, Aledort and Ferrera 2002). A lack of services provided, and negative experiences encountered throughout their time in care, may also discourage LGBTQ2S+ youth from agreeing to continued support after they leave care.

Immigrant and Refugee Youth

Like many countries in the Western world, Canada has a growing immigrant and refugee population (Kufeldt and McKenzie 2011). The CPS system, in turn, has been required to respond to a changing population and address the unique needs and challenges associated with the experience of living and parenting in a new country. Newcomer children and youth may come to the attention of CPS for a number of reasons. For example, conflict within a family may occur due to issues of autonomy for youth (contradicting family-of-origin beliefs), while for others, contact with the CPS system may be triggered by inappropriate discipline measures

— leading to allegations of abuse based on Canadian laws and customs (Kufeldt and McKenzie 2011). Some newcomer youth also come to the attention of CPS due to entering Canada without a parent or legal guardian. Once brought to the attention of CPS, newcomer families can encounter further obstacles. For many families this is often their first encounter with any type of social service system, and the difference in cultural norms and behaviour (between worker and new family) and inability to communicate effectively may cause caseworkers to apprehend children more hastily, with similar barriers further delaying case planning. As a result, newcomer children often experience longer stays in out-of-home care (Earner 2007). Children and youth in these circumstances not only experience separation from their family, but with prolonged out-of-home care face further disconnection from language and cultural roots (Kufeldt and McKenzie 2011). As previously discussed, this disconnection from culture and identity, particularly for youth transitioning from the CPS system, can have significant consequences in emerging adulthood.

For immigrant and refugee youth, once in the care of CPS they are provided access to education, health care services and other supportive resources that might otherwise prove challenging to access as a minor and refugee claimant (Hare 2007). However, this access and support is not necessarily permanent, and if work is not done to ensure a youth in care is a permanent resident or, ideally, full citizen prior to their transition from care to adulthood, then youth may be left in a vulnerable and precarious position. In particular, refugee youth in care may be unaware of their legal immigration status simply because they assume their CPS social worker to be taking care of their citizenship or permanent residency filing process on their behalf. If their social workers fail to process their claims (unbeknownst to youth), these youth may not discover their vulnerability until after they leave care and attempt to continue education, obtain legal aid, apply for a job, cross the border, visit a doctor, apply for a loan — or do any other routine activity that most people would take for granted (Hare 2007).

Being unable to work or obtain a higher education will undoubtedly contribute to income insecurity, putting immigrant and refugee youth at risk of poverty and homelessness. Research indicates that newcomer youth in Canada may already be over-represented in the "hidden homelessness" population, accessing formal shelter services and supports far less than their Canadian peers (Sauvé et al. 2018). Refugee youth transitioning out of care, in particular, may also be at risk of poor health as they may not be able to access health care supports, or may be fearful of accessing services, in part, due to their legal status (Salehi 2010). This is especially dire given that refugee youth may enter Canada with pre-existing medical conditions stemming from their experiences of war and violence.

Compared to immigrant youth, refugee youth experience unique challenges when coming to Canada. As an example, immigrant youth are more likely to arrive in a new country with their family, who can often support them emotionally and financially. Refugee youth, in contrast, are often fleeing war, violence, persecution or natural disasters and are more likely to be separated from family members during or prior to their escape (Guruge and Butt 2015). Refugee youth, therefore, are at greater risk of experiencing ongoing psychological concerns related to these pre-migration experiences. Studies on refugee children and youth affected by war indicate the presence of post traumatic stress disorder and other psychological affects resulting from war-related trauma, including sexual assault, forced labour, child soldiering, material deprivation and other forms of torture (Yohani 2010). Therefore, refugee youth who have been affected by the trauma of war and violence can face a more difficult transition, requiring additional supports and resources.

Lack of policy directing CPS agencies to ensure permanent residency or citizenship for youth reaching the age of majority while in care has been noted more recently — with calls to reform this area of agency discretion. For example, the Youth Leaving Care Working Group (2013) in Ontario recommends immediate action to several transition-related items for youth, including that immigration status is resolved by CPS agencies prior to age 18 (in order to access employment, education and health care). Whether oversight, confusion or lack of clear policy, the transition of undocumented youth in care to adulthood creates significant vulnerability related to health and well-being and requires further attention from policy-makers to minimize the risk of negative outcomes.

Policy for Youth Leaving Care — Gaps and Recommendations

With the exception of children and families living on First Nations reserves/communities, provinces and territories have legislative jurisdiction and responsibility for the provision of child and family services

(Schibler and McEwan-Morris 2006). Each province and territory has its own legislation and policies regarding the termination of CPS services for youth in care upon their reaching the age of majority. While there are some provisions for extensions of care, most provincial CPS legislation terminates care at age 18 or 19 (Mann-Feder 2011). As a result, policy and programs for youth aging out of care are largely focused on preparing youth for adulthood (e.g., independent living and self-sufficiency) (Avery 2010). Most provincial aging-out-of-care policies appear to be predicated on the idea that parents are no longer legally responsible for the well-being of their children after age 18 (Ontario Office of the Provincial Advocate for Children and Youth 2012). In reality, however, most parents continue to provide support to their own children beyond the age of 18, often well into adulthood.

Since the latter half of the twentieth century, the transition to adulthood has become longer, more complex and more uncertain for young adults (Avery 2010). This transition period has been marked, in part, with increased post-secondary education and training and changing relationship structures, including more co-habitation, often delaying marriage and parenthood. The period between adolescence and adulthood has, therefore, evolved into a distinct period of life between the ages of 18 and 25 that Arnett (2007) defines as "emerging adulthood," a time in which young people seek freedom and embrace experimentation following adolescence. In contrast, youth in the care of CPS systems are expected to largely bypass this period and assume a self-sufficient adult role upon emancipation from care. Ending CPS involvement between ages 18 and 21, or in some cases as early as 16, often means a loss of vital supports in the midst of key life stages, including finishing school, which, as described, is an important indicator of future independence and well-being. During a time when many youth have the opportunity to focus on their studies, youth leaving care are taking on significant responsibilities, including establishing and managing households and trying to ensure basic financial security with minimal support and guidance (Ontario Office of the Provincial Advocate for Children and Youth 2012).

Data on youths' living arrangements, educational achievement and entry into the workforce indicate that few young people, not just those who are exiting from care, are ready to assume adult roles before their mid-20s (Avery 2010). Within Canada, approximately 60 percent of young adults age 20–24 were living with their parents in 2011 (either not yet left home or returned after living elsewhere) while thirty years earlier the proportion was only 41 percent (Statistics Canada 2011). Young adults who have not grown up in care, in addition to enjoying an often stable upbringing with their natural family, are further able to transition through emerging adulthood with support where needed and over a longer period of time. In contrast, many youth leaving government care do not have this same option and are directed by CPS policy to transition from care, whether self-sufficiency has been attained or not.

Outlined in provincial CPS legislation, extensions of care or support services beyond the age of majority are often available only to youth in the *permanent* care of a CPS agency (Ontario Office of the Provincial Advocate for Children and Youth 2012). This excludes a number of youth in care by voluntary agreement (between parent and agency) or youth who are temporary wards of an agency. Together, youth with these legal statuses can comprise nearly half of the number of youth exiting care (McEwan-Morris 2012). In addition to a reduced number of youth in care eligible for continued support, extensions of care are often granted for a specific purpose, including completion of an educational, independent living or treatment program, or with the expectation of youth being employed or actively seeking employment (McEwan-Morris 2012). As previously identified, the experience of preparing for and transitioning from care can re-awaken past traumas associated with loss and isolation, resulting in some youth resisting the planning process altogether. Therefore, youth who appear resistant or non-compliant in this preparation process, and in turn are at increased vulnerability for negative outcomes, may be first to have services and supports terminated at the age of majority — a time in which they likely need support the most. As described by one former youth in care, "we are torn between doing too well or too badly — you have to justify why you need assistance" (Alberta Office of the Child and Youth Advocate 2013). Not only is resistance or non-compliance often a disqualifying factor, the appearance of self-sufficiency in areas such as life skills and employment can also raise doubts regarding the need for continued support by CPS. There is significant discretion among social workers and CPS agencies in granting and terminating extensions of care, as this is not a mandatory program or defined legal right for youth (Ontario Office of the Provincial Advocate for Children and Youth 2012). Consequently, a number of youth may be unaware of the option for continued support beyond the age of majority, or whether or not they are eligible, or of their right to appeal should they not be provided an extension of care or if their extension is terminated by the CPS agency.

With some exceptions, there is commonly no provision in provincial legislation for youth to return to care if services have concluded upon reaching the age of majority. Government requirements and agency policy often preclude an option for youth to return to care if needed (Mann-Feder 2011). Consequently, youth aging out of care are rarely afforded the privilege of a gradual transition or safety net in comparison to their peers not in care should they be not yet prepared for self-sufficiency and independent living (Geenen and Powers 2007). In many provinces, extensions of care are also required by legislation to conclude upon a young adult reaching 21 years of age. Policy and legislation, therefore, largely disregards the concept of emerging adulthood, whereby most young adults are not fully prepared for independence and self-sufficiency prior to the age of 25. Since the process of leaving care encompasses both emerging adulthood and a process that may revisit traumatic histories, sufficient time and flexibility must be built into the transition process (Mann-Feder 2011).

Research has documented the benefits of continued CPS support for youth well beyond the age of majority. Courtney, Okpych et al. (2016), for example, found that young adults receiving continued CPS support enjoyed positive outcomes in areas such as education and social supports and were less likely than their peers who had departed care at an earlier age to experience economic hardships, food insecurity, homelessness, psychiatric hospitalization and criminal justice involvement. Further, there can be a significant cost saving when former youth in care are provided continued support, as they may be less dependent on income assistance or have less involvement with the criminal justice system. Additionally, an increased number of youth would likely finish both high school and post-secondary studies, increasing their earnings and tax contributions (Ontario Office of the Provincial Advocate for Children and Youth 2012).

Collective activism and engagement by young people currently and previously involved with CPS is also generating important systemic changes. For example, Ontario's Youth Leaving Care Working Group, inclusive of current and former youth in care created the action plan: *Blueprint for Fundamental Change to Ontario's Child Welfare System*

(2013). Recommendations from this plan included the need to raise the age of protection for youth in Ontario from 16 to 18, and critical supports needed for young adults beyond the age of 18 — including continued health benefits and other transitional supports. This led to the development of Ontario's Aftercare Benefits Initiative, allowing former youth in care to continue receiving health benefits and life skills related support until, and in some cases beyond, the age of 25 (Ontario Association of Children's Aid Societies 2014). As of January 2018, Ontario also raised the age of protection for youth to age 18. The General Child and Family Services Authority's Youth Engagement Strategy (2009), an initiative led by former youth in care in Manitoba, also provided an important opportunity for young people currently and previously in the care of CPS to influence and determine how child welfare services could be improved, and what further supports are needed to successfully transition youth from care to adulthood. Recommendations from this initiative led to the development and launch of Building Futures (now known as Futures Forward). Bringing together a collaborative network of community partners, youth in and from care ages 15–29 can access important resources, including counselling, educational planning, employment preparation and financial services. Also in Manitoba, the grassroots movement "25 not 21," initiated and supported by current and former youth in care, has called for changes to the provincial Child and Family Services Act to better support youth transitioning from CPS to emerging adulthood. This includes raising the maximum age in which extensions of care can be offered from 21 to 25, and that this continued support be offered to any current or former youth in care — regardless of legal status while involved with CPS. Manitoba's current child welfare legislative review, launched by the province in December 2017, is reviewing transition supports for youth in care including the maximum age in which extensions of care should be offered, potentially beyond the age of 21.

Conclusion

Increasingly, Canadian youth are remaining or returning home well into their 20s for support related to education, life skills and guidance navigating the responsibilities of young adulthood. The needs of youth in care reaching the age of majority are not dissimilar. In fact, youth departing the care of CPS systems often have needs requiring additional time, specialized services and increased support to ensure better health and well-being outcomes in adulthood.

Canadian CPS systems represent a site that often perpetrates (and perpetuates) structural violence against children and youth, especially those who are aging out of government care. Policy and legislation (mis)guiding the transition of youth from CPS is largely focused on preparing youth for independent living and self-sufficiency by the age of majority. However, the loss of critical supports in the midst of key life stages can contribute to youths' vulnerability, leaving them more susceptible to negative outcomes. Specific populations of youth in care, including Indigenous, LGBTQ2S+ and immigrant and refugee youth, are further marginalized and vulnerable to adverse outcomes through policy oversight and system inadequacies. Therefore, policy and legislation specific to youth transitioning from care to adulthood requires further examination and improvement to ensure readiness and to better meet the unique needs of this population.

References

Aboriginal Children in Care Working Group. 2015. *Aboriginal Children in Care: Report to Canada's Premiers.* <www.canadaspremiers.ca>.

Alberta Office of the Child and Youth Advocate. 2013. *Where Do We Go From Here? Youth Aging Out of Care Special Report.* <www.ocya.alberta.ca>.

___. 2017. *Speaking Out: A Special Report on LGBTQ2S+ Young People in the Child Welfare and Youth Justice Systems.* <www.ocya.alberta.ca>.

Arnett, J.J. 2007. "Emerging Adulthood: What Is It, and What Is It Good For?" *Child Development Perspectives*, 1, 2: 68–73.

Avery, R.J. 2010. "An Examination of Theory and Promising Practice for Achieving Permanency for Teens Before They Age Out of Foster Care." *Children and Youth Service Review*, 32: 399–408.

B.C. Representative for Children and Youth. 2014. *On Their Own: Examining the Needs of B.C. Youth as They Leave Government Care.* <www.rcybc.ca>.

Bennett, M. 2016. *On the Edge Between Two Worlds: Community Narratives on the Vulnerability of Marginalized Indigenous Girls.* Office of the Children's Advocate, Manitoba. <www.childrensadvocate.mb.ca>.

Brownell, M., M. Chartier, W. Au, L. MacWilliam, J. Schultz, W. Guenette, and J. Valdivia. 2015. *The Educational Outcomes of Children in Care in Manitoba.* Manitoba Centre for Health Policy. <www.umanitoba.ca/medicine/units/mchp>.

Courtney, M.E., A. Dworsky, A. Brown, C. Cary, K. Love, and V. Vorhies. 2011. *Midwest Evaluation of the Adult Functioning of Former Foster Youth: Outcomes at Age 26.* Chicago, IL: Chapin Hall at the University of Chicago.

Courtney, M.E., A. Dworsky, J.S. Lee, and M. Raap. 2010. *Midwest Evaluation of the Adult Functioning of Former Foster Youth: Outcomes at Ages 23 and 24.* Chicago,

IL: Chapin Hall at the University of Chicago.

Courtney, M., C. Maes Nino, and E. Peters. 2014. *System Pathways into Youth Homelessness*. <www.spcw.ca>.

Courtney, M.E., N.J. Okpych, P. Charles, D. Mikell, B. Stevenson, K. Park, B. Kindle, J. Harty, and H. Feng. 2016. *Findings from the California Youth Transitions to Adulthood Study (CalYOUTH): Conditions of Youth at Age 19*. Chicago, IL: Chapin Hall at the University of Chicago.

de Finney, S. and L. di Tomasso. 2015. "Creating Places of Belonging: Expanding Notions of Permanency with Indigenous Youth in Care." *First Peoples Child and Family Review*, 10, 1: 63–85.

Dworsky, A. 2013. *The Economic Well-Being of Lesbian, Gay, and Bisexual Youth Transitioning out of Foster Care*. Office of Planning, Research and Evaluation, Administration for Children and Families, U.S. Department of Health and Human Services: Issue Brief.

Earner, I. 2007. "Immigrant Families and Public Child Welfare: Barriers for Services and Approaches for Change." *Child Welfare*, 86, 4: 63–91.

Flicker, S., A. Guta, J. Larkin, C. Lo, S. McCardell, and R. Travers. 2010. "Service Provider Views on Issues and Needs for Lesbian, Gay, Bisexual, and Transgender Youth." *Canadian Journal of Human Sexuality*, 19, 4: 191–198.

Foster, R. 2018. "Reimagining" the Child Welfare System." *Journal of Law and Social Policy*, 28, 174-175.

Fraser, S.L., M. Vachon, M.J. Arauz, C. Rousseau, and L.J. Kirmayer. 2012. "Inuit Youth Transitioning out of Residential Care: Obstacles to Re-Integration and Challenges to Wellness." *First Peoples Child and Family Review*, 7, 1: 52–75.

Geenen, S., and L.E. Powers. 2007. "'Tomorrow Is Another Problem': The Experiences of Youth in Foster Care During Their Transition into Adulthood." *Children and Youth Services Review*, 29: 1085–1101.

General Child and Family Services Authority. 2009. *Youth Engagement Strategy: Phase 1. Final Report*. Winnipeg.

Gil, D.G. 1999. "Understanding and Overcoming Social-Structural Violence." *Contemporary Justice Review*, 2, 1: 23–35.

Guruge, S., and H. Butt. 2015. "A Scoping Review of Mental Health Issues and Concerns Among Immigrant and Refugee Youth in Canada: Looking Back, Moving Forward." *Canadian Journal of Public Health*, 106, 2: 72–78.

Hare, F.G. 2007. "Transition Without Status: The Experience of Youth Leaving Care Without Canadian Citizenship." In V. Mann-Feder (ed.), *Transition or Eviction: Youth Exiting Care for Independent Living*. Special issue of *New Directions for Youth Development*, 113: 77–88.

Kufeldt, K., and B. McKenzie. 2011. "Critical Issues in Current Practice." In K. Kufeldt and B. McKenzie (eds.), *Child Welfare: Connecting Research, Policy, and Practice*, 2nd ed. Waterloo, ON: Wilfred Laurier University Press.

Mallon, G.P., N. Aledort, and M. Ferrera. 2002. "There's No Place Like Home: Achieving Safety, Permanency, and Well-Being for Lesbian and Gay Adolescents in Out-of-Home Care Settings." *Child Welfare*, 81, 2: 407–439.

Manitoba Families. 2017. *Annual Report, 2016–17*. <www.gov.mb.ca>.

Mann-Feder, V. 2011. "Aging Out of Care and the Transition to Adulthood: Implications for Intervention." In K. Kufeldt and B. McKenzie (eds.), *Child Welfare: Connecting Research, Policy and Practice,* 2nd ed. Waterloo, ON: Wilfred Laurier University Press.

Matta Oshima, K.M., S.C. Narendorf, and J.C. McMillen. 2013. "Pregnancy Risk Among Older Youth Transitioning out of Foster Care." *Children and Youth Services Review,* 35: 1760–1765.

McEwan-Morris, A. 2012. *Strengthening Our Youth: Their Journey to Competence and Independence: A Progress Report on Youth Leaving Manitoba's Child Welfare System.* Winnipeg: Manitoba.

McKenzie, B., and C. Shangreaux. 2011. "From Child Protection to Community Caring in First Nations Child and Family Services." In K. Kufeldt and B. McKenzie (eds.), *Child Welfare: Connecting Research, Policy and Practice,* 2nd ed. Waterloo, ON: Wilfred Laurier University Press.

Narendorf, S.C., and J.C. McMillen. 2010. "Substance Use and Substance Use Disorders as Foster Youth Transition to Adulthood." *Children and Youth Services Review,* 32: 113–119.

Ontario Association of Children's Aid Societies. 2014. *Aftercare Benefits Initiative.* <www.oacas.org/>.

Ontario Office of the Provincial Advocate for Children and Youth. 2012. *25 Is the New 21: The Costs and Benefits of Providing Extended Care and Maintenance to Ontario Youth in Care until Age 25.* <http://www.provincialadvocate.on.ca>.

Our Voice Our Turn, Ontario Provincial Advocate for Children and Youth. 2012. *My Real Life Book: Report from the Youth Leaving Care Hearings.* Toronto: Provincial Advocate for Children and Youth.

Reid, C., and P. Dudding. 2006. *Building a Future Together: Issues and Outcomes for Transition-Aged Youth.* <www.cecw-cepb.ca/publications/568>.

Rutman, D., and C. Hubberstey. 2016. *Fostering Success: Improving Educational Outcomes for Youth In/From Care.* Victoria, BC: University of Victoria.

Rutman, D., C. Hubberstey, and A. Feduniw. 2007. *When Youth Age Out of Care — Where to from There?* <www.uvic.ca/hsd/socialwork/assets/docs/research/WhenYouthAge2007.pdf >.

Salehi, R. 2010. "'Young, but Older than 20': Better Practices in Enhancing Access to Services for Newcomer Youth in Toronto." *Canadian Social Work Journal,* 12, 1: 93–100.

Sauvé, C., C. Smith, A. Fawzi, T. Rose, J. Langille, K. Burkholder-Harris, and J. Kennelly. 2018. *Building Bridges: Perspectives on Youth Homelessness from First Nations, Inuit and Métis, Newcomer, and LGBTQ2S+ Youth in Ottawa.* <www.homelesshub.ca>.

Schibler, B., and A. McEwan-Morris. 2006. "*Strengthening Our Youth*": Their Journey to Competence and Independence: A Report on Youth Leaving Manitoba's Child Welfare System. <www.childrensadvocate.mb.ca>.

Serge, L., M. Eberle, M. Goldberg, S. Sullivan, and P. Dudding. 2002. *Pilot Study: The Child Welfare System and Homelessness Among Canadian Youth.* Ottawa, ON: National Secretariat on Homelessness.

Shpiegel, S. 2016. "Sexual Minority Youth Emancipating from Foster Care: Challenges and Opportunities during the Period of Transition to Adulthood." [PowerPoint presentation]. June 7. <www.partcanada.org>.

Shpiegel, S., and C. Simmel. 2016. "Functional Outcomes among Sexual Minority Youth Emancipating from the Child Welfare System." *Children and Youth Service Review*, 61: 101–108.

Sinha, V., and A. Kozlowski. 2013. "The Structure of Aboriginal Child Welfare in Canada." *International Indigenous Policy Journal*, 4, 2 (Article 2).

Sinha, V., N. Trocmé, C. Blackstock, B. MacLaurin, and B. Fallon. 2011. "Understanding the Overrepresentation of First Nations Children in Canada's Child Welfare System." In K. Kufeldt and B. McKenzie (eds.), *Child Welfare: Connecting Research, Policy and Practice*, 2nd ed. Waterloo, ON: Wilfred Laurier University Press.

Statistics Canada. 2011. "Living Arrangements of Young Adults Aged 20 to 29, 2011 Census." Ottawa, ON: Statistics Canada.

Tilbury, C., and J. Thoburn. 2011. "Disproportionate Representation of Indigenous Children in Child Welfare Systems: International Comparisons." In K. Kufeldt and B. McKenzie (eds.), *Child Welfare: Connecting research, Policy and Practice*, 2nd ed. Waterloo, ON: Wilfred Laurier University Press.

Tweddle, A. 2007. "Youth Leaving Care: How Do They Fare?" In V. Mann-Feder (ed.), *Transition or Eviction: Youth Exiting Care for Independent Living*. Special issue of *New Directions for Youth Development*, 113: 15–31.

Wall-Wieler, E., M. Brownell, D. Singal, N. Nickel, and L.L. Roos. 2018. "The Cycle of Child Protection Services Involvement: A Cohort Study of Adolescent Mothers." *Pediatrics*, 141, 6.

Yohani, S. 2010. "Nurturing Hope in Refugee Children During Early Years of Post-War Adjustment." *Children and Youth Services Review*, 32: 865–873.

Youth Leaving Care Working Group. 2013. *Blueprint for Fundamental Change to Ontario's Child Welfare System*. <www.children.gov.on.ca>.

4

Symbolic and Discursive Violence in Media Representations

Portrayals of Indigenous and Muslim Youth in the Canadian Press

Yasmin Jiwani

edia representations play a key role in influencing social policy and
everyday practices between minority and majority populations. As
media theorists note, the effects of such mediated portrayals are not direct,
but rather indirect, interwoven and textured into our everyday common-
sense knowledge (Hall 2007; Kellner 2003/1995). The media tell us what
to pay attention to and how to understand such representations within
the context of daily life. In so doing, the media are indelibly steeped in
and reproduce dominant ideologies. Such ideologies are, as Stuart Hall
contends, "images, concepts and premises which provide the frameworks
through which we represent, interpret, understand and 'make sense' of
some aspect of social existence" (1990: 8)

The news media are a prominent site of ideological production and
reproduction (Allan 2004; Bennett 1996; Gitlin 1979; Wykes 2001).
Through their stories, they narrativize the nation, drawing attention to
issues that demand attention and, in the process, the actions or inactions
of state agencies. They identify the threats to the nation and to citizen
well-being. At the same time, they reassure citizens about the stability of
their immediate world and of the problems "out there" affecting the rest of
the world (Kaplan 2003; Lull and Hinerman 1997). This chapter examines
media representations in the *Globe and Mail* of two marginalized groups:
Indigenous and Muslim youth As the oldest and most reputable of the
Canadian dailies, the *Globe and Mail*'s stories also represent an archival

repository of state practices and policies, as well as identifying topics that are relevant to society as a whole.

Symbolic violence and discursive violence in news accounts occur in various ways. Symbolic violence refers to the unconscious ways in which dominance is exercised, through language, comportment, habits and the like (Bourdieu 2001). As a form of violence, it legitimates dominance by naturalizing it as part of the way things are. Media stereotypes are one way in which symbolic violence is enacted, for they perpetuate certain normative behaviours that are often internalized even by those who are subject to such violence. However, when groups are absented from any form of representation in the media, they are symbolically annihilated. For instance, Gaye Tuchman (1978), a prominent feminist theorist, argued that the lack of representation of women in the media constituted a form of symbolic annihilation.

Discursive violence is yet another way in which stereotypes function to represent particular truth claims about different groups in society. Discourse refers to both the ways and the kinds of language used to describe groups. Since language is never innocent, the words used and their connotations seal particular interpretations and meanings (Coates and Wade 2007; van Dijk 1993). Discursive violence refers to how language is used to communicate symbolic violence. Put differently, it refers to how words are used to suggest particular interpretations that symbolically inferiorize, trivialize or demonize particular individuals or groups.

In examining representations of Indigenous and Muslim youth, we begin by situating these groups within the larger context of societal constructions of youth in general. While both Indigenous and Muslim youth are encompassed within the overall category of "youth," they are marked by the specific and historically inscribed mythologies that not only antedate them but also influence the ways in which they are seen and reported about. More specifically, these mythologies have to do with the ways in which Indigenous Peoples have been viewed historically through colonially inscribed race. For example, the myth of the savage has a long history and continues to haunt contemporary representations of Indigenous Peoples (Dhamoon and Abu-Laban 2009; Ross 1998). Similarly, the Muslim as the barbaric other is steeped in the encounter between the West and Islam (Said 1978; Shaheen 2003), but its spectral presence is apparent in the discursive constructions that permeate news discourse. As Michel Foucault contends, the savage was conceptualized in anthropological and juridical thought as the "natural" man — the noble savage, who is interested in exchange and can be redeemed. The barbarian, in contrast, is beyond redemption. Unlike the savage, the barbarian stands outside of civilization: "He does not make his entrance into history by founding a society, but by penetrating a civilization, setting it ablaze and groups respectively destroying it" (Foucault 2003: 195)

Common to both mythologies is the notion that neither Indigenous nor Muslim peoples "fit" within the body politic. Both groups engage in criminal behaviours, and both are construed as problematic. In the sections that follow, we trace how contemporary representations of youth in the *Globe and Mail* work to support these ideological mythologies, paying particular attention to the gendered dynamics at play. How are young women from these communities represented, and in what ways do these representations lend themselves to how the young men are viewed?

As a caveat, in tracing and documenting these representations, we do not wish to suggest that all journalists and reporters are racist. Rather, as per Stuart Hall's (1990) illuminating analysis of the media and racism, we argue that the systemic racism that structures society inevitably slips into the kind of reporting practices that inhere within news organizations, and if some do not do so, differences in individual articles do not shift the weight of sedimented discourses. In other words, to have some stories that are "positively" framed does not detract from a larger meta-narrative that governs such representations; instead, the positive representations become yoked to this narrative, leading to such stories being framed as stories of exceptional personalities. The dominance of whiteness positions differences at the margins, and in this sense, stories of Indigenous and Muslim youth are cast through a white lens. Hence, our focus here is not on the "positive" stories per se, but rather the ones that dominated the corpus of our data — the thematic clusters that were the most salient.

Situating Indigenous and Muslim Youth

If dominant characterizations of youth in general situate them at the interstices of societal troubles and as being troublesome, what is the portrayal of marginalized youth? According to Statistics Canada's 2018 Demographic Estimates program, there are seven million youth, between the ages of 15 and 29, in Canada. In 2017, 27 percent were categorized as visible minorities (people of colour), and they were mostly concentrated in large urban cities (Toronto, Vancouver and Montreal in that order). Indigenous youth comprise anywhere from 1 percent (in the Toronto area) to 18 percent of the population (in Thunder Bay), and the Aboriginal Statistics based on the National Household Survey, 2011, puts the 15–24 years category at 18.2 percent.

In 2011, the Muslim population in Canada constituted 3.2 percent (1,053,945) of the total population. Of this, youth as a category approximated 9.22 percent (97,160), a figure derived from the Muslim population enrolled in post-secondary education (Hamdani 2015). Daood Hamdani also points to the presence of Aboriginal Muslims, numbering 1,065 in 2011, which demonstrates the intersectionality of these identity categories. The structural violence experienced by both Indigenous and Muslim groups differs but overlaps. It includes poverty, under/unemployment, state violence, intimate partner and peer violence, dislocation and displacement, stereotyping and stigmatization (Abdi 2015; de Finney 2015; Harding 2006; Maira 2009, 2010; Markstrom 2011). These forms of violence also texture the lives of Indigenous and Muslim youth.

Methodology

In charting representations of marginalized youth, we focused on Indigenous and Muslim youth as they were represented in stories published in the *Globe and Mail* from 2010 to 2013. We compiled all the stories that focused on youth (2,338 stories), and from these, separated out stories that dealt specifically with Indigenous youth (200) and Muslim youth (160), respectively (see Table 4-1).

Table 4-1: Number of Stories about Indigenous and Muslim Youth per Year (2010–2013)

Year	Indigenous	Muslim	Other	Total
2010	40	53	444	537
2011	53	15	559	627
2012	48	38	512	598
2013	59	54	463	576
Total	200	160	1978	2338

Figure 4-1 shows the numerical representation of the stories focusing on these two groups of youth in a pie chart. Clearly, both groups are under-represented in news stories about them: 8.55 percent of stories represent the lived realities of 18.2 percent of the Indigenous youth population, while 6.84 percent of stories concerning Muslim youth symbolically represent their realities and lived experiences. However, this numerical under-representation denotes one dimension of the issue — namely, that a reader of the *Globe and Mail* is not likely to encounter many representations of these groups. More critically though, it is the kind of portrayals that the paper circulates about these groups that is cogent.

Figure 4-1: Stories Focusing on Indigenous and Muslim Youth in the *Globe and Mail*

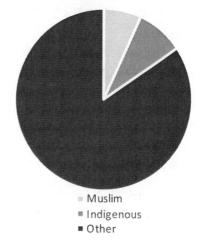

- Muslim
- Indigenous
- Other

Indigenous Youth Stories

> Indigenous peoples are just that: Indigenous to the lands they inhabit, in contrast to and in contention with the colonial societies and states that have spread out from Europe and other centres of empire. It is this oppositional, place-based existence, along with the consciousness of being in struggle against the dispossessing and demeaning fact of colonization by foreign peoples that fundamentally distinguishes Indigenous peoples from the peoples of the world. (Alfred and Corntassel 2005: 597, quoted in Barker 2015: 45)

Based on our census of all youth stories, we identified 200 stories that dealt specifically with Indigenous youth. We are cognizant of the fact that in categorizing all Indigenous youth under the umbrella term of "Indigenous" we do not address the numerous differences between Indigenous nations or their diverse geographies. Inuit youth in the North, for example, have different life circumstances than Mohawk youth in Montreal, whose experiences differ greatly from Haida youth growing up in Haida Gwaii, in the Pacific northwest. These different circumstances and experiences exercise considerable influence on how Indigenous youth see the world and view representations of themselves in that world. However, for our purposes, we collapsed these distinctions in order to observe the broader patterns that were cohering these different representations. In part, our rationale for doing so was informed by the existing literature on Indigenous youth, which highlights the common and widespread impact of colonialism and the stereotypical depictions of indigeneity that have and continue to circulate in popular culture and, until recently, in academic curricula (Arshad-Ayaz 2016; Harding 2006; Chartrand 1996; Steckley 2003).

Thematic Analysis of Indigenous Youth Representation

> Ask your average Canadian their impression of this country's indigenous people and their hopes for prosperity, stability and success in their communities. In all likelihood, you will hear about a story they read recently involving an aboriginal community's struggle with housing, education, youth motivation or even suicide.
>
> What you probably won't hear is an answer that demonstrates even a basic knowledge of Canada's indigenous people's involvement in the economic growth of this country; the initiatives they have under way for preparing the large numbers of indigenous youth poised to enter Canada's labour force; or even the names of two or three aboriginal organizations achieving remarkable success with their enterprises. (Calliou 2012: A15)

Brian Calliou's comment in the *Globe and Mail* stems from his experience as the director of Indigenous Leadership and Management at the Banff Centre. While speaking to the success of Aboriginal organizations, Cailliou's comment points to the realities of the stories that Canadians are apt to hear from their mainstream media. The stereotypes that are circulated in these stories are one-dimensional portrayals that lead to skewed interpretations of a complex reality.

The Royal Commission on Aboriginal Peoples also found that the media tended to exclude Indigenous voices and issues, and if covered, tended to frame them in stereotypical ways: "1) Pathetic Victims, 2) Angry Warriors and 3) Noble Environmentalists" (Harding 2005: 313). In his study of the coverage of Aboriginal people in three Canadian newspapers, spanning a period of four months in 2002, Robert Harding found the recurrence of many of these stereotypes, the predominant one being Indigenous Peoples as "pathetic victims" and as "angry warriors" (322). An emergent stereotype focused on "Aboriginal peoples as incompetent or corrupt financial managers" (324). Similarly, Frances Henry and Carol Tator's (2002) analysis of a case concerning a legal trial involving the sexual assault of a young Indigenous woman found that Indigenous Peoples were constructed as problems for society or as threats to the social order. While these studies do not focus on youth representations per se, their findings nonetheless reflect a continuity with the representations that we found in our corpus of news stories.

Representations of Indigeneity and race in general do not remain static. They evolve over time (Hall 1993). They are, as Stuart Hall puts it, "floating signifiers" (1997: 1) because they can be used to signify a range of different aspects of a group, which can then be harnessed to support a particular interpretation of that group. For example, a woman of colour can be represented as an exotic temptress or as a pathetic victim of male violence, or even as an evil, conniving other. How these characteristics are used depends on the logic of power that is being used to harness particular representations in order to communicate a certain perception or truth.

In our corpus of stories, we noticed an evolving narrative that began with a stark reminder of the growing population of Indigenous youth who were repeatedly cast as abject others, a stereotype that we discuss below. However, in the course of the four years of news stories that we examined, we noticed a definite difference — one that we link to the emergence of the Idle No More movement of Indigenous rights (2011–12). Subsequent to the birth of this movement, we observed a change in how Indigenous youth were represented; this time, they were portrayed as being more active, as reconnecting with Indigenous issues and politics, and as engaged political actors. See for instance, this news account:

> The youth know what's going on and they feel the pain and they don't want to live like that any more. So they are standing up. And they are backing up their chiefs. And the chiefs need to go

forward with their people and sit down with the government and the Crown. (Galloway 2012a: A1)

Nevertheless, the construction of Indigenous youth as in trouble, troubled and troubling for society continued to be a common thread throughout the stories we examined.

Indigenous Youth as Troubled, Troubling and in Trouble

Victims of a legacy of colonialism and the generation impacted by parents who were victimized by the residential school system, these youth were portrayed as a generation that had lost all hope, vulnerable and at risk of staggering rates of suicide, criminality and substance abuse and suffering from a range of medical conditions, which span the continuum from depression, diabetes, sexually transmitted diseases, teenage pregnancies, HIV and the like. However, in contrast to Harding's study, the news accounts consistently provided an explanatory frame for these conditions, linking them back to the structural violence of poverty, dispossession and the legacies of colonialism. Hence, rather than being "pathetic victims," as was the case in earlier representations, they tended to be framed as failed individuals. For instance, this story which focused on a low ranked school in Hazelton, BC, described the situation as follows:

> Hazelton has been in the news in recent years for having the highest youth suicide rate in the province. The 345 mostly aboriginal students enrolled at the high school come from surrounding first nations villages. Many have to travel more than an hour on a bus to get to classes in the morning. Too many haven't had a bite to eat by the time they get there. Who knows what they had to deal with the night before? Some have witnessed their mothers being beaten to a pulp by alcohol-enraged fathers. The last thing anyone's talking about at home is homework. With little supervision to speak of, many kids develop drug and alcohol problems. Many of the kids at Hazelton Secondary have had problems from the day they were born. By the time they were old enough to enter kindergarten, they were already falling behind. Most were "at risk" — meaning they didn't possess the language skills children should have at that age. Many didn't know colours, for instance. Or the difference between an apple and an orange. (Mason 2012: S1)

In another column, Indigenous journalist and author Richard Wagamese penned the following description:

> To be Indian in Canada today is to see your children suffer. On reserves, in Métis communities and in the cities, aboriginal children go hungry, lack warm clothing and solid educational resources, die as infants at a rate two to four times the national average and endure immunization rates 20 times lower than the general population. They suffer because different orders of government dispute who's responsible to pay or provide for a service.
>
> To be Indian in Canada today is to see youth languish in chronic unemployment and malaise, endure high rates of alcohol, drug and solvent abuse or die by suicide at a rate five to seven times higher than non-aboriginal youth. It is to see the future of your people fail to finish high school or get skills training; too often they become parents themselves at a frighteningly early age. This, despite Canada's being a signatory to the United Nations Convention on the Rights of the Child. (2013: A11)

Wagamese's description of Indigenous youth is not designed to feed into a construction of these youth as troubled or troubling, but rather to point to the stark reality of the issues that they face and the context in which they are situated; a context they have inherited as a result of the structural power relations that disadvantage them in multiple ways. However, consumed in a manner in which all news stories get read, the overall impression that a reader might have is that of a failed generation that is too damaged to be salvaged. There are constant references in the media to "tackling native problems" (Radwanski 2011: AS), and the "stubborn problem of aboriginal crime" (Everett-Green 2012: F1). Patricia Pearson insightfully notes:

> When remote reserves slide into crisis because of chronic poverty and a lack of training, Canadians respond by rearing up into high intellectual dudgeon about the "Indian problem." The chiefs are corrupt! It's the fault of the feds! The provinces are to blame! (2011: F3)

This evasion of responsibility on the part of government and its various agencies effectively casts the blame onto Indigenous Nations. In other words, one can tease through this fabric of stories a type of blame-the-victim logic. This is not to suggest that the reporters writing these stories take such a view. In fact, many of the stories are written in ways that are critical of both the government and industries and take the side of the Indigenous communities that are the subjects of the stories. However, what occurs in the cycle of the newspaper is that these accounts accrue a layered effect and the repetitions in the descriptions engender a frame of interpretation. Frames, as Robert Entman (2003) argues,

> that employ more culturally resonant terms have the greatest potential for influence. They use words and images highly salient in the culture, which is to say *noticeable, understandable, memorable, and emotionally charged*. Magnitude taps the *prominence* and *repetition* of the framing words and images. The more resonance and magnitude, the more likely the framing is to evoke similar thoughts and feelings in large portions of the audience. (417, emphasis in the original)

The magnitude and resonance of these frames is rooted in the historical memory of how Indigenous Peoples and Nations have been reported. Thus, the stereotypes identified by the Royal Commission on Aboriginal Peoples are not extinct; rather, their grammar remains in shaping incoming information and tweaking in ways that are legible within the contemporary context.

Failed Systems and Failed Youth

In the news stories we examined, there is a consonance between the failed generation and failed states and systems. Nowhere is this more apparent than in news accounts dealing with Inuit youth, as evident in this editorial:

> Nunavut belongs to the young, and the young are neglected. The most neglected of all are the most vulnerable, those children who have been sexually or physically abused or whose basic needs have not been met, owing to the substance abuse of their parents. And the Nunavut government, which should be protecting these children, is heaping more neglect on them. It is sending the message that no one cares about them.

The young people have sent their own message about how they feel about their lives, in the most vehement and devastating way available to them: Those aged 15 to 19 commit suicide at a rate 10 times the Canadian average. Neglect is surely not the only reason for this epidemic of self-destruction, but it is a dangerous message to send in such a community.

It is especially dangerous because Nunavut, created in 1999, has the country's youngest population, with 40 per cent of its 33,000 residents under 19. Of those, 633 receive some form of care or support service from the territory's Health and Social Services Department. (Editorial 2011)

And in another account, the same statistics are repeated, albeit in more detail, with a reference to Nunavut as a failed state:

With this kind of havoc and hardship, it's hard not to conclude that Nunavut is a failing state — that the bold experiment in domestic nation-building Canada launched in 1999 has gone deeply wrong. Is it at risk of becoming our own Haiti of the Arctic Circle, or can something be done to reverse the damage? (White 2011: F2)

This relationship between failed and failing youth and failed systems represents a significant departure from previous characterizations of Indigenous Peoples. Whereas previously, the failure was blamed on the victims, now the failure is based on failed systems, whether these be governments, agencies or systems of care. But central to such failure is the inability of the individual to fit, the inability to transcend the physical and psychological difficulties of the colonial legacy and the failure to become productive. Such failures are individualized, even while being attributed to external, structural forces, as evidenced in the repeated references to high suicide rates and high rates of incarceration and substance abuse. So, no matter how hard systems try, they fail because the people themselves are failing. Hence, the description one encounters in these news accounts read as follows: Aboriginals suffer from "debilitating cycles of problems" (Simpson 2011: A19), and despite "injections of money from Ottawa and the De Beers mining company," they are "unable to overcome deep-rooted problems" (Keevil 2011: A12).

Rescuing Youth: Extracting Labour

Leading from many of these accounts, especially those dealing with education, were stories about how different organizations, Indigenous and non-Indigenous, were stepping in by offering programs and services for youth. While some of these initiatives were clearly driven by religious organizations, for example, Youth for Christ in Winnipeg (White 2010: A3), others were predicated on the heighted awareness of Indigenous youth as an "untapped" source of labour for economic growth and entrepreneurship. For example, in a report in the business section, former Canadian prime minister Paul Martin writes:

> One of our programs in the schools is what we call the Youth Entrepreneurship Program. It's a program teaching young aboriginals how to start a business. We go into marketing and accounting, basically because it's important for them to understand how you start a business and how you become an entrepreneur. But also, it's been proven that there's a greater chance that they will stay in school and graduate if they can see a concrete reason for doing so. (Martin 2011: B5)

While Martin's motivations may have been instrumental, other educational initiatives were more cognizant of the potential of Indigenous youth as labour to be exploited:

> At stake are not only the social and economic fortunes of the country's aboriginal population, but the economic potential of the labour market, which affects all Canadians. Left unaddressed, this human capital deficit will only grow, as native youth are one of the fastest growing demographic groups in Canada. According to Statistics Canada, the aboriginal population is projected to reach 1.4 million by 2017, and is a relatively youthful group. The median age of aboriginals is 28, compared with 41 among the rest of the population. Eighteen per cent of aboriginal people are between the ages of 15 to 24, according to the 2011 National Household Survey, which is the most recent census data released Wednesday. (Tsaparis 2013: B11)

The connotations of stories that treat Indigenous youth as "human capital" are obviously grounded in a neoliberal logic that places the market first and views human labour purely as an exploitable resource. What is interesting is the underlying message that only through making these youth economically productive can their value as human beings actually be realized. Or, from a more cynical viewpoint, Indigenous youth are viewed in the same way that Indigenous lands have and continue to be — as exploitable resources. Anishinaabe scholar Leanne Simpson poignantly remarks:

> Extraction and assimilation go together. Colonialism and capi-talism are based on extracting and assimilating. My land is seen as a resource. My relatives in the plant and animal worlds are seen as resources. My culture and knowledge is a resource. My body is a resource and my children are a resource because they are the potential to grow, maintain, and uphold the extraction-assimilation system. The act of extraction removes all of the relationships that give whatever is being extracted meaning. (quoted in Barker 2015: 45)

It is no wonder that when faced with extractive logics of major corpora-tions, Indigenous youth become primary movers in protecting their lands.

Protecting the Land and Idle No More

The focus on Indigenous lands for resource extraction has not only led to companies investing in these communities, but also in many cases overriding Indigenous concerns and ownership of the land. This in turn has resulted in protests, and Indigenous youth have prefigured largely as being involved in attempts to stop such exploitation and reclaim their lands. However, these attempts have not always been viewed positively, with some stories, such as this one, focusing on the violence:

> Support has poured in for Elsipogtog First Nation from other native groups across the country after Thursday's violence, in which police cars were torched, rocks thrown and protesters pepper-sprayed. Over the weekend, the native leadership there called for calm — and an uneasy quiet has fallen, although pro-testers remain at the encampment. (Taber 2013: A5)

In many cases, stories about protests were linked to the emergence of

Idle No More (Galloway 2012: A4; 2013b: A1), signalling growing youth involvement in the movement. However, unlike the protests aimed around resource extractions, the Idle No More protests were generally framed as peaceful (Galloway 2013a: A4). Coverage of the movement also revealed the involvement of more young women (Friesen 2013: A4).

In our corpus of news stories, there was a fair amount of coverage of the Idle No More movement. Beginning with the hunger strike by Chief Theresa Spence, the coverage continued throughout the year. The news coverage highlighted women's contribution to the movement from its founders to the young women directly engaged in promoting its messages. As journalist Joe Friesen described it:

> [Ms. Lee] sees herself and the aboriginal friends she has made on campus as belonging to a new generation, one that will enjoy the benefits of university training, good jobs and an assurance about their place in the world. Like her, her friends are almost all the first of their family to go to university. They are determined to speak up against federal policies they see as wrongheaded and harmful to the environment. They are also aware of trying to live up to the expectations that come with their education. (2013: A4)

Thus, unlike the helpless and hopelessness depicted in the earlier news accounts, these later stories that focus on the Idle No More movement offer a more positive view of Indigenous youth, and particularly, of young Indigenous women.

Gendered Frames

Reference to gender in these accounts occur in various instances, from women's representation in the Assembly of First Nations (AFN) (Wagamese 2012: A11), to missing and murdered Indigenous women (Bailey and Tu Thanh Ha 2012: A7; Bailey and Dhillon 2012: S1; Galloway 2012: A4), as well as to the Idle No More movement, sparked by Chief Theresa Spence's hunger strike (Friesen 2013: A4). Central to many of these issues was the lack of police attention and intervention in the cases of the missing and murdered women, as well as the assault of Indigenous women by the RCMP (Mackreal 2013a: A3). The latter story focuses on a report released by Human Rights Watch, which noted:

Complaints documented … ranged from handcuffs being applied too tightly to an unwarranted attack by a police dog against a 12-year-old girl and allegations of sexual abuse and rape. The report did not include the full names of many of the alleged victims because it said they were too fearful of repercussions from police to allow themselves to be identified. (Mackreal 2013a: A3)

What this news article reveals is a rather common pattern: namely, that if an outside agency releases a report documenting the violations against Indigenous Peoples, it is more likely to get press attention, and the press in turn will seek responses from the government. If Indigenous Peoples were to report such violations without an intervening body that commands legitimacy, for example, the numerous demands made by the AFN to the government about violence against women, the response does not seem to be so immediate.

As with their male counterparts, women and girls were referenced in stories about their over-representation in prisons. However, for women, their victimhood was underscored by the realities that they were often subjected to violence both from men in their communities and males outside, as well as by institutions like the police and the prisons (Mackrael 2013b: A1; Seguin 2010: A6). Many of the stories referenced the deeply distrustful relations between Indigenous communities and the police. Similar to Indigenous young men, these women were also described in terms of their high levels of substance abuse, engaging in street prostitution and having a lack of support and access to resources. This is resonant with the "squaw" stereotype in contrast to Pocahontas (Green 2001). However, and in contrast to young men, young Indigenous women were more active in the Idle No More movement and were more likely to be educated.

Summary

For indigenous communities the issue is not just that they are blamed for their own failures but that it is also communicated to them, explicitly or implicitly, that they themselves have no solutions to their own problems. This view is exacerbated by media and politician rhetoric about the general hopelessness or corruption of indigenous communities and indigenous peoples. (Smith 1999: 92)

As Linda Tuhiwai Smith argues above, the issue of representations is not simply confined to a historical record-keeping or an archival repository of the stories of the nation, but one which indelibly also marks out those who are written about either as successes or as failures. Internalized, such representations have devastating consequences, and in the case of Indigenous youth, it also shapes the ways in which they are treated by societal institutions. As troubled, in trouble and troubling youth, Indigenous youth are confined to the negative end of the continuum. The only socially acceptable ways out are for them to conform to societal dictates and become "productive" members through participating in education programs, entrepreneurship initiatives and the like. However, the empowering effects of the Idle No More movement suggest that it is only through these indigenously rooted initiatives — which are informed by indigenous knowledge and accompanied by mobilizing action — that Indigenous youth find an expression of themselves and their realities that are outside of the constraints of normative expectations and values. Nevertheless, through the repetition of dominant frames, propagated often unwittingly, Indigenous youth representations continue to be subject to symbolic and discursive violence. In that sense, these representations are yoked to societal disturbances (through protest), criminality (prisons, gangs), substance abuse, ill health, government dependency and an ascribed inability to transcend the historical and contemporary circumstances forged by the colonial past.

Muslim Youth Stories

> We need to be extra nice just because we're Muslims. We need to go beyond certain limits, which is very unfortunate for people like me. Sometimes the media will call something Islamic terrorism — once you call it Islamic, you've brought me into the picture even though I haven't done something wrong. (Amin Elshorbagy, president of the Canadian Islamic Congress, quoted in Press 2013)

Even before the tragic events of September 11, 2001, Muslims have long been cast as a threat in the Western imagination (Karim 2000; Said 1978, 1981). However, since that time, the focus on Muslims as terrorists and of Muslim women as imperiled others has permeated popular culture (Boggs and Pollard 2006; Hirji 2011; Jiwani 2010; Morey and Yaqin 2011; Razack 2008a). And in that sense, it has also seeped into and textured stories presented in the news media (Byng 2010; Jiwani and Dessner 2016).

Our corpus of news stories consists of 160 accounts that specifically referenced Muslim youth or significantly referenced them in passing. In parsing through these stories, we grouped them around the dominant themes that emerged. These included radicalization and terror, surveillance, immigration, gang violence and honour killings.

Thematic Analysis of Muslim Youth Representation

In 2006, with the arrest of the "Toronto 18," a group consisting of young Muslim men based on their alleged involvement in a terrorist plot, the news media quickly embraced the template of home-grown terrorism (Miller and Sack 2010). Indeed, so swift was the condemnation of the attack and the connection with Islam that renowned veteran reporter Robert Fisk (2006) titled his report for the *Independent* "How racism has invaded Canada." Fisk was calling attention to the way in which the *Globe and Mail* referred to the alleged terrorists as "brown skinned." He noted that the term "'Home-grown terrorists' has become the theme of the month — even though the 'terrorists' have yet to stand trial." Arrested by 400 police officers, the Toronto 18 were subsequently sentenced. This sentencing spanned several years, culminating in one of the years in our survey of stories.

In their study of the news coverage in the immediate aftermath of the arrests of the Toronto 18, John Miller and Cybele Sack analyzed five dailies and *Maclean's* news magazine, including the opinions, letters to the editor and editorials. They found that all the dailies perpetrated a "moral panic" and a "homegrown terror" frame:

> "Moral panic" — the most extreme frame — casts this unproven case of apprehended violence as a profound crisis that imperils Canadians' way of life. It's seen as a wake-up call, forcing Canadians to re-evaluate larger issues such as our policies on immigration and multiculturalism. The "homegrown" frame, on the other hand, contains elements of the discourse of national unity (Muslims are ungrateful immigrants who do not identify with Canadian values) and the discourse of otherness (they prefer

their own alien cultural values and make unreasonable demands for accommodation from white society). Both these frames imply that Canadians have something to fear and that Muslim terrorists are in our midst. Both can be termed "alarmist" because they have the potential of causing attitudinal or legislative changes that penalize the target group. (2010:284–285)

It is not surprising that many of the stories in our corpus of articles echoed these alarmist tones, suggesting that only Muslim youth commit such crimes and only Muslims are vulnerable to radicalization. The critical aspect of this coverage was the emphasis on "homegrown" which suggests that these youth cannot be identified immediately because they camouflage themselves as "regular" youth. Here is one example of the kind of coverage describing a ringleader of the group:

An educated and affluent thirty something entrepreneur — born in the Middle East but raised in Canada — who allegedly saw an opportunity to profit from the chaos he would cause.… A decade older, better educated and far better off than most his co-conspirators, Mr. Abdelhaleem doesn't fit the profile of the teenagers and twenty somethings convicted to date. (Freeze 2010: A1)

The profile becomes important in terms of how it masks the "true" identity of these terrorists. Speaking to the acts of racial profiling, Sherene Razack (2008b) argues that this is the first step towards putting Muslims in a camp — a camp where they are denied rights and where they can be killed with impunity, or more to the point, excised from the body politic through deportation.

This theme of "homegrown terrorism" was explicitly linked to issues of immigration, whereupon the argument in many of these news accounts suggests that Muslims can't be assimilated and hence cannot be accepted in Canadian society. In a story titled "Son of Alleged Terrorist Faces Deportation," immigration and terrorism are connected in how the story is told, alleging a deep, if not biological connection, between the father's links to terrorist organizations and the son's proclivity to crime (Freeze 2012: A3). The end result is the son's deportation as he simply doesn't fit into Canadian society, which implicitly is considered law-abiding. The implication is that terrorism is imported, and though it is homegrown, it is because of immigration that it been transplanted onto Canadian soil. As Caroline Corbin (2017) astutely notes, Terrorists are always seen as Muslims!

The tie between young Muslims and terrorism was also evident in the coverage of Somali Canadian youth. The issue was how the youth were being recruited by the terrorist organization Al-Shaba in East Africa and were leaving Canada to participate in the terrorist activists abroad (Freeze 2010: A6). As Black and Muslim, Somali Canadians are poised at the intersections of two stigmatized identities. They experience a higher rate of unemployment than other groups, both white and racialized. Their level of poverty is higher, and they are the subject of surveillance, being stopped and searched, more frequently than other minoritized youth.

In the years of coverage that we examined, there were reports of Somali Canadian youth as victims of gang murders resulting from their involvement in the drug trade. In her analysis of the media representations of Somali Canadian youth, Sagal Jibril (2011) notes that the "words race and racism are almost always absent in these stories" (26) and further that "violent deaths involving Somali Canadian youth are being treated as an 'immigrant' problem, despite the fact that many of those who were murdered were born here" (20). In his analysis of Project Traveller, a police raid-and-seize operation in a Somali-concentrated neighbourhood of Greater Toronto, Kris Millett (2015) comments:

> The Somali folk devil has been made out to be a surplus "unproductive neoliberal subject," a racialized group requiring policing and surveillance due to proclivity to criminality; a "welfare fraudster" with a culture that does not align with Canadian values, and lastly, an "illegitimate subject," surveilled, incarcerated, and deported as a dangerous security threat. (2015: 59)

News accounts suggested that Somali Canadian youth were a lost generation, caught between the war-torn generation of their refugee parents and the structural violence of poverty and alienation that characterized their lives in Canada. Lured by the prospect of making quick money facilitated their involvement in the drug trade:

> The young drug dealer, originally from the East Mall area of

Etobicoke, thought he'd found paradise, but he needed help. He went home seeking recruits, and two Somali-Canadians were first to volunteer.... For a Somali community struggling with poverty, it was an attractive proposition. (Wingrove and Friesen 2010: A1)

Despite calls by the Somali Canadian community for resources and for an investigation into the killings of numerous Somali youths who had gone to Alberta in order to improve their economic prospects, there was little follow up on why the state and provincial authorities were not doing enough. Instead, the focus was on the criminality of these youth accompanied by pleas for help from the larger Somali Canadian community (Mackrael 2012: A15).

Surveillance is offered as a natural means to secure the nation, and in this regard, there were numerous stories of how the Somali community, in particular, but all Muslim communities in general, were asked to spy on their neighbours by the government and the Canadian Security and Intelligence Service (CSIS): "Ottawa urges immigrant communities to watch out for suspicious behaviour" (Chase 2010: A1; see also Chase and White 2010: A3). And in a subsequent editorial, the paper took the position that "Tipping off is a duty" (2010: A20), warning its readers that Al-Qaeda needs to recruit Muslims "and the West needs good Muslims, as the vast majority are." The comma separating out the "good Muslims" and the rest of the sentence — "the vast majority are" — connotes a separation signifying an afterthought. Further, the separation between "good" Muslims and "bad" Muslims, rests on a binary. As Mahmood Mamdani (2004: 24) points out, in Western discourse, "good Muslims are modern, secular, and Westernized, but bad Muslims are doctrinal, antimodern, and virulent."

The good/bad dichotomy is anchored in the notion of "culture talk"; it is a label often used to obfuscate power relations and structural violence and to offer culturalized explanations for differences. Davina Bhandar points out:

The present-day "culture talk" cannot be divided from the economic context of the intensification of uneven globalisation. The "good" Muslim is a version of a secular Jew, or a liberal Muslim, or a Muslim who celebrates and consumes western culture — an acceptable, tolerant modern subject, not bound by religious proclivities. The "bad" Muslim, as Mamdani illustrates, is the erroneously named "fundamentalist" Muslim, pre-modern and cast out of contemporary political and cultural civility (see also Razack 2008a). (Bhandar 2010: 339)

"Culture talk" is one way of dividing Muslims who are acceptable from those who fall outside the boundaries of normativity, where normativity is defined in the Foucauldian sense of the norm as "something that can be applied to both a body one wishes to discipline and a population one wishes to regularize" (Foucault 2003: 253; see also Riley 2009).

This culturalized frame has been used to explain away intimate partner and familial violence in Muslim families. In such cases, there is scant attention to the deskilling of Muslim immigrants and the pressures that unemployment and underemployment invokes within the household or even why clinging to faith and tradition becomes a way of salvaging one's dignity in the face of the racism, exclusion and Islamophobia that Muslims face (see Haque 2010).

Gendered Dimensions

Central to the construction of the bad Muslim is the tactical use of women's status under Islam. In the West, Islam is considered ultra-patriarchal and responsible for the oppression of Muslim women. From the hijab and niqab as imposed codes of dressing to the restrictions that women face in terms of their freedom of mobility and their forced confinement within the home where they are presumably subject to psychological, financial and physical violence, Muslim women are seen as oppressed. This is in stark contrast to the reality that Muslim women are more highly educated than their white Canadian counterparts, and young Muslim women are more present in non-traditional occupations and education programs like engineering (Hamdani 2015). Moreover, many young Muslim women voluntarily adopt the hijab and see it as a form of self-empowerment and assertion (MacDonald 2006; Rhys and Vashi 2007). This raises the question of whether Muslim women really need to be saved from the clutches of patriarchal Islam (Abu Lughod 2002). Yet, the generalized stereotype of oppressed Muslim women prevails, especially with regard to young Muslim women.

Within our corpus of news articles, stories about the murder of Aqsa Parvez, a young immigrant Muslim woman by her father and brother, and about three other young women and one older woman from the Shafia household who were killed by a father, mother and brother, were dominant. These stories, as Yasmin Jiwani (2014) details, offered an explanatory frame that clearly attributes these femicides to Islam and labels the murders as honour killings. In both cases, the media drew attention to how these young women were caught in a cultural bind — torn between the demands of their Muslim backgrounds and the demands of Western youth culture. One article surmised: "The youngest of eight in a family that had immigrated from Pakistan when she was 11, Ms. Parvez fought with her family over her desire to wear Western clothing, work outside the home and visit schoolmates" (Allan 2010).

In a column titled "Our daughters in peril; Forget Islamophobia, this comes down to speaking out against family violence," which would ostensibly draw attention to the widespread and transcultural phenomenon of gendered violence, popular columnist Margaret Wente opined:

> Intense conflict between conservative immigrant fathers and their modern daughters is nothing new. But this kind of violence — often premeditated, and condoned by the community — is driven by a *cultural belief that fathers ought to be able to control their daughters.* Daughters who act immorally — by talking to boys, or going to the mall, or wearing immodest clothes — bring shame and humiliation onto their entire families. Whatever punishment they suffer is widely thought to be their fault. (2010, my emphasis)

"Culture talk" becomes "cultural conflict" in this paradigmatic way of thinking. This notion of a conflict between cultures to explain femicides implicitly offers a logic that only by annihilating particular cultures, can these young women be saved. When they cannot be saved, it is because of their obsessive attachment to a misogynist culture. This was indeed the explanation used when Afghan women, during the so-called rescue missions by the West, refused to unveil (see Arat-Koç 2002). Jasmin Zine (2009) refers to this as the "death by culture" frame. Using culture in this way enables a form of cultural racism.

In her analysis of the western reactions to Muslim women's veiling practices, Alia Al-Saji argues:

> In cultural racism, culture becomes nature. Bodies are not only

perceived as belonging to a different culture, they are also seen to be culturally determined and inferior as a result.... The determinism that characterizes cultural racism goes along with a construal of the other culture or religion (here Islam) as static, "closed" and incapable of progress — in contrast to western cultures which are understood to be open and hence perfectible, to be spaces that enable, rather than determine and limit, individual expression. (2010: 890)

This is precisely the kind of explanatory framework that was advanced in the coverage of the Shafia murders. For here, the focus was on the "closed" nature of Islam versus the lure of the progressive West, to which the young women were attracted because of its promise of sexual liberation.

The prosecution's core theory is that the three teens were murdered in an effort to cleanse the Shafia family's "honour," supposedly stained by the daughters' independent, rebellious conduct, particularly Zainab's and Sahar's interest in dating boys and in eschewing traditional Afghan mores. (Appleby 2012: A3)

In her analysis of sixty stories that were reported in the *Globe and Mail* between July 2009, when the bodies were discovered, to March 17, 2012, when the verdict in the legal case against the father, brother and mother was announced, Jiwani (2014) argues that the Shafia women were constructed as "worthy victims" because they fit preconceived notions of Muslim women needing to be saved. They had shown agency by wanting to leave their home in the face of the abuse they experienced. They had turned to authorities, who had failed them. They were young, beautiful and photogenic (indeed, the accounts were replete with pictures), and they expressed a fervent desire to be like "us" — like the dominant society.

"These people were from Afghanistan, and they knew about the 'honour code'" wrote Lysiane Gagnon (2012), a reporter for the *Globe*. Even Muslim guest writers condemned the killings, but here too, the play on cultural racism was evident in how they construed Muslim cultures:

The father who feels let down, even inferior because his pretty young daughters have boyfriends, wear makeup and may not bag the right Afghan husband should emigrate not to Canada but to some backward country that can offer him face-saving solutions. Mr. Shafia should have stayed in Dubai, his previous home, and Canadian immigration authorities should have examined the family's financially leveraged entry criteria more thoroughly. (Sheik 2012: A13)

While Nazneen Sheik's article was written to cast light on the widespread misogyny against young women in Muslim cultures, it is her view that this misogyny is imported from elsewhere that is problematic. It implies that there is no misogyny in Canada and further, that such crimes against young women would not have been committed had there been no immigration or if the immigration process had carefully screened for misogynist men. This assumption is clearly spurious given that young women are vulnerable to male violence, regardless of their cultural background.

The labelling of these femicides as honour killings when it occurs in Muslim families can be traced to the criminalization of Muslims after 9/11. In her analysis of the press coverage of honour killings in Canada, Saima Ishaq (2010) notes that two murders that occurred prior to 2001 were not labelled honour killings; they were described simply as familial homicides. In contrast, after the bombings of 9/11, Muslim femicides have been described as honour killings.

Throughout the coverage on the Shafia killings, the identities of the perpetrators and victims were consistently raised in terms of their immigrant status. Readers learned about how Mohamed Shafia came to Canada via Dubai from Afghanistan, with stops in between in various countries. He was wealthy and entered the country through the entrepreneur-investment program, and he was constantly travelling leaving his family to be "governed," not looked after, by his second wife and his son. Mohamed Shafia had a first wife who he had brought over by concealing her true identity. She was treated as a slave in his home and bullied by the second wife. The first wife had been barren while the second had four children, three of whom were the young women who were killed.

What was scarcely mentioned in the news accounts is how the forces of assimilation work on youth as pathways to "fitting in." Assimilation works through consumption, through buying and wearing products that youth identify as styles that will make them more acceptable and allow them to conform to hegemonic codes (Deutsch and Theodorou 2010). Hence, buying one's way into acceptance becomes part of the strategy for fitting in. This is resonant with Angela McRobbie's (2008) observation that "the hyper-visibility of pre-teen girls as the ideal subjects of feminine consumption marks out the contours of new modalities of gender performativity now routinely required of young girls, *as a condition of their wider intelligibility*, so that they can in effect count as girls" (546, emphasis added). The issue around culture conflict wasn't so much about a conflict between two cultures as about the pressures of fitting into the dominant society, which demands a certain degree of conformity, while navigating a way of surviving.

Immigration

In both the coverage of young Muslim men as terrorists and young Muslim women as victims of honour killings, the news accounts implicitly and explicitly mentioned immigration. Immigration had permitted the importation of terrorism onto Canadian soil. Even though the stories about young Muslim men were examples of "homegrown terrorism," they were nonetheless associated with the immigration of the fathers or families. Similarly, in the case of young Muslim women, immigration is blamed for the importation of "barbaric" cultural practices, which is how the Conservative Party of Canada described it in Citizenship Guide for immigrants, which continues to be there despite the change in government (Stone 2009)).

Conclusion

In conclusion, while Foucault's notions of the savage and the barbarian are fitting, they fail to capture the nuances of how Indigenous and Muslim youth are positioned and perceived in contemporary news media. Rather than simply being represented as savages, the discourse of savagery gets translated into criminality (see Ross 1998). Moreover, as Foucault argued, the savage can be redeemed, and this is apparent in how entrepreneurship and education programs around the development of particular skills are encouraged in order to save Indigenous youth and put them on a path of upward economic mobility. That the programs mentioned in our corpus of stories usually referenced resource extraction — working in mines and industries — suggests that the extractive logic of capitalism prevails and is a direct impetus for the programs. On the other hand, funding for education is a key priority for Indigenous groups such as the Assembly of First Nations and is clearly needed on many of the reserves, along with other necessities of life, such as clean water, functioning sewage systems and the like.

Central, however, to both groups is the trope of criminality, within which one can group issues such as drug use/substance abuse, gangs and other criminal behaviours, as well as the over-incarceration of Indigenous and Muslim youth. While Muslim youth are in most cases tarnished with the connotation of terrorism, Indigenous youth are constructed as engaging more in street crime. The trope of criminality functions as a way to suggest a hopeless generation that can only be rescued through government (read white) interventions. For young Indigenous women, it is the portrayal as victims that captures attention, though less so for those involved in affirming movements such as Idle No More. Moreover, it is often suggested that these women can survive and thrive given the appropriate resources and direction.

In the case of young Muslim women who had been killed, their victimhood was portrayed as the result of being trapped under oppressive conditions — conditions brought on by the ultra-patriarchal nature of Islam. On the other hand, young Muslim women were also seen as agentic and their behaviour valorized if they were attempting to "fit in" to the norms of the dominant society. In other words, if they behaved like the normative teenager through dressing like them, expressing themselves in a similar manner through the use of cell phones and the like, they were deemed acceptable.

The representations we have examined are not new, but rather anchored in a historical genealogy of such representations. As such, they resonate with that sedimented history and in that way invoke associations that are deeply embedded in popular culture. This is not to suggest that such representations don't change over time, but rather that when they do, they tend to stick to the palimpsest of histories and are only uprooted through the force of social movements that move from the margins to the centre.

Note
The author is very grateful to Matthew Dessner and Jade How, Concordia University, for their research assistance.

References
Abdi, Cawo. 2015. "Disclaimed or Reclaimed? Muslim Refugee Youth and Belonging in the Age of Hyperbolisation." *Journal of Intercultural Studies,* 36, 5: 564–578. DOI: dx.doi.org/10.1080/07256868.2015.1072905.

Abu-Lughod, Lila. 2002. "Do Muslim Women Really Need Saving? Anthropological Reflections on Cultural Relativism and Its Others." *American Anthropologist,* 104, 3: 783–790.

Al-Saji, Alia. 2010. "The Racialization of Muslim Veils: A Philosophical Analysis." *Philosophy and Social Criticism,* 36, 8: 875–902.

Allan, Stuart. 2004. *News Culture,* 2nd ed. Maidenhead: Open University Press.

Allen, Kate. 2010. "Father, Brother of Slain Teen Sentenced to Life Without Parole for 18 Years." *Globe and Mail,* 16 June.

Appleby, Timothy. 2012. "Defiant Acts Led to Women's Deaths, Shafia Trial Told." *Globe and Mail,* 25 January: A4.

Arat-Koç, Sedef. 2002. "Hot Potato: Imperial Wars or Benevolent Interventions? Reflections on 'Global Feminism' Post September 11th." *Atlantis,* 26, 2: 433–444.

Arshad-Ayaz, Adeela. 2016. "Representations of First Nations in Quebec History and Citizenship Textbooks." In M. Ayaz Naseem, Adeela Arshad-Ayaz, and Jesus Rodriguez (eds.), *Representation of Minorities in Textbooks: International Comparative Perspectives.* Santiago de Compostella: University of Santiago de Compostella.

Bailey, Ian, and Sunny Dhillon. 2012. "Missing Women Inquiry: Compensation for Children Complicated, Oppal Concedes." *Globe and Mail,* 20 December: S1.

Bailey, Ian, and Tu Thanh Ha. 2012. "Killer named in 'highway of tears' case." *Globe and Mail,* 26 September: A7.

Barker, Adam J. 2015. "'A Direct Act of Resurgence, a Direct Act of Sovereignty': Reflections on Idle No More, Indigenous Activism, and Canadian Settler Colonialism." *Globalizations,* 12, 1: 43–65.

Bennett, Lance W. 1996. *News, The Politics of Illusion,* 3rd ed. White Plains, NY: Longman.

Bhandar, Davina. 2010. "Cultural Politics: Disciplining Citizenship." *Citizenship Studies,* 14, 3: 331–343.

Boggs, Carl, and Tom Pollard. 2006. "Hollywood and the Spectacle of Terrorism." *New Political Science,* 28, 3: 335–351.

Bourdieu, Pierre. 2001. *Masculine Domination,* trans. By Richard Nice. CA: Stanford University Press.

Byng, Michelle D. 2010. "Symbolically Muslim: Media, Hijab, and the West." *Critical Sociology,* 36, 1: 109–129.

Calliou, Brian. 2012. "Let's Hear More Indigenous Success Stories." *Globe and Mail,* 15 October: A15.

Chartrand, Paul. 1996. *Bridging the Cultural Divide: A Report on Aboriginal People and Criminal Justice in Canada. Chapter 2, Current Realities.* Royal Commission on Aboriginal Peoples. <https://qspace.library.queensu.ca/bitstream/handle/1974/7729/Bridging%20The%20Cultural%20Divide.pdf;jsessionid=592015FE79503841CDB44A1AA443A489?sequence=1>.

Chase, Steven. 2010. "Ottawa Urges Immigrant Communities to Watch Out for Suspicious Behaviour." *Globe and Mail*, 27 August: A1.

Chase, Steven, and Patrick White. 2010. "Be on the Lookout for Radicalized Youth, Toews Says." *Globe and Mail*, 4 October: A3.

Coates, Linda, and Allan Wade. 2007. "Language and Violence: Analysis of Four Discursive Operations." *Journal of Family Violence*, 22: 511–522.

Corbin, Caroline Mala. 2017. "Terrorists Are Always Muslim but Never White: At the Intersection of Critical Race Theory and Propaganda." *Fordham Law Review,* 86, 2: 455–485.

de Finney, Sandrina. 2015. "Playing Indian and Other Settler Stories: Disrupting Western Narratives of Indigenous Girlhood." *Continuum: Journal of Media and Cultural Studies,* 29, 2: 169–181.

Deutsch, Nancy L., and Eleni Theodorou. 2010. "Aspiring, Consuming, Becoming: Youth Identity in a Culture of Consumption." *Youth and Society*, 42, 2: 229–254.

Dhamoon, R., and Abu-Laban, Y. 2009. "Dangerous (Internal) Foreigners and Nation-Building: The Case of Canada." *International Political Science Review,* 30, 2: 163–183.

Entman, Robert M. 2003. "Cascading Activation: Contesting the White House's Frame After 9/11." *Political Communication,* 20, 4: 415–432.

Everett-Green, Robert. 2012. "Law and Disorder." *Globe and Mail*, 18 February: F1.

Fisk, Robert. 2006. "How Racism Has Invaded Canada." The *Independent.* <http://www.aljazeerah.info/Opinion%20editorials/2006%20Opinion%20Editorials/June/11%20o/How%20Racism%20Has%20Invaded%20Canada%20By%20Robert%20Fisk.htm>.

Foucault, Michel. 2003. *"Society Must be Defended," Lectures at the Collège de France 1975–1976,* trans. by David Macey. New York: Picador.

Freeze, Colin. 2010. "EXTREMISTS. Canada Adds Al-Shabab to Its Terrorist List; Crown Can Now Seize Money and Assets of Fronts Operating Here." *Globe and Mail*, 8 March: A7.

___. 2012. "Son of Alleged Terrorist Faces Deportation." *Globe and Mail*, 4 January: A3.

Friesen, Joe. 2013. "Idle No More: The Future Belongs to the Young." *Globe and Mail*, 19 January: A4.

Gagnon, Lysiane. 2012. "In Search of Red Flags." *Globe and Mail*, 6 February: A13.

Galloway, Gloria. 2012. "As Protests Well, Spence Stands Firm on Hunger Strike." *Globe and Mail*, 27 December: A1.

___. 2013a. "Chiefs Divided Over Value of Protests." *Globe and Mail*, 17 January: A4.

___. 2013b. "Harper, Chiefs to Meet Amid Chaos, Protests." *Globe and Mail*, 11 January: A1.

Gitlin, Todd. 1979. "News as Ideology and Contested Area: Toward a Theory of Hegemony, Crisis and Opposition." *Socialist Review,* 9, 6: 11–54.

Globe and Mail. 2010. Editorial. "Tipping Off Is a Duty." 5 October: A20

Globe and Mail. 2011. Editorial. "Nunavut: Young and Neglected." 12 March: F8.

Green, Rayna. 2001. "The Pocahontas Perplex, The Image of Indian Women in American Culture." In Susan Lobo and Steve Talbot (eds.), *Native American Voices, A Reader,* 2nd edition. Upper Saddle River, NJ: Prentice Hall.

Hall, Stuart. 1990. "The Whites of their Eyes, Racist Ideologies and the Media." In Manuel Alvarado and John O. Thompson (eds.), *The Media Reader.* London: British Film Institute.

Hall, Stuart. 1993. "What Is This 'Black' in Black Popular Culture?" *Social Justice,* 20, 1–2: 104–114.

___. 1997. "The Work of Representations." In S. Hall (ed.), *Representation, Cultural Representation and Signifying Practices.* Sage in association with The Open University.

___ (ed.). 2007. *Representation, Cultural Representation and Signifying Practices.* London: Sage, in association with The Open University.

Hamdani, Daood. 2015. *Canadian Muslims: A Statistical Review.* <https://muslimlink. ca/pdf/Canadian-Muslims-A-Statistical-Review-Final.pdf>.

Haque, Eve. 2010. "Homegrown, Muslim and Other: Tolerance, Secularism and the Limits of Multiculturalism." *Social Identities,* 16, 1: 79–101.

Harding, Robert. 2005. "The Media, Aboriginal People and Common Sense." The *Canadian Journal of Native Studies,* 25, 1: 311–335.

___. 2006. "Historical Representations of Aboriginal People in the Canadian News Media." *Discourse and Society,* 17, 2: 205–235.

Henry, Frances, and Carol Tator. 2002. *Discourses of Domination: Racial Bias in the Canadian English-Language Press.* Toronto, London, Buffalo: University of Toronto Press.

Hirji, Faiza. 2011. "Through the Looking Glass: Muslim Women on Television — An Analysis of *24, Lost,* and *Little Mosque on the Prairie.*" *Global Media Journal — Canadian Edition,* 4, 2: 33–47.

Ishaq, Saima. 2010. "Killing in the Name of 'Honour': The South Asian Community in the Canadian Context." M.A., Concordia University, Montreal.

Jibril, Sagal. 2011. "'Cashberta': Migration Experiences of Somali-Canadian Second-Generation Youth in Canada." Master in Environmental Studies, York University, Toronto, Canada.

Jiwani, Yasmin. 2010. "Soft Power — Policing the Border through Canadian TV Crime Drama." In J. Klaehn (ed.), *The Political Economy of Media and Power.* New York: Peter Lang.

___. 2014. "Posthumous Rescue: The Shafia Young Women as Worthy Victims." *Girlhood Studies,* 7, 1: 27–45.

Jiwani, Yasmin, and Matthew Dessner. 2016. "Barbarians in/of the Land: Representations of Muslim Youth in the Canadian Press." *Journal of Contemporary Issues in Education,* 11, 1: 36–53.

Kaplan, Richard L. 2003. "American Journalism Goes to War, 1898–2001: A Manifesto on Media and Empire." *Media History,* 9, 3: 209–219.

Karim, Karim H. 2000. *Islamic Peril.* Montreal: Black Rose Books.

Keevil, Genesee. 2011. "'We Don't Understand Who We Are Dealing With — So We're Not Able to Catch Up.'" *Globe and Mail*, 10 December: A12.

Kellner, Douglas. 2003/1995. *Media Culture: Cultural Studies, Identity and Politics between the Modern and the Postmodern*. London and New York: Routledge.

Lull, James, and Stephen Hinerman. 1997. "The Search for Scandal." In James Lull and Stephen Hinerman (eds.), *Media Scandals*. New York: Columbia University Press.

Macdonald, Myra. 2006. "Muslim Women and the Veil, Problems of Image and Voice in Media Representations." *Feminist Media Studies*, 6, 1: 7–23.

Mackrael, Kim. 2013a. "RCMP Under Review Over Native Women." *Globe and Mail*, 16 May: A3.

Mackrael, Kim. 2013b. "Number of self-Injuring Female Inmates Triples, Report Says." *Globe and Mail*, 1 October: A1.

____. 2012. "Concerned Somalis Push to Fix Gang Crisis: 'Discussions with Public Safety Minister Vic Toews Comes Less Than a Week After Ahmed Hassan Was Killed in Toronto's Eaton Center.'" *Globe and Mail*, 9 June: A15.

Maira, Sunaina. 2009. "'Good' and 'Bad' Muslim Citizens: Feminists, Terrorists, and U.S. Orientalisms." *Feminist Studies*, 35, 3: 631–656.

____. 2010. "Citizenship and Dissent: South Asian Muslim Youth in the US after 9/11." *South Asian Popular Culture*, 8, 1: 31–45.

Mamdani, Mahmood. 2004. *Good Muslim, Bad Muslim: America, The Cold War and the Roots of Terror*. New York: Pantheon.

Markstrom, Carol A. 2011. "Identity Formation of American Indian Adolescents: Local, National, and Global Considerations." *Journal of Research on Adolescence (Wiley-Blackwell)*, 21, 2: 519–535. DOI: 10.1111/j.1532-7795.2010.00690.x.

Martin, Paul. 2011. "Transformational Canadians/Moms, Dads, Aunts, etc." *Globe and Mail, Report on Business*, Canadian Special Report. 4 January: B15.

Mason, Gary. 2012. "Right-Wing Think Tank Flunks When It Comes to Grading Schools." 1 May: S1.

McRobbie, Angela. 2008. "Young Women and Consumer Culture: An Intervention." *Cultural Studies*, 22, 5: 531–550.

Miller, John, and Cybele Sack. 2010. "The Toronto-18 Terror Case: Trial by Media? How Newspaper Opinion Framed Canada's Biggest Terrorism Case." *International Journal of Diversity in Organizations*, 10, 1: 279–295.

Millett, Kris. 2015. "Project Traveller and the Criminalization of Somali Canadian Youth." M.A. major research paper, Trent University, Peterborough, Ontario.

Morey, Peter, and Amina Yaqin. 2011. *Framing Muslims: Stereotyping and Representation After 9/11*. Cambridge and Massachusetts: Harvard University Press.

Pearson, Patricia. 2011. "A Christmas Wish List for Our Many Attawapiskats (Constitutional Debate Not Required)." *Globe and Mail*, 17 December: F3.

Press, Jordan. 2013. "National Household Survey Shows Muslim Population Fastest-Growing Religion in Canada." *Ottawa Citizen*. <https://o.canada.com/news/nhs-religion-hedy-hed-hehd>.

Radwanski, Adam. 2011. "Defeatist Attitude Obstacle to Tackling Native Problems." *Globe and Mail*, 9 June: AS.

Razack, Sherene. 2008a. *Casting Out, The Eviction of Muslims from Western Law and Politics.* Toronto: University of Toronto Press.

___. 2008b. "The Camp: A Place Where Law Has Declared That the Rule of Law Does Not Operate." *RaceLink*, 9–17.

Rhys, William H., and Gira Vashi. 2007. "Hijab and American Muslim Women: Creating the Space for Autonomous Selves." *Sociology of Religion*, 68, 3: 269–287.

Riley, Krista Melanie. 2009. "How to Accumulate National Capital: The Case of the 'Good' Muslim." *Global Media Journal — Canadian Edition*, 2, 2: 57–71.

Ross, Luana. 1998. *Inventing the Savage: The Social Construction of Native American Criminality.* Austin: University of Texas Press.

Said, Edward W. 1978. *Orientalism.* New York: Vintage Books.

___. 1981. *Covering Islam: How the Media and Experts Determine How We See the Rest of the World.* New York: Pantheon Books.

Seguin, Rheal. 2010. "Vigil to Mark Two Years Since Native Girls Went Missing." *Globe and Mail*, 6 September: A6.

Shaheen, Jack G. 2003. "Reel Bad Arabs: How Hollywood Vilifies a People." *The Annals of the American Academy*, 588: 171–193.

Sheik, Nazneen. 2012. "Culture Experts Not Required." *Globe and Mail*, 1 February: A13.

Simpson, Jeffrey. 2011. "For Kashechewan, Read Attawapiskat." *Globe and Mail*, 7 December: A19.

Smith, Linda Tuhiwai. 1999. *Decolonizing Methodologies: Research and Indigenous Peoples.* London and New York and Dunedin: Zed Books Ltd and University of Oregon Press.

Steckley, John L. 2003. *Aboriginal Voices and the Politics of Representation in Canadian Introductory Sociology Textbooks.* Toronto: Canadian Scholar's Press.

Stone, Laura. 2009. "No 'Barbaric Cultural Practices' Here: New Citizenship Guide; 'When You Become a Citizen, You're Not Just Getting a Travel Document into Hotel Canada,' Minister Says." *Canwest News Service.* <http://www.montrealgazette.com/story_print_html?id=221740andsponsor_>.

Taber, Jane. 2013. "Premier Vows to Press on Despite Fracking Opposition." *Globe and Mail*, 22 October: A5.

Tsaparis, Paul. 2013. "We Don't Waste Resources. Why Squander Native Talent?" *Globe and Mail, Report on Business*, 10 May: B11.

Tuchman, Gaye. 1978. "The Symbolic Annihilation of Women by the Mass Media." In Gaye Tuchman, Arlene Kaplan Daniels, and James Benet (eds.), *Hearth and Home: Images of Women in the Mass Media.* New York: Oxford University Press.

van Dijk, Teun. 1993. "Principles of Critical Discourse Analysis." *Discourse and Society*, 4, 2: 249-283.

Wagamese, Richard. 2012. "We Want an AFN of the People; Too Many Important Voices Are Lost When Chiefs Are Called to Elect a National Leader." *Globe and Mail*, 18 July: A13.

___. 2013. "To Be Indian in Canada Today." *Globe and Mail*, 14 January: A11.

Wente, Margaret. 2010. "Our Daughters in Peril; Forget Islamophobia, This Comes Down to Speaking Out Against Family Violence." *Globe and Mail*, 8 May.

White, Patrick. 2010. "Grant to Faith Group for Youth Centre Sparks Debate." *Globe and Mail*, 22 February: A3.

___. 2011. "Death at the 64th Parallel." *Globe and Mail*. 2 April: F2.

Wingrove, Josh, and Joe Friesen. 2010. "Hopeful of Quick Cash, Ontario Somalis Walking in on Alberta's Fatal Drug Wars." *Globe and Mail*, 24 March: A1.

Wykes, Maggie. 2001. *News, Crime and Culture*. London: Pluto Press.

Zine, Jasmin. 2009. "Unsettling the Nation: Gender, Race and Muslim Cultural Politics in Canada." *Studies in Ethnicity and Nationalism*, 9, 1: 146–193.

PART 2

Voices against Violence:
Youth Stories Create Change

5

Indigenous Youth Use Art in the Fight for Justice, Equality and Culture

Catherine Richardson/Kinewesquao, Kate Elliott, Michelle Brake

> My people will sleep for one hundred years but when they awake it will be the artists who give them their spirit back. (Louis Riel, cited in Wyman 2004: 85)

Canadian Member of Parliament Charlie Angus reminds us that "far too many innocent youngsters have been needlessly ground up in a bureaucratic meat grinder. There isn't anything accidental about such a waste of potential and life." In his 2015 book, *Children of the Broken Treaty*, Angus describes the legacy of Cree youth Shannen Koostachin and the other children in Attawapiskat. After suffering decades of colonial neglect, Shannen was heartbroken and outraged that so many of her peers were leaving the education system prematurely. In addition to a lifetime of polluted water and broken infrastructure, the classrooms in her school contained toxic mould, and rats were running across the desks. Some children did not have enough to eat and, unlike in some schools in the south, there were not enough resources to provide lunches. As Angus makes clear, the children of Attawapiskat live in "Third World" conditions here in Canada. Although these conditions have been called out by United Nations rapporteurs, nothing is really improving at the level of addressing the structural violence. Shannen realized that learning under these conditions was impossible, so she launched a political campaign in which youth sent pencils and sparkles (e.g., art supplies) to the prime minister. Shannen died in a car accident before her 16th birthday, and the Campaign for Indigenous Education was renamed Shannen's Dream. A new school was eventually built and opened in 2014. After her tragic death in 2010, Shannen Koostachin of the Attawapiskat First Nation, was named one of the 150 greatest Canadians for her outspokenness regarding the neglect-ful conditions of schools in her community. On a global scale, she is not completely alone in her activism as young people across the world have taken leadership to contest injustice, whether that be Malala Yousafzai educating about rape in Pakistan or Greta Thunberg from Sweden waking up the world about climate change. As far back as 1992, twelve-year-old Severn Cullis-Suzuki spoke out at a United Nations summit in Rio; it seems that her words were largely ignored then as they are today.

In Canada, the disregard for Indigenous families, including their youngest members, continues. While discussing critical issues such as climate change and Indigenous rights, Canada advances its oil and gas extraction and pipeline agenda despite protest on the basis of ecological destruction and the violation of Indigenous lands and sovereignty. The federal government supports the criminalization of Indigenous protesters and their allies and fails to implement the required redress to Indigenous communities after losing the Supreme Court challenge initiated by Cindy Blackstock of the First Nations Child and Family Caring Society. And, although this challenge may be a victory on paper for status First Nations youth, often living on reserve, this fight must be expanded to include other Indigenous Peoples, such as the Métis, the Inuit and the non-status and urban youth in Canada.

In this chapter we refer to the racist neglect, mistreatment and crimi-nalization of Indigenous youth as structural violence, a form of violence that operates through multiple aspects of everyday life. This could include, for example, child welfare as a form of "human trafficking," the process of placing Indigenous children with non-Indigenous families under the guise of protection. Here, the youth face cultural assimilation and various forms of abuse and exploitation (Corcoran 2012). It is this type of colonial action that the youth in the Voices against Violence project raised for dis-cussion and called for action to address. As part of this national initiative, a number of participatory research groups involving arts-based practices were conducted with Indigenous youth across the country. This chapter describes the processes undertaken and shares key learnings that resulted from our group discussions. The focus of these groups was to examine how Indigenous youth experience and resist structural violence and how it relates to their health. Additionally, youth were given the opportunity to explore processes that can be used to overcome structural violence.

The Historical Context

There are three Indigenous groups recognized by the Canadian government (Constitution Act, 1982) and neglected on the ground. These are the Inuit, the Métis and the First Nations. These groups are heterogenous, based on their multiple distinct cultural and sometimes legal sub-groups, including status and non-status First Nations. British Columbia, where the Métis youth research group was facilitated, is home to 203 First Nations communities and 98 spoken Indigenous languages. The Métis have experienced unique forms of discrimination based on the perception that they do not belong to either the First Nations or the Euro-Canadian population.

The Métis are a unique First People due to their fur trade background. Métis communities existed around many of the fur trade communities, where the Métis traded their labour for sustenance with the Hudson's Bay or the Northwest Company. The Métis do not possess their own sovereign land base for their nation. The federal government allotted 1.25 million acres of land known as Métis settlements in the prairies (Government of Canada, The Indian Act, 1867). During the time of conquest and then settlement, Indigenous land in Canada was reduced from 100 percent to less than 1 percent in a relatively short historical period. Despite the existence of treaties in some parts of Canada, most of this "transfer of ownership" took place illegally or using treachery. Indigenous Peoples did not cede their lands to the colonizers when they signed treaties, but rather agreed to share the land and resources with them. However, in reality the colonial governments ignored the treaties (where they existed) and took the land, with the assistance of the police and the military. The Indian Act was established in 1876 to expedite these acts of disenfranchisement and the assimilation of Indigenous Peoples as well as the extraction of resources on traditional Indigenous lands. After 1922, the Indian Act dictated that the state no longer needed permission to take land out of the reserves, and Indigenous Peoples were then criminalized as "squatters" or "poachers" when residing or hunting on their own lands. Today on reserves and in some Indigenous communities, many Indigenous youth feel hopelessness at the lack of opportunity. In their research, Michael Chandler and Christopher Lalonde (1998) drew parallels between lack of sovereignty and self-governance in Indigenous communities and the rates of suicide in those communities. Like many First Nations and Inuit youth, the Métis suffer from a lack of access to land, to nature, to Earth's forests, lakes, rivers and natural sites. This was the basis of the ground-breaking Powerly case (1993) over Métis' hunting rights, a case that was eventually successful in the Supreme Court. There have been few cases granting rights to the Métis in Canada, a notable exception being the Daniels Decision in 2016, stating that the Métis and non-status Indians are "Indians" in regards to Section 91(24) of the Constitution Act (1862). Rather than granting rights, the federal government has been more occupied with removing them since Confederation. Changes have mostly come through the courts.

The Canadian government has developed, over time, strategies for gaining access to Indigenous land. Similar to perpetrators of violence, governments anticipate resistance and seek to suppress it in advance, which was one of the objectives of residential school and Sixties Scoop policies. The kidnapping and imprisonment of Indigenous children in residential schools was one strategy used to eliminate the Indigenous population in order to facilitate the theft of land and resources. This strategy was entrenched in 1936 when changes in the Indian Act transferred jurisdictional power for Indigenous Peoples from the Ministry of the Interior to the Department of Lands, Mines and Resources. Policies of assimilation encouraged enfranchisement (the removal of status), which would mean the termination of land rights on the reserve. Canadian churches of several denominations took federal contracts to run the schools, and many pupils died from malnutrition, disease, violence, broken hearts, suicide or trying to escape. Disease was sometimes achieved through deliberate transmission, constituting genocide through germ warfare (Annett 2001; National Inquiry into Missing and Murdered Women 2019). The film *Kuper Island: Return to the Healing Circle* (Thomas 2005) tells about how children died on logs trying to escape the school by ocean; many school survivors later died by alcohol, drugs and violent deaths as a result of the trauma they suffered at the schools.

Virtually everything of value was taken from Indigenous communities, including the children, and translated into wealth for the ruling classes. Land theft funded the development of logging, fishing, railroads and industry in British Columbia, and bankers and land brokers (who count members of parliament among their numbers) accrued massive wealth (O'Keefe and Macdonald 2001). As a result of these kinds of activities,

First Nations, Métis and Inuit were forced onto increasingly smaller land parcels (Nungak 2017), or enclosures, far from their traditional and ancestral lands and with inadequate housing and services. Métis families were forced to live, impoverished, on the road allowance in the prairies, and all Indigenous individuals needed a pass to exit their reserves and travel to other centres. The 1950s saw changes in child welfare legislation resulting in mass removals of Indigenous children from their communities. These children were placed with white middle-class families, where their culture would be stripped from them. Child "trafficking," facilitated by the social work profession, became a business in itself, developing into one of the largest enterprises in Canada. Today, there is a massive social service industry managing the lives of Indigenous Peoples in Canada, with a lot of the profits going to Euro-Canadian members of the civil service (Richardson, McInerney, Carrier and Maje-Raider 2017). It is this civil service that manages the structural violence which is embedded in social systems and policies.

Structural Violence Today

Despite growing awareness of Canada's colonial violence, the education system continues to invisibilize Indigenous students and perpetuate white privilege. This constitutes one form of structural violence. Assimilationist curricula focuses on a benevolent Canadian history, hides violence and does not offer teachings that reflect culture back to Indigenous students or celebrate Indigeneity. Métis perspectives in particular are noticeably absent from curricula (Richardson, Carriere and Boldo 2017). When Indigenous People suffer, they tend to use the available discourse and remedies that are available to them in Canada. Right now, this means they speak of themselves in psychiatric discourses (e.g., we are traumatized/ have damaged brains) and that they sometimes use alcohol and drugs (both pharmaceuticals and illegal street drugs) to numb pain and fill the gaps of their fragmented identity and ruptured belonging. Tragically, many Indigenous youth overdose and sometimes die, with varying degrees of intentionality, seeking an end to their suffering (Jongbloed, Pearce, Pooyak, Zamar et al. 2017). However, Indigenous youth who are connected to culture have other means available to them for dealing with emotional and spiritual pain. Thus, one goal of the research group we conducted with Métis youth was to assist with the connection process and to reflect on the ways the youth have tried to stay strong in the face of structural violence.

The Y-PAR groups with Indigenous youth provided an opportunity for participants to engage with artistic processes to explore historical experiences, as well as responses and resistance to racism and mistreatment. These youth were committed to forging a path forward against, and in spite of, the many obstacles they face. The participatory arts-based approach in this study helped to amplify the voices of Indigenous youth, indeed, helped them piece back together lives that have been fractured by structural violence in Canada. Engaging youth in respectful adult/youth collaborations is an important place to start. Youth engagement or youth consultations are usually tokenistic, constructed in ways that offer no real threat to the people in positions of power (Ginwright and James 2002). But a sincere and successful PAR process creates safe spaces for sharing.

In an Indigenous context, this means co-creating a sense of cultural safety. Cultural safety is the sense of security and belonging that tells us we are free from racism and prejudice in any particular space. Creating cultural safety involves, in part, creating a space that reflects the values of the people involved (Richardson and Blanchet-Cohen 2016). Cultural safety can be increased through the integration of some Indigenous language and art, and references to nature and the natural world. It is also achieved by ensuring that the space does not become dominated by non-Indigenous individuals, especially in positions of relative power. Cultural safety is also achieved when participants, including non-Indigenous researchers, self-locate and speak about their experiences and their limitations in regards to working with Indigenous communities, and when people organize themselves around accountable allyship and social justice rather than job descriptions and socially constructed ideas about qualifications (Richardson and Reynolds 2015).

Catherine Richardson, Jeannine Carriere and Vicky Boldo (2017) write about the importance of Indigenous pedagogy and teaching in circle for creating cultural safety. Their suggested methods parallel those used in the research groups with Indigenous youth. For example, at a Métis youth research retreat on Vancouver Island, youth sat in a circle together with Elders to talk, listen and share stories. This storytelling methodology has been elaborated as culturally appropriate and ethical by Indigenous researchers such as Margaret Kovach (2010), Robina Thomas (2015, 2005) and Shawn Wilson (2008). The circle also serves as a safe space where in-group conversations of identity and resistance can take place, as we experienced in our Métis research group on Vancouver Island.

Working with Métis Youth

After putting out a call for Métis youth participants through a local Métis organization, a list of youth was created. The youth were invited to an orientation session about the research retreat, and some basic screening took place. The youth research facilitator decided to exclude one person from the group after it was clear the youth was not emotionally stable at the time and could not commit to being drug-free throughout the retreat. The psychological safety of the whole group was considered. The group met a few times to prepare for the research retreat.

Once at the retreat, an arts-based approach to research was used to give youth an opportunity to express and document their perspectives and experiences in a way that created meaning for them. Arts-based approaches make room for different learning styles and the strengths of the individual participants. They provide space for those who prefer to express themselves non-verbally, through image, metaphor, colour and themes, rather than speaking aloud. This process can also be safer and more soothing for individuals who have been traumatized by violence in their lives. Many therapeutic practices include meditative activities such as creating art. Depicting life experience through mastery also allows an individual's presentation to remain strong, whereas there can be pressure in dialogue for an individual to join in a consensual perspective, some-times diluting their own voice in favour of the group voice.

As is typical in culturally informed Indigenous learning processes, Elders were included in the research retreat. Their role was to act as a stabilizing force, transmitting culture and stories as well as treating the youth with love and care. The group dynamic was harmonious and eve-ryone genuinely enjoyed their time together. Research activities included sessions for brainstorming, drawing and painting, as well as circle discus-sions. In addition to a counsellor, Métis guest presenters came to facilitate sessions with the youth, including Kathi Camilleri, who led an activity called "The Village" to demonstrate the historical conditions related to residential schools and the harm done to Indigenous communities. She described the typical roles held by family members — including those of nurturing, teaching, working, playing and enjoying each other — and how communities today are trying to re-establish themselves as sovereign, self-governing nations.

Many of the youth reported that they had never felt safe enough to open up like they did during the retreat. At one point, we were all working on crafts in silence for over thirty minutes, demonstrating the level of comfort, safety and trust that was achieved by the group. This is especially noteworthy as most of the youth were strangers to each other prior to the retreat. The youth all commented on the incredible experience, which underscores the importance of ceremony and the building of relationships as research outcomes. Researcher Shawn Wilson reminds us that "the purpose of ceremony is to build stronger relationships" (2008: 137). Indigenous research is a life-changing ceremony because, Wilson says, "if research does not change you as a person, then you have not done it right" (153). We believe this was achieved within our research group.

The goal of the research facilitators was to create a safe space in which the youth could come together and bond, explore, share experiences and receive support from Elders. Many of the youth had never been able to discuss their lives in a safe space and with support. At least one of the participants was a parent, and they were all struggling with the mainstream university system where they learn little to nothing about their own culture and people. This Métis-focused opportunity allowed them to experience a "third space" of Métis culture and the kinds of opportunities that may be found in such a space (Richardson 2016).

Another goal was to create opportunities for depicting their stories through artistic media, both individually and collectively. In relation to the objectives of the study, the group explored the ways in which the youth overcome, resist and prevent structural violence. As part of this, the youth discussed what structural violence looks like in their own lives and in the lives of their parents and grandparents. Some talked about their experiences in foster homes and away from their family of origin. Much of this talk took the form of "how they have been affected," but the art creations tended to represent more how they responded to, survived, dealt with or overcame structural violence and certain aspects of their suffering. The youth also strategized together about how to contest this violence, how to speak out and articulate their preferred forms of treatment in Canada.

Shared Learnings

The youth articulated four main themes: faces of structural violence, culture, health/well-being and change. These themes were important to the youth for a number of reasons, but mainly because more attention needs to be paid to the experience and the needs of Métis people. For example, structural violence needs to be contested and ended; social policy needs to be fair and restorative. Indigenous communities, including the Métis, want land back and the opportunity to live together in ways that express their collective aspirations. Culture was a main vehicle or process for articulating how people should live together, how they should feed and clothe themselves, and how they should celebrate birth, life and death. Participants stated that they feel "culture" in their bones when they live in the mainstream in a culture that is "not them." The youth expressed the importance of living together and having the feeling of an embodied Métis cultural experience. For the youth, health and well-being are linked to living free from racism, from deprivation and from the things that harm them. The youth expressed a knowledge that many young people, as well as others in community, are using substances to manage pain. The way to address this collectively is to put a stop to the violence, including structural violence, which is often painful and traumatizing. They expressed grief and realized that loss is inseparable from life, and they stressed the importance of having the Métis community to assist them in processing their grief and loss. The last theme, change, related to the ending of structural violence. Change means change for the better, for conditions that are more just in Canada and for processes that uplift the Métis, as well as other Indigenous Peoples. The main themes and subthemes are listed in Table 5-1.

The relationship between the themes is always complex and multi-faceted, embodying layers of meaning or layers of reality. Indigenous worldviews often discuss themes or processes as part of holistic models that include a spiritual, intellectual, physical and emotional aspect. Moreover, these aspects exist inside a context, which often covers the "environmental," "social," "financial/economic" and "political." Indigenous reality exists within a world of complex and multi-layered family and kinship relationships, and experience must be understood within this context.

After the study, a young man who had been involved in the research as

Table 5-1: Participant Themes and Sub-Themes

Themes	Sub-Themes		
Structural Violence	Defining	Implications for Identity	Threat to self
Culture	Values	Traditions	Way of being
Health and Well-Being	Health is holistic	Belonging	Barriers
Change	Empowerment	Resistance	Métis 101

an arts advisor and group facilitator curated an art show at a conference in Toronto, highlighting the youths' art. With the help of another member of the National Youth Advisory Board, he also created postcards out of the art that explored the voices and views of the youth. While some of the cards depict visual images whose meanings are left to the interpretation of the viewer, others include powerful written messages, such as the following three examples:

> We all have experiences and stories to learn from one another. When we realize we're not alone in our struggles, we can work together and create something that impacts the world in a beautiful way. Our differences will help in the future.

> People laugh big feminist, you are.

> Trop de contrôle donne envie de fuir, au detriment de notre sécurité. [Being controlled makes you want to run away, but that can also undermine our safety.]

After being a part of circle discussions in the Métis youth research retreat, the participants continued to make numerous links between today's suffering and historical events. They were "connecting the dots" between government policies, historical events, resistance, government suppression of resistance and the marginalization experienced today. One participant stated: "Structural violence has made me more aware of why my family has hidden their ancestry." Another said: "I think structural violence has a huge component of history that's tied in to it and completely unable to be removed from it." A few made statements about Métis identity: "Most Canadians may not understand or recognize what being Métis is … and when a person lacks that identity how do they feel

good about themselves and have positive self-esteem and self-efficacy?"
And "In our primary and secondary education we are taught to devalue
ourselves. We are taught that Métis people means Riel and that's it." Some
of the youth linked their personal and collective well-being to that of the
Earth/environment and shared a critique of the colonial/capitalist resource
extraction projects which they see as harming the Earth and its citizens.
On one of the drawings, a participant wrote: "Nature Forever!" Another
spoke of how fossil fuel extraction violated Indigenous teachings about
having respect for Mother Earth and pointed to Alberta's "tar sands" as
an example. One of the participants was working in a sustainable First
Nations logging industry on Vancouver Island and was proud that they
align harvesting methods with care of the Earth.

The youth created an art project that identified and celebrated their
values. These are the words they used: kindness, respect, love and gen-
erosity. Another word collage strung together the following verbs: hope,
pray, laugh, inspire, work, dream, learn, play, parlé, wish and dance. They
also included the word "forever."

Analyzing Acts of Resistance

A difference between PAR and psychological research, which is often
couched in deficit terms, is that PAR findings are "situational" and embedded in context. This means they are not mere abstract mental states
detached from a particular reality. Psychological findings often overlook
the larger social context and focus only on the mind of the individual.
For example, within some trauma-informed practices, trauma is trauma
regardless of whether that trauma resulted from a sexualized assault or
an earthquake, and the quality of the social responses to survivors is
not considered. But in PAR we recognize that, while it may be painful
or traumatic to be a victim of structural violence, especially repeatedly
and consistently, understanding this under the psychiatric construction
of "trauma" conceals the intentionality and deliberateness of structural
violence and its legislators. As Catherine Richardson and Allan Wade
(2008) argue, the psychological professions often categorize responses
to violence and injustice as deficits or symptoms of mental illness, which
invisibilizes social injustice and can shut down activism. For example,
labelling someone's sadness in the face of this violence "depression"
individualizes the problem and obscures the very real hurts that this

violence causes. While Marx believed that religion was the opiate of the masses, today it might be psychiatry, where people are diagnosed and drugged rather than encouraged to engage in activism. In this study, the behaviour and actions of the youth are understood as a response to the larger social context of colonization and oppression, rather than as signs of mental illness.

Participant Definitions of Structural Violence

The participants identified and described historical and ongoing structural violence embedded in practices of governance and civil society. They talked about the effects of various aspects of structural violence, such as racism, colourism, exclusion, land theft and impoverization, segregation, internment (residential schools) and forced displacement (foster care). However, it was sometimes difficult for youth to define structural violence due to its ubiquitous and insidious nature. With no easy target to hold accountable, structural violence is easy to hide and deny. Aspects of structural violence, such as colonialism, may enter the public consciousness for a short period of time after government commissions or apologies, but this doesn't necessarily lead to social change (Macias 2014).

The youth discussed structural violence in term of colonialism, institutional racism and systemic violence, and were able to identify the power imbalances that they experience. As one youth said, "when I think of structural violence I think of ... the colonial framework that structures our society today." They recognized "othering" — "a process that identifies those that are thought to be different from oneself or the mainstream, and it can reinforce and reproduce positions of domination and subordination" (Johnson et al. 2004: 253) — as another form of structural violence. The youth also noted that relationships between different forms of structural violence are complex and challenging to disentangle. One youth shared:

We have talked a lot about structural violence and I think that even though it's an education term we need to like kind of define it. It's really important to put a name on it, so its these inequities, or injustices that are placed on us from a system perspective, it's not necessarily people being directly mean to each other or spreading violence that way. It's almost scarier in a sense 'cause it's from this unnamed system and it's these things that are placed on us that are preventing us from really flourishing to the fullest extent that we can.

Non-Indigenous people's ignorance of Indigenous cultures and histories is both a form of structural violence and a means by which it is perpetuated. Another youth said:

> It's hard sometimes, because I feel like I'm constantly fighting to educate people on who the Métis are. It is really frustrating ...it's hard to make progress because you have to keep teaching everybody about who you are as a person. In order to educate others, one needs to have strong sense of identity. Unfortunately, structural violence has played a large role in the loss of identity for Métis people.

Colonial Violence, Structural Violence and Identity

The youth held up colonialism as one particularly powerful example of structural violence and one that led to significant losses in areas such as language, identity, culture, ways of being and livelihood. One participant said:

> When you remove a people from their land and all's they know is how to hunt off the land, how to fish, how to harvest food and live like that, and it's very connected to community. When you completely disrupt that, people are left wondering "what do we do? Where do we go from here?"

Similar responses have been found in various studies, such as the report of the Truth and Reconciliation Commission (Government of Canada 2015), the report of the National Inquiry into Missing and Murdered Indigenous Women and Girls (2019) and the Native American Health Organization's model of historical factors that have damaged Métis health and identity (NAHO 2008). The participants confirm that they, their families and their communities continue to feel these losses today.

A common narrative of the Métis youth was being told by older family members to hide their ancestry in order to avoid further racism and persecution. This was a form of resistance designed to increase their safety, even though it left people feeling less dignified. Going underground was a typical Métis way of dealing with discrimination (Richardson 2006). Some of the youth discussed their own families' experiences of hiding their ancestry.

[This] has made me more aware of why my family has hidden their ancestry and has made me want to make sure that it does not continue ... in the past structural violence has made people become ignorant about who the Métis people are because everyone went underground and hidden and been ashamed.

Although hiding your identity in order to avoid becoming the target of racialized violence is understandable, there are consequences to this denial. Speaking to self-esteem, self-worth and self-efficacy, the youth noted that structural violence not only fuels power imbalances and inequities within systems, it threatens youth's sense of self. One youth noted: "I can definitely say that institutionalized racism or structural violence does affect our health and well-being. It affects our self-esteem."

Another youth described how she was often misunderstood or silenced as a Métis person:

Like people ... most Canadians do not understand or recognize what being Métis is, and when a person lacks identity ... how do they feel good about themselves and have positive self-esteem and self-efficacy? ... that can create problems around peers who are non-aboriginal, not Métis. That all relates to structural violence. How can someone be healthy and do well at school if they are not whole as a person? And I think it has a rippling affect, I think structural violence has a rippling effect on people and I think that leads to problems like alcoholism and drug abuse with Métis youth.

This youth points to how Indigenous youth must fight to preserve their dignity, identity and well-being in the face of racism. It is important to note that resistance is not only about fighting back in ways that are visible and aggressive; any act serves as a silent protest to violence, and oppression can also be construed as violence. These acts are what Wade called "small acts of living" (1997).

Resistance

While colonization and other forms of structural violence have done enormous damage to Indigenous Peoples, it is important to remember that Indigenous youth and their families are not merely passive victims being acted upon, but have at various points and in various ways responded to these forms of violence and theft. Tom McCallum, a Métis Elder, states: "The Métis are in an era of resurgence in reclaiming their identity, but this does not come without struggle" (NAHO 2008).

Depictions of Indigenous Peoples as being "broken" and beyond repair (e.g., having brain damage related to neuro-psychological discourses of trauma) can, at times, constitute structural violence against Indigenous People, including Métis youth. Stories told about Indigenous trauma and victimization can also be an example of structural violence. For example, deterministic intergenerational transmission theories often argue that Indigenous Peoples have lost their parenting skills as a result of their experiences in residential schools and foster homes. And while it may hold some truth in certain circumstances, it is certainly not true in all. And yet this perspective is frequently deployed by social service agencies as they proactively "save" Indigenous children from their traumatized families and communities. In court settings, Métis youth who are mothers and victims of intimate partner or family violence are often cast as psychologically unwell and unfit to parent (Richardson and Wade 2008). However, a different discourse, such as one of survivance, resistance or strengths/resilience, would shed a different light on the population and may not remove their children (Brown and Strega 2005). In some circumstances, youth may need support, but child removal serves the purposes of assimilation and cultural destruction; it is one form of ongoing racist practice. The young people in this study asserted their right to belong, to have access to their culture and to experience opportunity. Many of the Métis youth were also dealing with grief, in some form, about people or aspects of culture that were lost or taken.

Grief, Remembering and Stories

Many Métis participants in this research group were grieving the losses of their past. The youth expressed sorrow and compassion for their ancestors, people who lived through multiple forms of attack and mistreatment. The youth spoke of participating in rituals and ceremonies to help them process grief both individually and collectively. Expressions of grief are often transmitted through storytelling and Elders' teachings, such as the stories shared by Métis Elders and facilitators at the research gathering. Circle processes and pedagogies offer opportunities for healing and integrating experience (Richardson, McInerney et al. 2017), both generally

The drawing of a canoe was a collective project of all the youth in the group.

and as part of this research methodology. Those who are made safe, who are cared for and empowered by the loving-kindness of others, adapt better to the relational commitments of parenting and social relationships in general. Many of the Métis youth in the group expressed the importance of hope, understanding the context of their parents' lives and making good decisions for the future. The feeling of "travelling together" helped reduce feelings of loneliness and isolation.

Concluding Thoughts

Sharing stories in a safe space with other youth who have had similar experiences was powerful for Indigenous youth. As trust was built, the youth shared their understandings and experiences with increasing openness and questioning. There is an aspect of healing that can come from having one's stories received supportively and compassionately. Opportunity to depict these experiences through art and artistic forms, individually and collectively, helped the youth to map out their hopes and plans for the future. There is much from this research that can be used to inform social policy. While society often says that "children are the future," the mainstream lack of attention to the rights of young people — socially and politically, in terms of decision-making power — shows that we do not always act on this adage. At a minimum, Métis youth desire recognition, restoration, and policy that supports their return to culture, values and land-based communities. The youth in this group believe that, if the Canadian population could take in the stories related to Métis historical experience, there would be more movement to restoring the wrongs of the past. Kay Schaffer and Sidonie Smith write that retelling is "one of the most potent vehicles for advancing human rights claims" (2004: 34). Some of this work has begun to take place in the aftermath of the Truth and Reconciliation Commission that was established in 2008, but further attention to Métis-specific concerns is merited. The Powley supreme court victory also served to advance Métis rights.

The youth noted that a push from the "ground-up," guided by the Métis, together with a "top-down" movement to restore rights, opportunities and land, will improve the lives of Métis youth. Events and nations across the world have demonstrated that social justice is possible. The end of apartheid in South Africa, the dismantling of the Berlin Wall, the official end of the Cold War and the election of an African-American president in the United States showed the world that progressive change is possible. Métis leader Louis Riel predicted that the arts and Métis artists would be the ones to prompt the advancement of Indigenous rights all across Canada. The young people in this group contributed to this important task, in their own way, and find art to be an important part in the fight for justice and equality in their country.

References

Angus, C. 2015. *Children of the Broken Treaty: Canada's Lost Promise and One Girl's Dream*. Regina: University of Regina Press.

Annett, K. 2001. "Hidden from History: The Canadian Holocaust: The Untold Story of the Genocide of Aboriginal Peoples by Church and State in Canada." Truth Commission into Genocide in Canada 2001. <http://canadiangenocide.nativeweb.org/genocide.pdf>.

Brown, L., and S. Strega. 2005. *Research as Resistance: Critical, Indigenous and Anti-Oppressive Approaches*. Toronto: Canadian Scholars Press/Women's Press.

Chandler, M., and C. Lalonde. 1998. "Cultural Continuity as a Hedge Against Suicide in Canada's First Nations." *Transcultural Psychiatry*, 35, 2.

Corcoran, R. 2012. "Rethinking 'Foster Child' and the Culture of Care: A Rhizomatic Inquiry into the Multiple Becomings of Foster Care Alumni." Victoria, BC:

Unpublished Masters thesis in the School of Child and Youth Care at the University of Victoria.

Ginwright, S., and T. James. 2002. "From Assets to Agents of Change: Social Justice, Organizing, and Youth Development." *New Directions for Youth Development,* 96: 27–46.

Johnson, J.L., J. Bottorff, A. Browne, S. Grewal et al. 2004. "Othering and Being Othered in the Context of Health Care Services." *Health Communications,* 16, 2: 255–271. Retrieved from Google database.

Jongbloed, K., M. Pearce, S. Pooyak, D. Zamar et al. 2017. "The Cedar Project: Mortality Among Youth Indigenous People Who Use Drugs in British Columbia." *Canadian Medical Association Journal,* 189, 44: 1352–1359. DOI: https://doi.org/10.1503/cmaj.160778.

Kovach, M. 2010. *Indigenous Methodologies: Characteristics, Conversations and Contexts.* Toronto: University of Toronto Press.

Macias, T. 2014. "'Tortured Bodies': The Biopolitics of Torture and Truth in Chile." In S. Perera and S. Razack (eds.), *At the Limits of Justice: Women of Colour Theorize Terror.* Toronto: University of Toronto Press.

National Inquiry into Missing and Murdered Indigenous Women and Girls. 2019. *Reclaiming Power and Place: Final Report.* Ottawa.

NAHO (Métis Centre, Native Aboriginal Health Organization). 2008. *In the Words of Our Ancestors: Métis Health and Healing.* <http://www.naho.ca/documents/metiscentre/english/TK_IntheWordsofOurAncestorsMetisHealthandHealing.pdf>.

Nungak, Z. 2017. *Wrestling with Colonialism on Steroids: Quebec Inuit Fight for Their Homeland.* Montreal: Véhicule Press.

O'Keefe, B., and I. Macdonald. 2001. *Merchant Prince: A Story of Alexander Duncan Macrae.* Vancouver: Heritage House.

Richardson, C. 2016. *Belonging Métis.* Vernon, BC: John Charlton Publications.

Richardson, C. 2006. "Métis Identity Creation and Tactical Response to Oppression and Racism." <http://www.uvic.ca/hsd/assets/docs/publications/variegations/vol-2/richardson.pdf>.

Richardson, C., and Blanchet-Cohen, N. 2016. "Cultural Safety: Applications and Implications for Indigenous Children, Families and Communities." In K. Hele (ed.), *Survivance and Reconciliation: 7 Forward/7 Back: 2015 Canadian Indigenous Native Studies Association Conference Proceedings.* Aboriginal Issues Press.

Richardson, C., J. Carriere, and V. Boldo. 2017. "Invitations to Dignity and Well-Being: Cultural Safety Through Indigenous Pedagogy, Witnessing and Giving Back." <http://journals.sagepub.com/doi/abs/10.1177/1177180117714413>.

Richardson C., B. McInerney, R.C. Carrier, and A. Maje-Raider. 2017. "Creating Safety and Social Justice for Women in the Yukon." In D. Paré and C. Audet (eds.), *Social Justice and Counselling.* New York: Routledge.

Richardson, C., and V. Reynolds. 2015. "Structuring Safety for Survivors of Torture and Residential School." *Canadian Journal of Native Studies,* 34, 2: 147–164. <http://www.vikkireynolds.ca/documents/2014RichardsonandReynoldsStructuringsafetyIndi genoussurvivorsresschools.pdf>.

Richardson, C., and A. Wade. 2008. "Taking Resistance Seriously: A Response-Based Approach to Social Work in Cases of Violence Against Indigenous Women." In S. Strega and J. Carriere (eds.), *Walking This Path Together: Anti-Racist and Anti-Oppressive Child Welfare Practice*. Winnipeg, MB: Fernwood Publishing.

Schaffer, K., and S. Smith. 2004. "Conjunctions: Life Narratives in the Field of Human Rights." *Biography*, 27, 1: 1–24.

Smith, L.T. 1999. *Decolonizing Methodologies: Research and Indigenous People*. London: Zed Books.

Thomas, R. 2005. "Storytelling in the Spirit of Wise Woman: Experiences of Kuper Island residential school." Unpublished Masters thesis at the University of Victoria.

___. 2015. "Honouring the Oral Traditions of My Ancestors Through Storytelling." In L. Brown and S. Strega (eds.), *Research as Resistance: Critical, Indigenous and Anti-Oppressive Approaches,* 2nd edition. Toronto: Canadian Scholars' Press.

Truth and Reconciliation Commission of Canada. 2012. *Truth and Reconciliation Commission of Canada Report: Calls to Action.* <http://trc.ca/assets/pdf/Calls_to_Action_English2.pdf>.

___. 2015. *Honouring the Truth, Reconciling for the Future: The Summary of the Final Report*. Ottawa.

Wade, A. 1997. "Small Acts of Living: Everyday Resistance to Violence and Other Forms of Oppression." *Journal of Contemporary Family Therapy*, 19, 1: 23–39.

Wilson, S. 2008. *Research Is Ceremony: Indigenous Research Methods*. Black Point: Fernwood Publishing.

Wyman, Max. 2004. *The Defiant Imagination: Why Culture Matters*. Vancouver/Toronto: Douglas & McIntyre.

6

Structural Violence in the Lives of Youth Experiencing Homelessness

Abe Oudshoorn and Jessica Justrabo

"Children's aid failed me by taking my son away from me when I wasn't the parent to be concerned with."

"**S**treet kids," "runaways"; the language around youth experiencing homelessness is often pejorative and most frequently reflects perceptions of homelessness as a choice of youth who are rebelling from their home environment. These are the "bad kids," the "dropouts," perhaps current or future gang members and criminals who have chosen the streets over good society, aren't they? What if homelessness for youth is not about personal choice but more about policies, systems and structures that marginalize particular groups and particular individuals? The purpose of this chapter is to review the results of five research groups conducted across Canada with youth experiencing homelessness. These groups were focused on experiences of structural violence — what one participant called "damage from a system that isn't set up to face individuals' needs" — and this chapter focuses particularly on policy issues and policy implications. Guided by an intersectional framework, with particular attention to issues of the criminal justice system, child welfare system and housing system, consideration is given to policy intersections across various government programs and services. Ultimately, our goal is to highlight policy challenges and opportunities and ways that policy may be altered to eliminate structural violence in the lives of youth experiencing homelessness.

At 20 percent, the proportion of those experiencing homelessness in Canada who are youth is significant (Gaetz, Gulliver and Richter 2014). A national survey of homelessness demonstrates the importance of institutional and systemic factors as causes of youth homelessness (Gaetz, O'Grady, Kidd and Schwan 2016). These include poorly supported transitions from institutional care such as child welfare, corrections and in-patient mental health, as well as barriers to living wages and affordable housing. These include structural biases, such as the lack of accessible services for LGBTQ2S youth (Abramovich 2012), who are vastly over-represented in the population of youth experiencing homelessness. While family breakdown and instability are often cited as key causes of youth homelessness (Barker 2016), it is important to question why adequate and affordable housing options for youth are not available in the case of such disruption, pointing to considerations beyond the personal or familial, to structural dysfunctions and violence.

Who We Talked With

The research groups covered in this analysis were formed in five cities across Ontario and Quebec, with youth ranging in age from 15 to 28. The average number of youth per group was fourteen and a total of sixty-two youth were considered co-researchers for the projects. Twenty-four youth self-identified as male, thirty self-identified as female, and eight self-identified elsewhere on the gender spectrum. Eleven participants described themselves as parents, with custody status not being assessed. The participants self-described as a varied range of ethnicities, including Indigenous, Caribbean, Polynesian, Hispanic, Italian, Portuguese and Hungarian, although most identified as being Canadian-born. The youth co-researchers had all experienced homelessness, either currently or in the past, or were close to someone who was or is experiencing homelessness. Many had experiences with the justice system, the child welfare system, emergency shelters and alternative education programs. Most of the participants reported that they had dropped out of school at one time and persistently experienced a lack of money to pay for basic needs like food and medicine. Youth lived mostly off income support programs offered by different levels of government, such as social assistance, employment insurance and student financial aid.

Of the five groups included in this chapter, four were formed through recruitment processes at drop-in centres or emergency shelters. The youth co-researchers all had previous affiliation with the centres and programs but had not necessarily attended structured programming prior to these

As a group, youth created art to share their experiences.

particular research groups. The fifth research group was formed from a previously established therapy group focused on creating art. Staff from the host centres attended groups most of the time, although the research participants made it clear that they preferred the staff to check in but not stay for group topics and discussions, particularly when the group was formed from a drop-in centre or shelter. The youth preferred this independence because of the power dynamic between themselves and the staff, and because they wanted to speak freely about the structural violence they had experienced or were currently experiencing, which may sometimes be at the hands of the institution the staff represented.

The examples pictured demonstrate some of the art created by the youth that served as a platform to discuss the differences and similarities of their experiences. Arts-based approaches to dialogue varied from site to site. Some sites chose to use the same approach consistently through their time meeting together, while other sites used different arts-based approaches in different weeks. These activities included poetry writing, painting, collage, body mapping, drama, portraiture, mask making and creating comic strips. The consistency across project sites was using the arts activities as a springboard for dialogue regarding structural violence in the lives of youth. Some of the arts activities were individual and others were conducted in a group. Many of the sites retained a portion of the

The use of art for self-reflection and dialogue.

art that was created on site and displayed it for a period of time after the group was concluded.

Our findings are organized by the three policy sectors that were discussed in each of the groups: criminal justice, child welfare and housing. In each section, we explore themes arising from the groups and potential areas for policy reform.

No Justice in the Justice System

Youth across groups spoke about interactions with the criminal justice system, from police, to courts, to jail and beyond. The two areas most frequently discussed were police contacts, particularly in regard to ticketing, and post-incarceration with regard to orders, probation and bail conditions. It was clear that policing was a frustration for the youth, being an explicit experience of disempowerment, marginalization and discrimination. One member of the research group in Quebec expressed anger at the "surveillance and suppression to which they were subjected by police," specifically in relation to social profiling or being known by police for having a criminal record. The youth felt they were frequent victims of police harassment and subject to arbitrary stops and even arrest. Although research on youth homelessness has spoken to some positive interactions with police, this was not the way that experiences were framed by youth in any of our groups. Youth lived their lives in public, with constant exposure to risks of violence and lack of privacy, and policing often felt like the formal application of this exposure. Youth at times expressed feelings of helplessness and hopelessness around ticketing and felt punished for behaviours that they did not want to be conducting in public in the first place. One participant spoke about sleeping on the street and having to move locations every hour due to policing. Another participant discussed how sometimes when living rough they would have liked police to stop and assist them, yet they were ignored unless getting into trouble.

Much of the ticketing experienced by youth was based on the Safe Streets Act, but also represented general nuisance laws and "carding," constant challenges for youth forced to conduct their private lives in public spaces. Although legislation is currently changing with respect to random police checks, historically in most provinces police can approach and ask any person to provide personal information, or answer questions about other persons of interest, or about their current activities (O'Grady, Gaetz and Buccieri 2011). These interactions, based on no observable crimes, lead to a documentation of appearance, age, gender, location, mode of transportation and skin colour (O'Grady, Gaetz and Buccieri 2011), all of which is then recorded in police databases, making it more likely that an individual would be subject to further arbitrary stops in the future: an exponential effect. Nuisance laws — such as those against loitering, loud noises and public urination — also disrupt the lives of youth, particularly in light of efforts to find stability within a consistently unstable living environment. Fines related to nuisance laws and petty crimes are "both expensive and unhelpful. Youth face fines that they are unable to pay and the system wastes resources in trying to pursue the matter" (Springer, Lum and Roswell 2013: 17). These tickets can build up and affect youth later in life, creating emotional stress and debt. They can lead to jail time or prevent youth from seeking job prospects, with fine-related court orders often preventing youth from leaving the province for better prospects (Bryant 2014).

Policy Analysis

In Ontario, the Safe Streets Act (SSA) came into effect in January 2000 with the stated purpose of addressing public concerns regarding *aggressive* panhandling and squeegeeing. The Act defines aggressive behaviour as "a manner that is likely to cause a reasonable person to be concerned for his or her safety or security" and prohibits anyone from soliciting in such a way. Section 2(3) of the Act gives examples of aggressive solicitation:

1. Threatening the person solicited with physical harm, by word, gesture or other means, during the solicitation or after the person solicited responds or fails to respond to the solicitation.
2. Obstructing the path of the person solicited during the solicitation or after the person solicited responds or fails to respond to the solicitation.
3. Using abusive language during the solicitation or after the person solicited responds or fails to respond to the solicitation.
4. Proceeding behind, alongside or ahead of the person solicited during the solicitation or after the person solicited responds or fails to respond to the solicitation.
5. Soliciting while intoxicated by alcohol or drugs.
6. Continuing to solicit a person in a persistent manner after the person has responded negatively to the solicitation.

However, in a review of ssa tickets handed out by the Toronto Police between 2004 and 2010, only 20 percent were for aggressive solicitation, while 80 percent were for non-aggressive acts such as soliciting a captive audience (O'Grady, Gaetz and Buccieri 2011). This extensive use of the ssa for non-aggressive acts, in opposition to the stated reason for the legislation, results in the eradication of alternative forms of income generation for youth (O'Grady, Gaetz and Buccieri). As well, while research highlights a significant decline in panhandling and squeegeeing since 2000, the number of ssa tickets has increased exponentially over the past decade. As youth in our study noted, this suggests that the ticketing is not in response to behaviours of public concern but is being used to manage and control youth who are forced by their homelessness to live their lives in public. In Toronto, for example, the number of ssa tickets rose from 710 in 2000 to 15,324 in 2010 (O'Grady, Gaetz and Buccieri). Exempted from these tickets are canvassers and fundraisers, meaning that only the most vulnerable and visibly homeless receive tickets for asking for financial donations.

Experiences with police and ticketing are not the same for all homeless youth. Rather, social locations of ethnicity and homelessness often overlap, leading particular groups of youth to be most susceptible to ticketing. Racialized youth, especially Indigenous and African Canadian youth, are significantly over-represented among populations experiencing homelessness and those that are involved with the criminal justice system (Goraya 2015). Regardless of the stated intent, current applications of the SSA and nuisance laws result in the criminalization of homelessness and become other ways in which racialized youth are criminalized.

Policy Recommendations

Homelessness is the root issue, forcing youth to live their lives in public and exposing them to excess police interaction, but rather than addressing this root issue, public nuisance laws actually further entrench youth homelessness. If homelessness is the root, then housing youth is the solution. Programs that adopt the philosophy of "housing first" have shown positive outcomes in this regard (Gaetz 2014). Housing that is safe, permanent, affordable, adequate and of one's choice is good for health and well-being, and a part of this for youth is avoiding negative and unnecessary police interactions.

Youth who participated in our research groups recommended a number of policy changes related to the criminal justice system. Extensive work has been done through the Homeless Hub regarding policy recommendations for the SSA, and many of these same recommendations were echoed by participants. Primarily, participants were adamant that the government of Ontario should eliminate the Safe Streets Act. Bill O'Grady, Stephen Gaetz and Kristy Buccieri (2011) recommend that this repeal should be immediate and that governments should instead focus on more effective ways to end homelessness, such as prevention and rapid re-housing, including discharge planning supports from correctional facilities.

Youth participants also felt strongly that restrictions and conditions around bail hampered their efforts to progress. One youth stated: "Often unnecessary conditions are assigned that have no relevance to the alleged crime or keeping the person on bail away from trouble." This might include participation in schooling at a time when youth are not actively enrolled in school or a condition may be in conflict with their most recent school location. They further commented that bail conditions make sentencing and the trial take longer. The youth felt that conditions of bail should serve to allow them to rehabilitate back into the community, but conditions often imposed unnecessary barriers that hindered attempts at rehabilitation. For example, bail may restrict access to certain areas of the community, resulting in youth losing vital support systems. Conversely, youth may be forced to reside in a shelter as their address at release, which can lead to delays in finding more permanent housing and integrating into the broader community.

Governments and inter-ministerial committees need to work together to develop innovative strategies and solutions for homeless youth involved in the criminal justice system. Provincial governments are well situated to produce integrated plans as they are responsible for relevant services, such as child welfare and housing (O'Grady, Gaetz and Buccieri 2011). These plans need to recognize that not all youth experience homelessness in the same way, and they must offer tangible long-term supports relating to such issues as the continuation of school, interaction with child welfare, and services particular to the LGTBQ2S+ community and those focused on the needs of racialized youth. Existing services, such as shelters, housing and drop-in programs, are advised to re-evaluate their own policies — for example policies that lead to youth being labelled "problematic" and banned from programs and services — and understand how such policies disrupt youths' efforts to find long-term stability.

The Harms of "Protecting Children"

Many of the youth researchers involved in this project had experiences with child protection services, specifically the Children's Aid Society (CAS) and the Director of Youth Protection in Quebec (DYP), some as children and some as both children and parents. As with the criminal justice system, homelessness and child welfare services are very much interconnected, with approximately 40 percent of youth who are homeless having been involved with child welfare (Dworsky and Courtney 2009). In one of the research groups, all of the participants "turned to the street around the age of 15 or 16 to escape rehabilitation centres affiliated with the Director of Youth Protection." Youth report challenging experiences with the child welfare system, both as children in care and as parents. As well, some youth connect these two experiences explicitly, having had children while themselves still in contact with CAS. In defining what made these experiences challenging, the common trend was an overwhelming sense of powerlessness. Whether as a child in care or a parent involved with the system, youth felt unable to make decisions they considered to be in their (or their children's) best interests.

Youth who are parents and experience homelessness are highly likely to be investigated by child welfare services as neglect is notoriously hard to distinguish from poverty (Swift and Parada 2004). Similarly, familial experiences of poverty are often what led youth themselves to be taken into care as children. With social assistance rates in Ontario well below the low-income cut-off line since 1995 (Swift and Parada), families in poverty struggle to provide adequate shelter, food and clothing for their children. Therefore, familial cycles of poverty are intertwined with persistent surveillance by child welfare services. One youth in our study echoed these particular sentiments as she had experienced involvement with CAS as a child and now as a mother herself, and had recently had her children apprehended. She attributes this apprehension to poverty, explaining that she has been living in transitional housing and trying to make ends meet on social assistance. With only $100 monthly to pay for electricity and buy basic necessities and clothing, and living in unstable housing, her children were apprehended under the accusation of neglect. She stated: "I've been doing what I've been asked to, and still it wasn't good enough. Story of my life, I don't understand why they [CAS] are so concerned with my life."

The sense of powerlessness was ubiquitous among youth who had been involved with child welfare services, either as children or parents, or often both. Youth expressed frustration over lack of control and "feeling unaware of decisions that affect our own lives." Some youth stated that being apprehended and removed from their parents' home as children, most often due to experiences of abuse, was a positive thing; however, "how it was done was always a negative experience." Many youth described a feeling of instability related to foster care and the desire to "go home." Powerlessness was experienced when their thoughts and ideas for their own plan of care were not taken into consideration. In the context of zero choice, several youth chose to leave adoptive or foster families, resulting in perpetual re-placements and thus continuing a cycle of instability. And moving from home to home also means attending new schools and trying to meet the expectations of new classrooms, which is especially difficult if mental health or learning disabilities are factors. Eventually, many of the

youth were formally discharged from the care of child welfare services
or signed themselves out prior to aging out of care.

Ending care with child welfare services, often referred to as "signing
out of care," can be quite problematic for the youth involved. This process
involves youth between the ages of 16 and 18 years old applying to the
courts to terminate a Society or Crown wardship order (Nichols 2013).
Although CAS and DYP offer financial support, education opportunities,
life skills workshops, direct access to a care worker and opportunities for
extended care and maintenance (financial support past the age of 18),
those who sign out of care relinquish these supports. In many cases this
process precipitates a young person's first stay within the emergency shelter
system. Although the powerlessness mentioned above was a frequently
identified reason for youth in our study exiting care, entering the emergency shelter and homeless serving sector involved a new set of complex
relationships with systems of surveillance and control. While youth
spoke of experiences of couch surfing and sleeping rough upon leaving
care, they suggested that the easiest pathway into their own housing was
through the shelter system. In sum, the youth identified two major areas
of concern: the complex interaction between child welfare and housing
systems, and the difficult compromises they had to make between access
to services and personal autonomy.

Policy Recommendations

Although child welfare services in Ontario have seen reform in recent
years, such as the 1997 amendments to the Child and Family Services Act,
the 2006 Transformation Agenda and the introduction of the Commission
to Promote Sustainable Child Welfare in 2012, youth researchers unani-
mously wished to advocate for continued significant reform to child
welfare services. They experienced firsthand a disconnect between CAS
or DYP and other related systems, such as education, housing and social
assistance. Scholars argue that child welfare services need to be understood
as one of multiple policy systems that affect the lives of vulnerable youth,
so that the interactions between those different systems can be managed
more effectively (Swift and Parada 2004) and a more coordinated systems
approach to addressing youth homelessness can be developed. Rather than
single system reviews and reforms, youth promoted a process of reform
that involves multiple provincial ministries, such as education, housing

and justice. The Quebec research group offered a promising model, called the "Law to Fight Poverty and Social Exclusion" (Swift and Parada). This inter-ministerial approach would consider the deeper root issues that lead vulnerable youth to be engaged with multiple governmental systems, addressing the poverty and exclusion that were significant areas of focus for youth researchers.

In child welfare policies in particular, the issue of powerless as felt through the lack of decision-making control, whether as a child in care or as a parent engaged with the system, needs further consideration. Child welfare services exist in an ethical grey zone where rights of safety and rights of choice often play off against each other. Youth acknowledged that workers were making logical decisions that prioritized the youths' safety or the safety of their children, but lamented what they perceived as often over-prescribed solutions rather than collaborative decision-making. Particularly regarding taking children into care, there is an opportunity to build policy that more actively includes the perspectives of minor children in their own care plans. If the goal is to keep youth engaged in systems of care, and yet current policies leave them feeling powerless, and often to signing out of care, then it is best to be inclusive and potentially seek compromise at the outset of care planning.

Housing Held Out of Reach

Homelessness is a complex experience, with pathways into homelessness being unique for each individual. However, the commonality of the experience is that housing is the only solution for homelessness — particularly, housing that is safe, affordable, permanent, adequate, of choice and supported as needed. Youth face two particular barriers to accessing housing over and above those of adults experiencing homelessness: age discrimination and policy limitations, such as the inability to sign a lease. Although the Ontario Human Rights Commission forbids discrimination based on age, youth face barriers in entry into the rental housing market (Ontario Human Rights Commission n.d.). Youth researchers spoke to perceived discrimination, noting that upon meeting with a landlord they rarely received further contact or lease offers, even when they met the requirements of demonstrating an income or passing a police check. That said, barriers to employment and the likelihood of interaction with the criminal justice system, noted above, did at times make such conditions difficult to fulfill. Youth noted experiences of overt discrimination, but also that their life experiences of homelessness led to systemic discriminatory barriers to housing in a market context where landlords can freely screen out applicants without providing any reason.

In addition to discrimination, youth highlighted practical barriers to accessing housing. These included preconditions, such as attending school, sobriety or stability of mental health, which proved difficult to achieve in the context of the transient nature of homelessness. Additionally, youth are far more likely than adults to have absolutely no income, as most have not been independent and primary recipients of social assistance prior to an experience of homelessness. The time required to qualify for social assistance, particularly when under the age of 18, delays access to housing and lengthens shelter stays. Those under 18 also face practical barriers associated with signing a lease, as some provinces require legal emancipation before minors can do so. In provinces such as Ontario, where no such requirement for legal emancipation exist, landlords are often unfamiliar with the law. Youth in our groups spoke of landlords incorrectly asserting that they couldn't sign their own lease. Youth aged 16 or 17 also find that many housing services for homeless youth, such as transitional housing programs, are geared for those aged 18–24. Youth of all ages experiencing homelessness and trying to enter into the private sector for the first time also struggle to provide a reference from a former landlord. Many leave home in the context of family conflict and/or abuse and simply have no past housing history from which to obtain a reference. Finally, youth spoke at times of being caught in a catch-22 situation, where they had to have a lease to receive the housing portion of social assistance, but landlords required demonstration of income before entering into a lease.

A concern raised by youth researchers in one of our groups, which is not frequently considered, is pets as an obstacle to obtaining housing. Several youth spoke of pets as a priority for their well-being, providing a sense of security or actual protection if they were sleeping rough: "Oh I know my dog will protect me. If it's someone I know she'll stay in her corner ... but if it is someone she doesn't know she won't shy away!!" A pet was also a symbol of significant attachment at a time of estrangement from family and many friends. Two participants stated very strongly that their dog literally gave them a reason to live, preventing them from making a suicide attempt and allowing them to keep pushing for solutions to their homelessness: "Yeah me too that's why I bought my dog, I was screwed. In my head it was ... I had no life, I didn't want to go on, I needed ... a reason to hold on ... You have to take care of a dog, you have to be there, feeding it ... you have no choice but to be there." Finding housing that would accommodate both themselves and their pets was challenging, and youth were frequently forced to turn to grey market options, which refer to a variety of non-legal, non-conforming, unlicensed living options that might be found through informal channels or falsely advertised as legal units.

While the refusal of pets in rental housing is not uncommon, youth noted that this refusal was often added when they met with a landlord, even if it was not listed in the online advertisement; youth interpreted this as landlords being specifically suspicious of young people with pets. While some youth chose housing at the cost of separation from pets, others refused to leave exploitative or violent housing situations out of fear of losing their pet. Still other participants chose to delay leaving life on the streets in order to keep their pet in their custody: "There are some who decide to stay on the streets simply because they don't have to be apart from their dog." The youth in one of our research groups felt so adamantly about no-pet policies that they decided to petition area landlords to reconsider such policies. The group also engaged in political action, asking the general public to sign a petition on the National Assembly of Quebec website in order to nullify any clause on a lease that forbade dogs and cats. Two landlords contacted by the group stated they were flexible on the pet policy but maintained the policy on the lease in order to inspect the pet in question. The youth then wondered if the pet inspection was used as an excuse to refuse people who seemed marginal or appeared young or untrustworthy.

Policy Analysis

There is a notable incongruence between policies prohibiting discrimination based on age and the experiences of homeless youth. Although youth are able to report discrimination based on age, race and being in receipt of social assistance to their provincial human rights commission, the paperwork involved is extensive and the process does not prevent a delay in access to housing and exit from homelessness. Although human rights commissions in Canada and many community legal clinics provide educational resources for landlords, these preventative tools are insufficient in the immediacy of a housing crisis. In fact, what was noted by youth was that bureaucratic processes, whether accessing housing or social assistance, entering a youth-specific transition program or others all serve to delay the move from homeless to housed. This calls into question the vision of "rapid rehousing" within "housing first" policies, when it is as much systems as it is the youth themselves that are making rehousing less than rapid.

Policy Recommendations

Timely access to adequate income is a foundational factor in supporting youth to move into housing. Social assistance is meant to fill this need, yet both the adequacy and the timeliness of access are open for improvement. Social assistance rates were cut drastically in Ontario in the mid-1990s, and since have either been held stagnant or have increased at a rate lower than inflation for almost all years. This means that year-over-year, the discrepancy between the housing portion of social assistance and average market rents increases. Ontario's Social Assistance Review Commission highlighted the inadequacy of rates, yet since that time any focus on growth has been for the basic needs portion of social assistance rather than the housing portion. In such a context youth are left on wait lists for affordable housing that stretch from months to years, so they are forced to turn to grey market housing, remain stuck in a shelter or complete for a limited number of rent supplements. To make housing possible for youth exiting homelessness, social assistance housing components must be increased to reflect market realities. Additionally, there is room for simplifying the application process for youth who are newly independent, such as youth exiting the child welfare system, youth leaving home or youth under the age of 18 no longer in the care of an adult. Proving independence from family is often a challenge, especially when it is conflict with this family that precipitated homelessness. Systems that expedite payment and require subsequent follow-up paperwork to continue payment would better support youth in meeting basic needs.

In addition to income policies supporting youth in accessing market rental housing, affordable supportive housing geared specifically to youth is needed for those requiring something in addition to independence. In particular, youth researchers recommended supportive housing with

minimal rules and requirements, allowing them to build skills for independent living and acknowledging their resilience. Youth were frustrated
by presumptions within some housing services that they needed to be
taught how to be tenants and preferred that services were available upon
request rather than forced upon them. It is noted in particular that policies
about curfews or guests may inhibit the ways youth survive on their own.
Decreasing their ability to have social supports might lead to failure of
the tenancy in transitional supportive housing. Rather, if youth are supported in understanding the tenant responsibilities of their housing, they
should be autonomous in deciding how they meet these responsibilities.

A final practical note of a policy that forces youth into homelessness are
discharges from a provincial institution to no fixed address. Youth exiting
mental health care, the criminal justice system, child welfare services or
residential treatment programs should be supported into permanent housing options. Where discharge is made to no fixed address, you simply have
one provincial service moving the burden of care to another provincial
service. And, it is likely that the discharge goals of any of these services will
be compromised if youth enter a state of homelessness. "No discharge to
no fixed address" should be a policy for youth services across the country.

Conclusion

To return to the questions we posed in opening this chapter, it is clear
that homelessness for youth is about much more than personal choice.
Indeed, youth were trying to choose housing but it was held out of reach.
In speaking with youth about their experiences of structural violence,
we sought to explore the policy landscape that either assists or hinders
youth from achieving their long-term goals for stability. What we heard
were frustrations with the justice system, child welfare system and
housing system. Although at times youth identified policies they found
problematic within specific systems, it was often the overlapping effects
of policies across systems that proved challenging. These systems are
primarily within provincial jurisdiction, and we note that nearly identi-
cal challenges were faced by youth in all provinces within our project.
Therefore, we see significant opportunity for change both within provinces and territories themselves, but also with national oversight. We
recommend that provincial reviews be conducted to seek policy reforms
to support homeless youth across systems, and that these be conducted

within a national collaboration so that practices and knowledge can be shared across provinces and territories. In this process, it will be essential that the voices of youth with lived experiences of homelessness be central to decision-making.

References

Abramovich, I.A. 2012. "No Safe Place to Go–LGBTQ Youth Homelessness in Canada: Reviewing the Literature." *Canadian Journal of Family and Youth/Le Journal Canadien de Famille et de la Jeunesse*, 4, 1: 29–51.

Barker, J. 2016. "Conceptualisations of Youth Homelessness and the Role of the Family." In Andy Furlong (ed.), *Routledge Handbook of Youth and Young Adulthood*, 219.

Bryant, M. 2014. "Squeegee Law Hurts the Poor. I Should Have Abolished It." *Globe and Mail*, 27 Nov. <http://www.theglobeandmail.com/opinion/i-didnt-repeal-the-squeegee-law-it-hurts-the-poor-and-should-be-abolished/article21809521/>.

Dworsky, A., and M.E. Courtney. 2009. "Homelessness and the Transition from Foster Care to Adulthood." *Child Welfare*, 88, 4: 23.

Gaetz, S. 2014. "A Safe and Decent Place to Live: Towards a Housing First Framework for Youth." Canadian Homelessness Research Network. <https://homelesshub.ca/sites/default/files/attachments/HFFWYouth-FullReport_0.pdf>.

Gaetz, S., T. Gulliver, and T. Richter. 2014. "The State of Homelessness in Canada: 2014." Toronto: Canadian Observatory on Homelessness Press. <https://homelesshub.ca/sites/default/files/attachments/SOHC2014.pdf>.

Gaetz, S., B. O'Grady, S. Kidd, and K. Schwan. 2016. "Without a Home: The National Youth Homelessness Survey." Toronto: Canadian Observatory on Homelessness Press. <https://homelesshub.ca/sites/default/files/WithoutAHome-final.pdf>.

Goraya, J. 2015. "The Overrepresentation of Minority Youth in Canada's Criminal Justice System." <https://ppgreview.ca/2015/03/09/the-overrepresentation-of-minority-youth-in-canadas-criminal-justice-system/>.

Nichols, N. 2013. "Nobody 'Signs Out of Care': Exploring Institutional Links Between Child Protection Services and Homelessness." In S. Gaetz, B. O'Grady, K. Buccieri, J. Karabanow and A. Marsolais (eds.), *Youth Homelessness in Canada: Implications for Policy and Practice*. Canadian Observatory on Homelessness, Toronto: Canada. <https://www.homelesshub.ca/sites/default/files/YouthHomelessnessweb.pdf>.

O'Grady, B., S. Gaetz and K. Buccieri. 2011. "Can I See Your ID? The Policing of Youth Homelessness in Toronto." Toronto: JFCY and Homeless Hub. <https://homelesshub.ca/sites/default/files/CanISeeYourID_nov9.pdf>.

Ontario Human Rights Commission. n.d. "Prohibited Grounds of Discrimination." <http://www.ohrc.on.ca/en/human-rights-and-rental-housing-ontario-background-paper/prohibited-grounds-discrimination>.

Springer, J., J. Lum, and T. Roswell. 2013. "Policy Challenges to Homelessness Among Caribbean Youth in Toronto." In S. Gaetz, B. O'Grady, K. Buccieri, J. Karabanow and A. Marsolais (eds.), *Youth Homelessness in Canada: Implications for Policy and Practice*. Toronto: Canadian Observatory on Homelessness. <https://www.homelesshub.ca/sites/default/files/YouthHomelessnessweb.pdf>.

Swift, K.J., and H. Parada. 2004. "Child Welfare Reform: Protecting Children or Policing the Poor." *Journal of Law and Social Policy*, 19, 1.

7

Newcomer Youth Seeking Inclusion
and Caring Responses

Rita Isabel Henderson, Anshini Shah, Lynda Ashbourne, Rachel
Ward, Alex Werier, Cathryn Rodrigues, Wilfreda E. Thurston

"Canada can never be your own country. It is a foreigner's country."

In this chapter, we ask what "structural harms" newcomer youth in Canada experience as they navigate education, employment and service sectors, at times accepting and at times resisting social exclusion in their struggles to adjust to Canadian society. We examine how members of seven Voices against Violence participatory action research groups conceptualized steps needed to mitigate structural harms impacting their well-being.

Structural violence involves "invisible manifestations of violence or any harm ... built into the fabric of society — political and economic organization of our social world — and [it] creates and maintains inequalities within and between different social groups, gender and ethnic-cultural groups" (Montesanti and Thurston 2015). The emphasis here is on systemic and structural factors that perpetrate oppression. While structural violence is widespread, determining how these oppressive influences are enacted and what form solutions could take is less straightforward. This complicates efforts by policy-makers and service providers to develop effective action plans for overcoming many barriers to well-being impacting new Canadians. After all, the forces impeding equitable health and social services are often so commonplace that the harm produced is normalized by those delivering services. One effect is that those harmed may come to feel as though they caused their own injury.

From Arts-Based PAR to Policy Implications

The research teams anticipated that youth in the PAR groups may make limited reference to actual policies affecting them, such as schooling or housing policies, and that direct exploration of policy at any level could be challenging. After all, youth may not be exposed to much by way of social life beyond their families and immediate networks, and marginalized youth face consistent barriers to participation in decision-making processes that affect them. On top of that, newcomer youth may be constrained by rules about their immigration status that restrict their capacity to fully participate in social life (e.g., schooling, work), limiting their ability to name and mobilize around specific policy issues. Nevertheless, the Voices against Violence team affirmed from the outset that limited capacity to explicitly name policy quandaries does not mean marginalized youth are necessarily ignorant to the ways wider "social arrangements ... put individuals and populations in harm's ways" (Farmer, Nizeye, Stulac and Keshavjee 2006: 1686). Importantly, such arrangements are "*structural* because they are embedded in the political and economic organization of our social world; they are *violent* because they cause injury to people" (Farmer et al. 2006: 1686). While they are often beyond the immediate control of individuals, they can be empirically observed and acted upon.

The synthesis presented here draws on analysis generated from a scoping review of the literature and seven Y-PAR groups with newcomer youth in four Canadian provinces: Nova Scotia, Quebec, Ontario and Alberta. It includes an overview of themes identified by youth participants, culminating in a policy analysis and recommendations for achieving systemic change. It builds from concept maps generated by youth and is guided by questions from scholar Carol Bacchi's *What's the Problem Represented to Be?* (WPR) model for policy analysis (2009). Via the WPR model, we explore how policy "problems" affecting newcomer youth are talked about and represented by youth themselves and by those who support them. This approach uncovers the taken-for-granted nature of social and structural factors that may limit our imaginings of other ways of living and achieving equity. The authors of this chapter include two newcomer youth (Shah, Rodrigues), two youth of settler-Canadian backgrounds (Ward, Werier) and three academic researchers (Henderson, Ashbourne, Thurston).

Context: Known Challenges to Integration for Newcomer Youth

The documented experiences of newcomer youth, who form one of the fastest growing populations in Canada (Kunz and Harvey 2000), raise questions around the legitimacy of Canada's proclaimed multicultural status. These youth experience subtle and overt discrimination based on race, ethnicity, language and religion, indicating that structural violence is indeed a reality for many upon settlement in this country (Anisef and Kilbride 2000; Phinney, Berry, Sam and Vedder 2006). Reception of immigrant and refugee youth is influenced by the way in which the post-migration society judges newcomers (Khanlou 1999, 2004). This judgement is often based on historical relationships between particular cultural groups or mass media portrayals of the global, political and economic positioning of diverse groups. This is important to newcomer youth in Canada, as prevailing perceptions among dominant society of one's cultural group influences identity and consequently self-esteem (Khanlou, Koh and Mill 2008). Newcomer youth of 13 years and older face the additional risk of not finishing secondary school (Schroeter and James 2014), because systemic biases, the challenges of normal developmental transitions (Anisef and Kilbride 2000) and a lack of resources to help manage adversities (Gouin 2016) can lead to negative educational experiences, from which youth often decide to flee. The literature establishes that structural violence permeates many aspects of life for newcomer youth, limiting and in some cases denying successful integration. In particular, youth face both subtle and overt racism — such as stereotyping, racial profiling, discrimination and bullying — throughout multiple social spheres. Here, we identify broad themes around which structural factors constrain or may support youth well-being in Canada.

Educational Imperatives amid Experiences of Exclusion

The Organisation for Economic Co-operation and Development (OECD) positions Canada first among English-speaking countries with regards to education (2019). Despite this ranking, structural violence punctuates schooling experiences for immigrant and refugee youth, particularly for those who are racialized. Students in both elementary and high school perceive racism and exclusion on the part of teachers (Kayaalp 2014; Phillion 2000) and may feel as though teachers do not believe in or care about them and doubt their ability to pursue post-secondary education.

Some youth requiring extra assistance felt teachers are either unwilling or unable to help them and interpret this perceived lack of attention as apathy on the part of teachers (Kayaalp 2016). Some students found that teachers suggest vocational programs and trade schools to be a best fit for them after high school (Schroeter and James 2014). This perceived lack of attention for their growth was experienced by some as micro-aggression, that is "words and interactions *perceived as racist* by racialized targets that rarely reflect vindictive intent yet inadvertently inflict insult or injury" (Fleras 2016: 1). Theory on micro-aggression puts into question what forms of racism are widely considered to matter by positioning those who experience and perceive it in their lives as the experts on defining it. Therefore, this seeming apathy on the part of educators was felt to limit the potential seen in racialized youth, leading many youth to feel that they were denied equal opportunity to pursue professional programs and leading some to internalize low expectations directed at them within the Canadian education systems (Taylor and Krahn 2013).

Youth recognize both overt and subtle racism from not only teachers but from peers as well (Clancy 2007; Kanu 2008; Kayaalp 2014; Li 2009; Phan 2003). Stereotyping by peers and harmful jokes or racialized assumptions about their countries of origin are not uncommon, with youth being repeatedly asked "What are you?" (Kayaalp 2014) or "So where are you from? … No, where are your parents from?" (Khanlou, Koh and Mill 2008). Racialized language and name-calling or more subtle forms of exclusion such as eye-rolling when newcomers attempt to express themselves in English (Kumsa 2006; Li 2009) are among more general forms of bullying experienced (Clancy 2007; Khanlou, Koh and Mill 2008; Phan 2003). Those who stand up to harassment often face undue punishment as a result and feel they are disciplined more harshly than peers, especially when lacking the ability to defend themselves in the English language.

Some youth report frustration with being placed in classrooms based on their age rather than academic experience (Kanu 2008) or facing different expectations from educators regarding aspirations or capabilities (Schroeter and James 2014). Such challenges are exacerbated for some refugees whose education has been disrupted by war or other traumatic experiences (Kanu 2008; Pajouhandeh 2004; Wilkinson, Yan, Ka Tat Tsang et al. 2012). English as a second language (ESL) classrooms are noted by some youth as harmful to successful integration, as placement within an ESL program distances them from peers, hampering their ability to spend time with those outside of ESL programs. This leads to feelings of isolation (Kayaalp 2016; Li 2009, 2010), and, for some, further enforces language barriers. Students who do not receive continuous integrated and strong ESL support often have negative educational outcomes, evident through comparably high dropout rates (Baffoe 2006; Madibbo 2008). Further, lacking proficiency in the official language of their region may incite newcomer youth to choose non-academic courses, which in turn limits post-secondary opportunities and chances to pursue professional careers (Karanja 2007).

Employment, Precariousness and a Not-So-Welcoming Environment

Canada has one of the highest inflows of permanent residents among OECD countries (Government of Canada 2012). In some provinces, immigrants contribute greatly to the labour force, with some cities projecting a 100 percent dependence on immigration for labour force development (Murphy 2010). Despite encouraging national trends, newcomer youth identify finding work to be difficult and see their parents facing a similar struggle (Lauer, Wilkinson, Yan et al. 2012; Zaami 2015). Upon arriving in Canada, youth and their parents do not receive adequate support for the development of linguistic and cultural skills valued within Canadian society and necessary to secure fulfilling employment (Baffoe 2006; Clancy 2007). Education, experience and credentials achieved in countries of origin are often not recognized or are deemed less valuable, resulting in considerably less lucrative employment opportunities. Lack of recognition or devaluation of prior achievements contributes to youth feelings of isolation and lack of integration (Baffoe 2006; Kanu 2008; Lauer et al. 2012; Rousseau, Hassan, Measham et al. 2009; Shakya, Guruge, Hynie et al. 2010; Taylor and Krahn 2013; Wilkinson et al. 2012), particularly when linked to lower socioeconomic opportunity (Taylor and Krahn 2013). At the same time, newcomer youth, through exposure to Canadian education systems, may gain a stronger command of English and Canadian cultural norms compared to their parents, and are often unfairly positioned to take on the additional responsibility of acting as guides and caretakers of their parents and other family members. This requires youth to work long hours on top of academic responsibilities (Kanu 2008; Shakya et al. 2010), which can be stressful for parents and children alike. Further, some youth grieve a lack of parental support, due to a need for parents to work long hours just to achieve a living wage (Mondain and Lardoux 2013; Shik 2003). Still others feel their parents' lack of linguistic or cultural knowledge limits ability to provide support for youth in certain situations, such as attending parent/teacher interviews (Bisson 2012; Kanu 2008).

Access to Services in the Face of Multiple Barriers

Other services that may assist newcomers in gaining social and cultural knowledge for life in Canada relate to housing, health care, legal systems and diverse social supports, though youth may often be at a loss as to how to access these (Quirke 2014). While systems to serve immigrant youth do exist, many youth note that counselling, housing or employment services are difficult to access and are otherwise underfunded or unable to adequately provide assistance (Madibbo 2008; Van Ngo 2011). Other difficulties noted may be more challenging to capture and mitigate, such as previous trauma (Kanu 2008) or negative past experiences with authority figures, both in their countries of origin and in Canada (Busby-Sham Choy 1998). Such experiences lead many newcomer youth to distrust the institutions designed to help them. Furthermore, racial profiling is widespread in Canada, affecting youth at airports and border crossings (Khanlou, Koh and Mill 2008) and in towns and cities (Baffoe 2006; Madibbo 2008; Zaami 2015). Such experiences often leave an enduring sense of being treated differently because of one's racialized, newcomer status. Cultural differences, including stigmatization around seeking help and language limitations, constrain the ability or desire of newcomer youth to ask for help or accept resources (Quirke 2014).

Resilience through Culture, Identity, Relationships and Leisure

Nazilla Khanlou, Jane Koh and Catriona Mill (2008) highlight the strength of cultural identity in helping youth maintain a positive outlook on multiculturalism in Canada, arguing that it can allow minority groups to recognize the possibility of maintaining their own culture while obtaining higher social status. Still, newcomer youth face several contradictory expectations. The labels of "immigrant" and "refugee" are often racialized and experienced as stigmatizing, causing some youth to feel pressured to act "white" or "Canadian" (Phan 2003) and to downplay their own cultural identities. Others notice that their own cultural practices are deemed inferior (Baffoe 2006). At the same time, youth may feel unable to distance themselves from the labels and stereotypes placed on them, leading to desire among some to reject being labelled as immigrants or refugees and instead preferring to self-identify as simply Canadian. Perhaps due to frequent profiling as "at-risk" by diverse actors in their lives, newcomer youth also report sometimes being perceived as violent, drug users or gang members, or simply thought of as less civilized (Madibbo 2008; Phillion 2000). Other demoralizing stereotypes newcomer youth have reported feeling directed at them include being seen as delinquent when they are routinely monitored in stores while shopping or by police while on the streets (Phan 2003); being seen as comical when they are the butt of jokes by peers and co-workers (Kayaalp 2014); and being assigned certain types of work based on their cultural heritage (Rousseau et al. 2009). Such experiences may result in youth internalizing these negative perceptions of them, which then impacts their integration and self-esteem (Kayaalp 2014; Khanlou, Ko and Mill 2008; Kumsa 2006; Rousseau et al. 2009). Often, systems in place to support newcomer youth do not address the many nuanced cultural identities with which youth enter Canada (Deckers and Zinga 2012; Pajouhandeh 2004). This plays out for youth as they inhabit dissonant social spheres, often with different cultural expectations surrounding acceptance of religious diversity and LGBTQ2S+ rights (del Villar Nash 2011; Li 2009; Quirke 2014; Rousseau et al. 2009), parenting styles (Beiser 2015) and appropriate age to marry and start a family (Bisson 2012).

Doing YPAR with Newcomer Youth in Four Provinces

Between 2013 and 2015, each of the seven Voices against Violence groups convened with newcomers collectively decided on a final project for their group. The projects were all media-based and included documentary film-making, vox pop-style film production, digital storytelling, photovoice, poetry, zines and blogs (see Table 7-1). Each group also utilized a variety of arts-based activities to facilitate critical reflection and expression of thoughts, feelings and opinions about the impact of structural violence on their lives. The arts-based activities included visual representations of safe spaces, group rules, body maps and reflections on identity and systems; collages reflecting and critiquing gendered media representations; and sculptures, letter writing and murals. Activities sometimes led to public presentations of the work produced (e.g., the Calgary project culminated in a public screening of their documentary film in April 2014, attended by the city's mayor).

Table 7-1: Arts-Based Activities among Seven Newcomer Groups in Four Provinces

		Methods
1	Halifax	Collage, digital narratives
2	London	Mural, collage, zines, drawings, body maps, journaling, policy wheels, blog entries
3	Ottawa	Murals, collages
4	London	Identity maps, photovoice
5	Toronto GTA	Storytelling, poetry, short stories
6	Calgary	Murals, letters, sculptures, documentary film
7	Montreal	Collage, video interviews, magnets

Each of the seven groups engaged a different population of newcomer youth (i.e., of immigrant or refugee background; from diverse genders, ages, countries of origin and cities of current residence), drawing perspectives from urban centres in Halifax, Montreal, London (two groups), Ottawa, Toronto and Calgary. In total, fifty-nine participants across these groups contributed their voices, with forty-five being newcomer women and girls, fourteen men and boys, and four identifying as gender-fluid or from a sexual minority. Participant ages ranged from 13–29 years. Identified regions of origin included Central/South America, the Middle East, Northern and East Africa, Central Asia and Eastern Europe. In several groups, refugee youth in particular shared having spent months or years in intermediary countries before arriving in Canada, sometimes in refugee camps and other times following family networks to safety.

How Did the Groups Function?

Group facilitators employed several strategies to make participation as easy as possible for youth and to promote a positive experience despite emotionally charged topics. Strategies included convening regular meeting times and dates agreed to by youth, condensing the research timeframe when needed, providing youth-friendly snacks, paying remuneration in cash and by way of bus tickets, emphasizing a youth-focused approach

Wishing tree for resources, supports and challenges faced by newcomer youth.

(i.e., adapting facilitation plans to emergent priorities expressed by participants) and grounding explorations in expressive arts-based activities.

Some projects reported conflicts or issues with group functioning, which varied between projects depending on the cohort makeup and group activities employed. In the Calgary group, for instance, the only female participant was less outspoken than male peers, who tended to dominate discussions, though the 15-year-old from Afghanistan did play a co-host role in the group's summative public event. In that same group, the research team initially found it difficult to encourage youth to be candid in articulating personal experiences with structural violence. Initially the youth seemed passive in conversations and nervous to speak beyond generic scenarios, such as regarding experiences at school, in sports and in other recreational settings. The research team eventually found that when facilitators of racialized backgrounds led activities, sharing became more candid. This suggests that the perceived ethnic-cultural background of facilitators affected how safe youth participants felt in sharing their stories.

Meanwhile, the Halifax group, which consisted of only female participants, did not have issues navigating gender dynamics, but facilitators found the timing of meetings affected participant engagement; the group gathered after school and many of the participants were tired as a result. It was also the end of the school year and many of the youth had extra-curricular activities and exams to study for, which limited participation. That group had already been established for other purposes, and because their prior activities had been mainly around social outings, it was difficult to shift expectations from a fun social experience to one that would involve some degree of mental and emotional work.

Key Themes and Findings

Each PAR group identified several key themes as part of their discussions and arts-based products. These included topics resonant in the literature, such as inclusion and exclusion; identity and belonging; media influences on identity; various forms of violence and oppression in their lives, including social inequality, racism and bullying; obstacles to acting against oppression; empowerment and resistance; and healthy relationships, development of self-esteem and seeking communities of support (see Table 7-2). Much like in the literature, a strong theme identified by youth across all groups involved problems with integration into school systems, with many of their peers showing ignorance to non-Christian religions and non-Western cultures. This played out in struggles to balance multiple identities; questions around what constitutes "belonging"; the nature of evolving relationships with families; experiences of racism and isolation; and identity changes made to adjust to Canadian society.

Table 7-2: Key Themes Identified by Each PAR Group

Group Location	Key Themes Identified by Participants
Halifax	Community-building, inclusion/exclusion (peer relations and student-teacher interactions), body image and media representation of girls and women
London	Apathy as a defence, identity, health, the need for time and space where youth can discuss youth issues
Ottawa	Structural misogyny and racism
London	Forms and effects of oppression, obstacles to acting against oppression, empowerment, health, inclusion and belonging
Toronto GTA	Intersectionality, historical racism, personal experiences of racism
Calgary	Racism, isolation, bullying, school and family as support systems
Montreal	Safe spaces, healthy relationships, seeking communities of support, women in the media, youth identity

Carol Bacchi's WPR policy analysis model draws attention to how youth represent the "problems" in their lives on which specific policies might act, problems that the youth understand to be systemic, or at least deeper than interpersonal or idiosyncratic in nature. Youth perspectives are organized here on a general progression from proximal or near forms of structural violence to more intermediary forms, for instance of personally mediated racism (Jones 2000) and experiences of injury structured by organizations and institutions.

Social Inclusion and Exclusion

Across the seven groups, youth repeatedly identified one process by which structural violence affects them daily, which is through pressure to "fit in" and integrate into "Canadian society." We put the latter in quotation marks, as the youth articulated that this was less about what they understood Canadian society to involve or represent, and more about what other people do to police newcomer youth with constrained ideas about what it means to be Canadian. These everyday processes of navigating social inclusion and exclusion were linked to issues of individual identity formation, which arose in discussions within every project, though in two instances youth participants were uneasy with a discussion of identity formation, requesting that it not be their primary focus and to instead target attention towards wider systems. Those who did explore it argued that their identities were multiple, as they felt a sense of belonging to their new country, but continued to identify with their countries of origin or homelands of their parents. As such, participants demonstrated how they actively work to forge new, intersecting identities for themselves in Canada, while still preserving values and beliefs connected to their cultural heritage.

Nevertheless, the youth discussed how some identities are assigned to them by others because of their newcomer status — these identities included "outsiders" and "foreigners," as well as simply "immigrants" and "refugees." To some degree, Voices against Violence was complicit in this by identifying eligible participants with these latter terms. All seven projects highlighted the struggle youth participants and researchers faced together when using such labels for marginalized youth; "newcomer" was often preferred by participants as an alternative term to immigrant and refugee, and one project used the term "racialized" instead, though this would not have suited all youth in other groups. The name of the documentary made in Calgary reflects this desire to change the way they are seen by others: *The New Citizens*. This indicates common discomfort with being labelled refugees and immigrants, terms linked to colonial roots and the unequal capacity of people to cross national borders. As several groups noted, these terms are used by the federal government as part of its immigration policy, which determines who is eligible for citizenship and rights under Canadian law.

Inclusion and exclusion also played out through religion or spirituality, which was important in the lives of many of the newcomer youth. They had difficulties practising their faith in public schools because they could not pray throughout the day and did not have their specific religious holidays observed or even recognized. Many Muslim girls spoke about how it was difficult to wear the hijab in school, with some even changing out of it as soon as they arrived at school. Some youth spoke about the

Storyboarding the film The New Citizens.

challenges of being immersed in a pluralist society and what tolerance meant for them. They said their beliefs were challenged on a regular basis, and it created some identity strain as members of a religious community. Broader differences between life in Canada and life elsewhere also formed a recurring theme, with multiple youth saying their least favourite aspect of Canadian life was the lack of street life or common spaces where families and friends could meet casually in public, leading to feelings of loneliness and social disconnection in Canada.

The youth represented the problems around inclusion and exclusion in the following ways:

- the policing of cultural identity comes from many corners, including from within newcomer communities;
- non-stigmatizing terminology around newcomer identities is an important anti-racism strategy;
- availability of spiritual resources within youth-focused systems (e.g., schools) may reinforce meaning and sense of belonging; and
- public non-commercial spaces for unstructured, social interaction mitigate isolation.

Racism and Personally Mediated vs. Structural Violence

Many youth pinpointed racism as a main vector of their oppression; however, some group facilitators noted multiple factors that made the sharing of experiences of racism challenging. One factor is that these experiences were often described as personally mediated between members of one's own social group or at the hands of members of other newcomer groups. Public health scholar Camara Jones identifies three levels of racism, where personally mediated is the most familiar kind, often concealing structural and internalized levels of racism. Personally mediated racism plays out as prejudice or discrimination and is "what most people think of when they hear the word 'racism' … can be intentional as well as unintentional, and it includes acts of commission as well as acts of omission" (2003: 8). The youth were perhaps reluctant to talk about these experiences for fear of contributing to or being further victimized by stereotyping or further marginalizing people from all racial and ethnic minorities. As an example, one youth identified how people in their city would not sit next to Black people on buses, including him: "Most people go on the bus, and they do not want to sit too close to you. They don't want to get close to you … in Canada, everywhere you go you see racism. And most of the time it is from people from other countries." Another youth from the Middle East spoke about how his mother would be subjected to racist taunts and insults because she wore her hijab. He mentioned that Indigenous youth yelled racist insults at her and even spat on her, which he felt he could do little to confront. Yet another participant reflected on having frequently witnessed immigrants bullying other immigrants; when asked if he would do anything to stand up to a bully for himself or another, the boy admitted that he would not. These examples demonstrate the pervasiveness and silencing of such violence and suggest that the youth have developed a degree of tolerance or passivity to racism in the moments they encounter it. The examples also highlight structural violence, in that wider social systems seem to enact marginalization by isolating those at the margins from one another.

Another factor, evident in all of the groups, was that the youth were not indignant about their experiences of racism, but instead many seemed to have internalized it and accepted it as a status quo. One youth who heard Islamophobic jokes about the September 11, 2001, terrorist attacks said that he simply went along with such humour because it helped leverage his transition into a new school. He said that in some cases, he would participate in making such jokes. This sheds additional light on the dynamics of structural violence in their lives, in that the youth described instances of being victims, perpetrators and bystanders to such forms of harm as a means of self-preservation. Such fluidity highlights that the violence at hand is not merely interpersonal in nature, but at times enacted as a coping mechanism that allows youth to navigate the social norms of networks and systems that offer inclusion on condition that they conform.

The reticence of youth participants to directly talk about racism perhaps demonstrates its mundanity in their lives. They often seemed to accept it as part of the immigration experience, despite its potential to inflict severe physical and emotional harm on them and their families. Most of the seven groups talked about experiencing some form of physical abuse or being physically threatened by family members and strangers for a multitude of reasons.

Sometimes the greatest physical harms were directed towards themselves. The female participants in the Halifax group identified experiences with eating disorders, while those in London spoke of suicidal thoughts, addiction and self-harm. Youth participants in Toronto spoke of mental health problems, while those in Calgary described feelings of passivity or coming to feel numb in the face of adversity. Many youth had escaped extremely challenging circumstances in their migration journeys and consequently felt that structural violence in Canada was a small price to pay for some freedoms and the security they now enjoyed. Accordingly, some felt that talking about any negative experiences or challenges while living in Canada would be perceived as ungrateful.

Despite diverse backgrounds and experiences among newcomer youth located across Canada, participants often shared one common response to structural violence, namely silence. Research team members note that this may itself be an internalization of structural violence. After all, it involves newcomer youth being conditioned not to speak up against racism in their lives for risk of being seen as something less than gracious recipients of Canadian benevolence and aid.

The following are several ways that the problems around personally mediated racism are represented:

- personally mediated racism among newcomer youth themselves

may be symptom of competing for limited resources and attention within wider society;

- self-harm, particularly among female youth, was often a conse-
quence of racism and stigma; and
- anti-racist education that prepares youth and their allies to confront micro-aggressions and discrimination has not been part of
their preparation for living in Canada.

Organizational and Institutional Violence

Youth frequently located systemic harm in services and organizations
catering to immigrant and refugee people. Participants talked about
an absence of knowledgeable, respectful and sensitive supports within
these organizations. They described multiple wants and needs and the
challenge of negotiating many access points, but they also point to the
patronizing and paternalistic undertones they sometimes encountered.
For example, at times the youth felt that they had to present themselves
as worthy subjects in order to access certain services, and they also felt
that these agencies often seemed to disregard the personal and collective
agency of newcomers.

When such organizations and services fail to meet youth needs, participants highlighted the importance of intra-group supports for their
resilience, in the form of informal social networks. However, informal
supports were limited in their capacity to help youth, particularly young
women, overcome their own marginalization. These could, for instance,
increase pressures within familial and migrant networks, because such
social support may be extended in exchange for meeting cultural expectations within the private sphere. The group in Ottawa described this
dynamic, noting that dependence on family and cultural community
networks for support may reinforce inequities around who does household
chores, how mothering is valued or not valued, and who makes choices
about women's bodies. All of these factors limited the nature of supports
that female participants might expect to leverage from their family and
cultural community networks. The importance of non-familial networks
was emphasized in one all-female group from London, whose members
noted that systemic arrangements beyond their immediate control often
dictated their ability to integrate into such networks. Addressing public school zoning policies that determine who may attend where and

affordable housing policies to promote ethno-culturally mixed neigh-bourhoods would go a long way to mitigating these systemic factors and reducing isolation within family and cultural community networks.

In terms of school policy, many youth expressed feeling safe and secure at school, but said that it was common for newcomer youth to be mocked for their lack of English-language skills. Participants argued that despite anti-bullying campaigns in their schools, bullying persisted mostly outside of the classroom during break times and before and after school. This highlights a need to explore the efficacy of anti-bullying programs. These need to be aligned with the evolving and multi-faceted nature of bullying and harassment, for instance as it manifests itself online via social media, through "sexting" and in emergent slurs and slang that escape anti-racist educator attention.

The following are several ways that the problems around organizational and institutional violence are represented:

- even newcomer-serving institutions are often ignorant to the particular needs of youth or different individuals within new-comer families;
- social supports outside of the family are important resources to diminish isolation among youth; and
- schools and other youth services should be nimble and respon-sive to the evolving needs of newcomer youth within diverse contexts.

Actions that Could Be Taken

The youth proposed a number of actions that could be taken to address the issues raised. For example, the youth suggested that creating supportive environments for newcomers within schools, encouraging a more general awareness and acceptance of multiple diverse experiences, and fostering changes in attitude around diversity and cultural traditions would promote emotional and mental well-being for newcomers. As the project itself demonstrated, just getting youth together to discuss structural violence, to share their experiences and discuss possible solutions, was a valuable and healing encounter. One participant from London described it as a positive experience, saying, "This made me realize how sharing experi-ence is important for us to live a happier life."

While some participants had specific calls for action for institutions (e.g., more flexible school zoning policies), some had difficulty identifying structural violence and developing the capacity to work against it. For example, though students within the Toronto group recognized racism, they had difficulty naming wider social forces (e.g., poverty) that drive their encounters with it. By expressing that they themselves were not "experts" on racism, the youth at times dismissed the possibility that they are *systemically* disadvantaged due to their newcomer status, focusing on its interpersonal rather than structural expressions. A young Calgarian believed standing up for themselves was "a waste of energy," and another argued that it was easier to take part in Islamaphobic jokes against themselves than stand up to the jokers. While this apparent acceptance of discrimination as the status quo may be disheartening, it reflects a reality for these youth that offers them limited options for confronting oppression. Whether youth are conscious or unconscious about the experiences of structural violence against newcomers, they clearly highlighted that there is a blurred line between being victims, complicit or active in the oppression of newcomers to Canada. While some students internalized aspects of their oppression, turning it towards themselves through self-harm, it should not signal that they are complacent or accepting of such realities.

As reflected in the literature, the capacity of a setting to adequately support youth development is greatly influenced by social relationships (Bronfenbrenner 1979). For youth entering an entirely new society, being around familiar faces — whether family, friends or even others of similar cultural background — is an important part of successful integration. Many youth indicate feeling less parental support in Canada because of avoidable discrimination within the systems in which their families are expected to participate. Schools and recreational facilities in particular emerge as significant venues for promoting the emotional and mental well-being of youth. While many of the youth said they felt safe in their school, all of the groups highlighted that to some extent bullying is among their biggest problems. Bullying rooted in xenophobic comments that attack their poor language skills or "different" cultural or religious practices were especially trying to endure. This invites added attention for the efficacy of anti-bullying programs to ensure their currency with the changing and multi-faceted nature of bullying and harassment.

References

Anisef, P., and K.M. Kilbride. 2000. *The Needs of Newcomer Youth and Emerging "Best Practices" to Meet Those Needs: Final Report*. Toronto: Joint Centre of Research on Immigration and Settlement. <http://atwork.settlement.org/downloads/Newcomer_Youth_Best_Practices.pdf>.

Bacchi, C. 2009. *Analysing Policy: What's the Problem Represented to Be?*, 1st edition. Frenchs Forest, N.S.W: Pearson.

Baffoe, M. 2006. "Navigating Two Worlds: Culture and Cultural Adaptation of Immigrant and Refugee Youth in a Quebec (Canadian) Educational Context." PhD thesis, McGill University.

Beiser, M. 2015. "Cultural Distance and Emotional Problems Among Immigrant and Refugee Youth in Canada: Findings from the New Canadian Child and Youth Study (NCCYS)." *International Journal of Intercultural Relations*, 49, 6: 33–45.

Bisson, M.A.S. 2012. "Successfully Adapting to Canada: Refugee Youths Share Their Expertise." PhD thesis, University of Calgary.

Bronfenbrenner, U. 1979. *The Ecology of Human Development*. Cambridge: Harvard University Press.

Busby-Sham Choy, C.A. 1998. "Interpersonal Trust in Teacher-Student Relationship: Meaning for Black Students (14–16 Years) of Caribbean Background in Secondary Schools in the Greater Toronto Area." OISE/University of Toronto.

Clancy, A. 2007. "An Exploration of Bullying as Experienced by Sudanese Refugee Youths." MSW thesis, Wilfred Laurier University.

Deckers, C., and D. Zinga. 2012. "Locating Home: Newcomer Youths' School and Community Engagement." *Canadian Journal of Education*, 35, 3: 30–47.

del Villar Nash, C. 2011. "Bullying, Ethnic Discrimination, or Both? A Phenomenological Study of the Experiences of Immigrant Adolescents." MSW thesis, University of Toronto.

Farmer, P.E., B. Nizeye, S. Stulac, and S. Keshavjee. 2006. "Structural Violence and Clinical Medicine." *PLoS Medicine*, 3, 10: 1686–1691.

Fleras, Augie. 2016. "Theorizing Micro-aggressions as Racism 3.0: Shifting the Discourse." *Canadian Ethnic Studies* 48, 2, 1-19. <doi:10.1353/ces.2016.0011>.

Gouin, R. 2016. "Facilitating the Integration of Newcomer Children and Youth." Boys and Girls Clubs of Canada. <https://sencanada.ca/content/sen/committee/421/RIDR/Briefs/BoysandGirlsClub_e.pdf>.

Government of Canada. 2012. "Trends in Economic Performance of Immigrants in Canada." < https://www.canada.ca/en/immigration-refugees-citizenship/corporate/reports-statistics/research/role-migrant-labour-supply-canadian-labour-market/section-5.html>.

Jones, C. 2000. "Levels of Racism: A Theoretic Framework and a Gardener's Tale." *American Journal of Public Health*, 90, 8: 1212–1215.

Kanu, Y. 2008. "Educational Needs and Barriers for African Refugee Students in Manitoba." *Canadian Journal of Education*, 31, 4: 915–940.

Karanja, L. 2007. "ESL Learning Experiences of Immigrant Students in High Schools in a Small City." *TESL Canada Journal*, 24, 2: 23–41.

Kayaalp, D. 2014. "Educational Inclusion/Exclusion of Turkish Immigrant Youth in Vancouver Canada: A Critical Analysis." *International Journal of Inclusive Education*, 18, 7: 655–668.

___. 2016. "Living with an Accent: A Sociological Analysis of Linguistic Strategies of Immigrant Youth in Canada." *Journal of Youth Studies*, 19, 2: 133–148.

Khanlou, N. 1999. "Adolescent Cultural Identity and Self-Esteem in a Multicultural Society." PhD thesis, McMaster University.

___. 2004. "Influences on Adolescent Self-Esteem in Multicultural Canadian Secondary Schools." *Public Health Nursing*, 21, 5: 404–411.

Khanlou, N., J.G. Koh, and C. Mill. 2008. "Cultural identity and Experiences of Prejudice and Discrimination of Afghan and Iranian Immigrant Youth. *International Journal of Mental Health and Addiction*, 6, 4: 494–513.

Kumsa, M.K. 2006. "'No! I'm Not a Refugee!': The Poetics of Belonging Among Young Oromos in Toronto." *Journal of Refugee Studies*, 19, 2: 230–255.

Kunz, J., and L. Harvey. 2000. *Immigrant Youth in Canada*. Ottawa: Canadian Council on Social Development.

Lauer, S., L. Wilkinson, M. Yan, R. Sin, and A. Ka Tat Tsang. 2012. "Immigrant Youth and Employment: Lessons Learned from the Analysis of LSIC and 82 Lived Stories." *Journal of International Migration and Integration*, 13, 1: 1–19.

Li, J. 2009. "Forging the Future Between Two Different Worlds: Recent Chinese Immigrant Adolescents Tell Their Cross-Cultural Experiences." *Journal of Adolescent Research*, 24, 4: 477–504.

___. 2010. "'My Home and My School': Examining Immigrant Adolescent Narratives from the Critical Sociocultural Perspective." *Race Ethnicity and Education*, 13, 1: 119–137.

Madibbo, A. 2008. "The Integration of Black Francophone Immigrant Youth in Ontario: Challenges and Possibilities." *Canadian Issues* (Spring): 45–49.

Mondain, N., and S. Lardoux. 2013. "Transitions to Adulthood among First Generation Sub-Saharan African Immigrant Adolescents in Canada: Evidence from a Qualitative Study in Montreal." *Journal of International Migration and Integration*, 14: 307–326.

Montesanti, S.R., and W.E. Thurston. 2015. "Mapping the Role of Structural and Interpersonal Violence in the Lives of Women: Implications for Public Health Interventions and Policy." *BMC Women's Health*, 15: 100. DOI: 10.1186/s12905-015-0256-4.

Murphy, J. 2010. *The Settlement and Integration Needs of Immigrants: A Literature Review*. Ottawa: Citizenship and Immigration Canada. <https://olip-plio.ca/knowledge-base/wp-content/uploads/2013/03/Olip-Review-of-Literature-Final-EN.pdf>.

OECD. 2019. *Education at a Glance 2019*: OECD Indicators. Paris, France. <https://doi.org/10.1787/f8d7880d-en>.

Pajouhandeh, P. 2004. "Living Between Two Cultures: The Acculturation Experiences of Young Iranian Immigrant Women in Canada." PhD thesis, University of Toronto.

Phan, T. 2003. "Life in School: Narratives of Resiliency among Vietnamese-Canadian

Youths." *Adolescence*, 38, 151: 555–566.

Phillion, R. 2000. "Culture, Identity and Change: The Experience of Southeast Asian Refugee Adolescents in Canada." PhD thesis, York University.

Phinney, J. S., J.W. Berry, D.L. Sam, and P. Vedder (eds.). 2006. *Immigrant Youth in Cultural Transition: Acculturation, Identity, and Adaptation Across National Contexts*. Mahwah, New Jersey: Lawrence Erlbaum Associates Publishers.

Quirke, L.C. 2014. "A Study of the Information Practices of Afghan Newcomer Youth in the Contexts of Leisure and Settlement." PhD thesis, University of Toronto.

Rousseau, C., G. Hassan, T. Measham, N. Moreau et al. 2009. "From the Family Universe to the Outside World: Family Relations, School Attitude, and Perception of Racism in Caribbean and Filipino Adolescents." *Health and Place*, 15, 3: 751–760.

Schroeter, S., and C.E. James. 2014. "'We're Here Because We're Black': The Schooling Experiences of French-Speaking African-Canadian Students with Refugee Backgrounds." *Race Ethnicity and Education*, 18, 1: 20–39.

Shakya, Y., S. Guruge, M. Hynie, A. Akbari et al. 2010. "Aspirations for Higher Education Among Newcomer Refugee Youth in Toronto: Expectations, Challenges, and Strategies." *Refuge*, 27, 2: 65–78.

Shik, A. 2003. "Battling Solitude: The Experience of Loneliness among Hong Kong Chinese Immigrant Youth." PhD thesis, University of Toronto.

Taylor, A., and H. Krahn. 2013. "Living Through Our Children: Exploring the Education and Career 'Choices' of Racialized Immigrant Youth in Canada." *Journal of Youth Studies*, 16, 8: 1000–1021.

Van Ngo, H. 2011. "The Unravelling of Identities and Belonging: Criminal Gang Involvement of Youth from Immigrant Families." PhD thesis, University of Calgary.

Wilkinson, L., M.C. Yan, A. Ka Tat Tsang, R. Sin, and S. Lauer. 2012. "The School-to-Work Transitions for Newcomer Youth in Canada." *Canadian Ethnic Studies*, 44, 3: 29–44.

Zaami, M. 2015. "'I Fit the Description': Experiences of Social and Spatial Exlusion among Ghanian Immigrant Youth in the Jane and Finch Neighbourhood of Toronto." *Canadian Ethnic Studies*, 47, 3: 69–89.

8

Trans Pirates for Justice

Gender and Sexual Minority Youth Resist Structural Violence

Mina Harker, Alex Werier, Cathryn Rodrigues,
Wilfreda E. Thurston, Rita Isabel Henderson

"[We] should be able to live authentically, just like people who are cisgender, who have lived their life ... People just want to go through life, get their stuff done, not have to worry."

This chapter is written with the intent to give space and voice to gender and sexual minority (GSM) youth who participated in Voices against Violence. As used in the context of this chapter, GSM is an encompassing phrase that typically includes gay, lesbian, bisexual, two-spirit and transgender persons. Results from this project reveal how GSM youth are marginalized and denied care in their social worlds and in Canadian systems. We also learned about the various tactics of resistance, survivance and "oppression management" used by the youth to deal with structural violence. In this chapter, we contextualize the youths' experiences of harm and make connections to their health and well-being in the face of this violence.

The term "structural violence" is discussed widely in this book. Pertinent to this particular chapter are forms of structural violence that arrive by way of homophobia, heterocentrism and the privileging of cisgender people over people who are gender-non-conforming and belong to GSMs. In terms of medical and health services, GSM discrimination often frames the body itself as political and the ways that mainstream expectations of the physical human body are imposed on GSM service users and facilitated by a general lack of cultural safety in systems for GSM individuals. These practices are played out through verbal, linguistic and psychological abuse and may even be enacted through treatment protocols. In this study, definitions of health, well-being, care and quality of life were expanded and linked to social justice as well as to human rights. Working within a social determinants of health framework, an analysis of the health care system includes an analysis of how dominant social, political and economic structures, policies and institutions contribute to and interrupt good health and create unnecessary suffering.

Description of Our Research

We engaged fourteen GSM youth using an arts-based participatory action research (PAR) methodology over two initiatives to examine structural violence, exploring action steps youth take to develop survivance capacity and action steps policy-makers can take to improve health outcomes for GSM young people. The research question decided upon by the youth participants was: *What are the experiences of LGBTQ2S+ youth with structural violence and what barriers do LGBTQ2S+ youth identify to their well-being?* The umbrella term "GSM" was later adopted to be more inclusive of the wide variety of sexual and gender identity markers used by the youth. This initial process involved ten youth identifying as *LGBTQ2S+* (i.e., lesbian, gay, bisexual, transgender, transitioning, queer and Two-Spirit) who participated in a weekly arts-based workshop over a four-month period in winter 2014. During workshops, the group collaborated to produce diverse art pieces analyzing gender and sexual-based violence embedded in wider systems. A subsequent process to enrich the perspectives generated engaged an additional four youth who identified as transgender, who preferred to be engaged one-on-one and who also produced art analyses that could be disseminated in public art exhibits. While the former group addressed structural violence throughout their lives and social worlds, the latter focused attention primarily on health care systems. While the medical system's problematically limited approach to health caused difficulties for the GSM youth overall, interactions with this system were necessary in particular for the transgender youth seeking services related to their transitioning. They looked to the medical system to offer life-saving treatments such as hormone therapies, gender-related surgeries and mental health supports while on the path to gender self-actualization. Some of the things needed by the youth, such as breast augmentation for trans women, were denied to them if considered by providers to not be basic health care needs. The youth pointed to the absence of safe spaces and/ or communities of care outside of simple practitioner-based health care.

The GSM youth also shared examples of challenges outside the medical system, including verbal assaults from strangers in public. In these cases, witnesses were described as not always intervening to increase the safety — or even just the dignity — of the GSM youth. Often in such cases, the perpetrators pointed to the youth's outward appearances as grounds for the attack and for the harm inflicted upon them. Very often, the targets of such attacks would not report violence to the police or other authorities within a system (e.g., schooling).

This particular research group was conducted in Calgary, the "cowboy town" known for its oil and gas production and situated in Treaty 7 Territory and Alberta's Métis Region 3. The GSM community is spread throughout this geographical region and does not function as a cohesive, singular or politically discrete unit. The youth reported that in Calgary, GSM youth can be found in community centres, in one particular bar with a complicated history and at multiple pop-up parties. The few organizations reported to offer resources for GSM youth in Calgary include the Camp fYrefly, a yearly camping retreat promoting self-esteem through a positive camp experience for GSM youth, and Skipping Stone, a transfocused organization working tirelessly to help trans youth reach their gender goals. A vibrant cultural GSM scene was felt by many to flourish in the city, with organizations such as the Fairy Tales Queer Film Festival, which has launched youth-focused queer media projects since 2011, as well as a few all-ages drag nights promoting contemporary forms of drag with an interest in performance-art.

Current Understandings

A review of relevant literature reveals that rates of suicidal and self-destructive behaviours are significantly higher among gender and sexual minority youth than among cisgender and/or heterosexual youth — often because of actual or perceived mistreatment and discrimination from others:

- Three-quarters of Canadian lesbian, gay and bisexual youth and 95 percent of transgender youth feel unsafe at school (Taylor and

Peter 2011), and it was found that a non-supportive school environment is correlated with depression and suicidality for sexual minority youth (Denny et al. 2016).

- In a meta-analysis of suicide risk among GSM people, the majority of large studies of youth risk behavior indicate that sexual orientation creates disparities in suicide attempts as well as increases rates for more serious forms of suicide-related behaviour, measured for instance by greater need for medical attention (Plöderl et al. 2013).

- From the 2009–2010 TransPULSE survey of 433 trans Ontarians age 16+: 20 percent had been sexually or physically assaulted for being trans and 43 percent had history of attempted suicide.

- In 2015 nearly two-thirds of trans identifying youth reported self-harm within the past year; a similar number reported serious thoughts of suicide; and more than one in three had attempted suicide (Veale et al. 2015).

A significant suicide rate among GSM youth is partially attributable to experiences of structural violence in everyday life, such as misgendering from heterosexual, cisgender people or, worse, peers. In these instances, everyday language can be seen as something that contributes to chronic stress, which can be connected to negative health outcomes for GSM youth. This kind of chronic stress has been termed "minority stress" by Ilan H. Meyer (2003). Meyer describes the chronically high levels of stress faced by marginalized individuals in the social conditions of everyday life and attributes this stress to experiences of daily prejudice and discrimination, a lack of social support and low socioeconomic status. He emphasizes that minority stress can lead to poor mental and physical health because prejudice or discrimination often causes a stress response in the individual (e.g., high blood pressure, stomach pain, headaches, anxiety) which may compound over time into a serious health condition. The GSM youth in our project described to us how they often resist chronic sadness and suicidality despite this stress and what they recommended to institutions to support young people like themselves.

The Young People with Whom We Worked

As indicated, our activities were carried out over a four-month period during which ten of the fourteen GSM youth between the ages of 18 and 25 were recruited for weekly activities in a church basement in central Calgary. As a means of enhancing transgender perspectives that were identified by the research team to be marginalized in the original sample, an additional four transgender youth were subsequently recruited for interviews and to share their art. Each youth specified their preferred gender pronouns, and participants included individuals who used the gender pronouns she, he and they. The workshop group was culturally diverse and included individuals who had immigrated to Canada. One person indicated that they were of uncertain Indigenous origin, but due to entering the child welfare system at a young age, they were no longer connected to any specific Indigenous background and expressed that they were experiencing spiritual rupture. Three group members were in secondary school during the workshops. Participants were either unemployed or their employment was precarious, indicating that employment precarity is a key contextual reality affecting GSM young people in Calgary. Participants lived with friends or at their family home.

One key theme shared by participants was their calculated decision to not report violence — structural or interpersonal — when it was done to them. The GSM youth anticipated that reporting would invariably go badly and that they would be blamed and made to feel even worse. They stated that they were embarrassed to report because the justification for attacks was supposedly their GSM outward presentation and the fact that they did not pass as a cisgender person. They feared similar hostility when interacting with the police. An openly queer person was felt to be at risk for being assaulted for holding hands with a same-gender partner, for instance. These perspectives are not unfounded; they are well covered in the media, which reports that it is still dangerous in many Western countries to hold hands in public with a same-sex person (Bielski 2018; Blair 2019; Holden 2019). The youth highlighted that not only before and during an attack, but also after an experience of interpersonal violence, structural violence comes into play. They described system indifference or dismissal of the violence as constituting "negative social responses" towards victims and increasing suffering (Richardson and Wade 2008).

When victims of violence experience unsupportive responses from the system, from professionals and from family and/or friends, they are more likely to suffer for extended periods, to receive a mental health diagnosis and to experience suicidal ideations (Richardson and Wade 2008).

GSM youth often avoid seeking help from institutions, such as the medical system, out of not wanting to experience further stigmatization from the policies or professionals within. The GSM youth reported that, at times, their privacy had not been respected in such institutions, thus increasing the chance of stigmatization and judgement. These overwhelming forces of stigma and harm impede equitable access to health and social services for GSM youth and are often so commonplace that the harm produced was felt to be normalized as acceptable.

In opposition to this harm, GSM youth may engage in tactics for "survivance," which is defined as individual or community-based resistance to death and dying, and an ability to resist, survive and even thrive despite intensely harmful circumstances. Indigenous scholar Emerance Baker (2007) describes survivance as moving beyond traumatic circumstances to build a better life for yourself and your friends despite structural violence from the past and present consistently presenting itself as reality. Survivance is typically considered a tactic of resistance against state oppression, in which the individual or group continues living, against all odds.

Challenging Structural Violence through Art

In the early weeks of the project workshop, the participants used artistic media to express personal experiences of structural violence by individually decorating journals and making individual sculptures out of clay. For instance, the youth were given clay and invited to sculpt anything that makes them feel strong in the face of adversity. While the sculptures focused on sources of "resilience," this activity was co-facilitated by a psychologist and had a therapeutic and formal undertone from which some youth participants withdrew. These early activities saw participants identify structural violence at personal levels, but were not very effective at challenging systems and their effects. In subsequent weeks, participants expressed a concern that singular activities ran counter to collaborative engagement and seemed counter-intuitive to the aims of the project.

Following this, youth participants were asked to make a double-sided trading card that on one side reflected the harmful external forces bearing down on them, and on the other side reflected the internal forces that push back and protect against harm. The activity concluded with the group discussing the underlying logic of their own cards. While this activity proved more engaging than prior activities and was successful at identifying and challenging the impact of structural violence, it continued a therapeutic approach that the participants hoped to disrupt. Upon the request of youth participants, an effort was then made throughout the rest of the project to work on the same artistic pieces together, for the purposes of mapping collective experiences of structural violence. The group moved beyond the early focus on identifying and challenging the impact of structural violence at a personal level to begin addressing systemic harm and proposing collective solutions through collaborative poetry, group murals and a group-produced zine (i.e., small-circulation, self-published magazine).

Developing Resistance Against Structural Violence Through Arts-Based Activities

The first collaborative initiative was an idea provided by a youth participant: writing poetry using the surrealist "exquisite corpse" technique, whereby each participant adds a line to a poem based on a line written by a previous person, in this case sitting next to them. Seven poems initiated by group members addressed themes of self-esteem, love, anger, coping strategies, mental health, rights and resistance, though there was some disagreement about the extent to which these themes tackle structural violence. This disagreement, itself, led to interesting discussions. For instance, the person who advocated for "love" as a theme credited their survival to finding a loving partner, while others felt that idealized forms of love were harmful.

The use of the exquisite corpse method advanced the collaborative potential of the group by resisting individualizing experiences or taking a therapeutic approach. While group members' opinions about how to confront structural violence varied substantially, which can be seen in the contrasting serious and humorous tones that participants applied to each poem, the youth broadly considered this exercise as an opportunity to avoid a singular narrative, to make space for quieter personalities, to create space for different perspectives and to allow disagreements to exist unproblematically.

Exquisite corpse poem "Anger,"
written collectively by participants

ANGER
fire burning, choking me out, i need to make the ache in my belly stop,
let the words pass my lips and scream the truth. the power of anger
is strong, it makes the victims of its power forever scarred, one must
surrender his anger to stop the harm.

angry for the way i was treated, angry because this world is not fair,
angry is not who i am. that's how i like it, when you judge me, don't get
to have a voice, it became a scream without an audience, a mute beast.

can't sleep, won't sleep, not cheap, can't sleep, throw words, eat feelings,
purge, purge, purge, let fury have the hour, anger can be power, did you
know you could use it?

Exquisite corpse poem "Survival Strategies,"
written collectively by participants

SURVIVAL STRATEGIES
survival. how we make it through each day. whatever gets us through
each day. your strategy for enduring. may not work for someone else.
but it may help them find their own. dance, sway, rock a baby. grow a
beautiful flower from seed. have a picnic and celebrate. dance. coping
is the way the mind survives.

just as the food we eat is needed to survive for our bodies. doggy kisses,
butterfly kisses. long lingering hugs, warm baths, cool colours. dancing
to loud music, walks in nature, ocean waves, silence. my fears. my love,
my shield, my secret place, help. cope, escape, escalate, scale, scope, cop,
copy, cope. i've eaten up my whole life, want to be a wife.

While the poetry activity proved effective for identifying structural
violence and developing arts-based methods for challenging this harm,
it became clear that poetry did not resonate with everyone.

Proposing Solutions to Structural Violence at Community or Public-Policy Levels

The group subsequently dedicated two weekly gatherings to painting a large poster-style mural inspired by graffiti. The image, of a wall with a piece of wallpaper torn back to reveal what is underneath, is intended to convey the idea that beneath a surface of harm and distrust, a better world is possible. The mural proposed multiple solutions to structural violence, including activism, enjoying nature, loving animals, intersectionality and collaboration.

For a final activity, the group created a zine. Each participant created a page addressing structural violence and resistance. Themes that emerged included diversity education, overcoming negative self-talk, mental health, speaking out, support for gay-straight alliances in schools and the notion of "trans piracy" as a subversive movement for justice. The idea of trans piracy comes from the book *Testo Junkie* by Paul B. Preciado (2008) and involves stealing back the rights to bodily autonomy and the right to love

Mural created collectively by youth participants.

who one wants to love and to make one's own choices about gender and sexuality. Transitioning between genders was also referred to as piracy and the youth compared switching gender codes in online video game or movie piracy, and described their understanding of gender as something we can splice, cut up, download and "pirate" from one another or the medical establishment and entertainment industries.

Sharing in the art of zine-making.

Key Learnings

Indicators of Structural Violence Experienced by GSM Youth

Using an iterative process, the team of adult and youth co-researchers coded interview transcripts and workshop texts for everyday forms of structural violence, for institutional forms of structural violence and for coping, healing and thriving mechanisms identified by youth. This coding recognizes that the harm impacting the health of GSM youth is part of everyday *and* institutional life, but it also recognizes that youth often already carry valuable resources for confronting or coping with the structural violence they endure. The youth in the workshop identified forms of oppression such as gender mislabelling, lateral violence, judgement, assumptions and silencing. Participants identified issues such as stigma, gender binarism, lack of knowledge, general transphobia within institutions and an absence of trans-friendly health care.

Healing and Thriving Strategies Identified by GSM Youth

The youth in our project identified strategies similar to those reported in the literature, indicating that strategies used by GSM youth to resist structural violence in Calgary are also used by the wider population of GSM youth. They described using yoga practices, meditation and cognitive or dialectical forms of behavioural therapy to engage with oppression. Structural oppression was so overwhelming to many that any kind of freeing mindfulness practice was used by these youth "like a healing balm."

Demonstrating empathy for themselves and the other. Empathy for the other was also regarded as a positive mechanism for dealing with stigma. For example, understanding why a cisgender person might ask inappropriate personal questions (e.g., "Have you had 'the surgery'?"). One youth said:

> [I] look in their shoes and be like "Why would they want to know that?" … Just being able to have that reflexive self … You could have been their first gender-fluid person or transgender person ever so how would you react if you were that person and you were working with them … It does give you a sense of strength because you're able to look at it and just be like "Okay, this is what happens, this is what could be improved on, this is what I'll know for next time,

*maybe not say certain things" but then of course you're restricting
yourself to appease society.*

Having empathy for the other despite the oppressive circumstances
faced by GSM youth was understood as a form of activism focused around
education, communication, conversation and friendliness. It could provide youth an opportunity to give context to their lives and to educate
and engage with people. It was visualized as a practice to be moderated
so one could still maintain self-respect while accepting the other where
they are at.

*Being vigilant in social situations and in public; social media activism;
and building a chosen family.* Hypervigilance was a common theme with
most participants. One youth felt they were always on edge about what
is known about their sexual identity in different contexts (e.g., at work,
at church, in public etc.). For them, this constant preoccupation with
controlling public perception was tied to feelings of depression and
anxiety. As a coping method, they made efforts to be in GSM-friendly
contexts where they could be their authentic self and have the support
needed to ensure their mental well-being. One participant identified
social media as a place where they needed to be less vigilant about their
identity, although not all youth participants felt the same because family
members followed their accounts. Identity vigilance was also a theme
in the art, where some participants depicted feeling caged, trapped or
scribbled over. "Chosen family" was a concept mobilized by many youth,
who described themselves and their friends as a ragtag "family" as opposed
to the normative, biological and sometimes oppressive families many of
the youth came from.

Self-expression and creativity. As can be seen in the artistic imagery,
youth were also concerned with social issues beyond those of the GSM
community. For example, one youth tagged the group mural with "food
not bombs" and "grow your own food," reflecting activism around non-
commercial public spaces and self-sufficiency, especially in the inner-city
neighbourhood where this person lived. Another message on the group
mural read "migration is life" and another in Spanish added "*sin fronteras
ni gobiernos*" ("without borders or governments").

For many youth participants, art was more than just a means to an end.
Art was both the medium and the message for resisting structural violence.

Youth emphasized this collaboration of activism and creativity as a strategy for confronting oppression. Because of this, researcher-driven discussion questions that focused on influencing formal avenues of decision-making (i.e., participating in civic politics) were seen by youth to emphasize normative ideas about social change, neglecting more anarchist and intimate forms of resisting oppression and overcoming structural violence (e.g., correcting gender pronouns, creating survivance-focused art).

Participating in activism and challenging the structure. Contesting transphobic attitudes within social structures, such as health care, policing and education, was overwhelming for many of the youth, who explained that they often simply wanted to be included in society and to participate in these structures as best they could while maintaining self-respect. Advocating for similar rights and opportunities within these systems was a way for GSM youth to push back and create space for themselves. Simply existing in spaces previously denied to them (i.e., the institution of marriage, the education system, the health care system) was a form of taking up space for these youth. Even existing or thriving in the workplace or the hospital was a way to do activist work and resist while still maintaining a sense of self as "different." However, because this work of managing stigma all by themselves is so overwhelming and exhausting, the youth also spoke to the importance of allies. Allies were seen by these youth as people who needed to step up for young people too intimidated or overwhelmed by the pressures of everyday life to thrive for themselves as well as do activist work, policy work or administration for activist issues.

Disrupting systems using collaboration and intersectional analysis. Youth did not restrict their search for justice to gender and sexual minorities only, but equally addressed other forms of harm experienced more broadly because of capitalist systems, mass consumption, systems of governance and the rights and justices associated with other minority groups in Canadian society (i.e., Indigenous land rights, feminism, disability justice). This strategy for resisting structural violence uses Kimberlé Crenshaw's (1991) "intersectional" form of analysis, which recognizes that individuals inhabit multiple identities (i.e., poor, racialized, trans, gender fluid) and that these identities intersect in unique ways to the benefit or harm of the individual. Youth understood their oppression as interrelated to the structural harm experienced by all minorities in institutional systems and they actively wanted to mitigate violence experienced by all minorities.

Discussion and Policy Recommendations

Arts-based activities had mixed results for identifying and confronting structural violence among this group, but were most effective when youth collaborated to work towards common artistic products. The youth did not always agree on solutions to structural violence — some hoped to resist wider capitalist systems, others advocated self-actualization and tolerance above collective societal transformation — but the youth did work in collaboration with the lead researchers to find policy recommendations.

The transgender youth participants believe that a coordinated effort across systems, mobilizing allies and forging alliances are necessary for addressing systemic violence. Critical trans-education is important for all service providers to help achieve greater social care, as well as to subvert leadership within systems in order to challenge inequities, even when there is no mandate to do so. More generally, an acknowledgment of the existence, lived experiences and histories of GSM people, at the practice and policy levels, was a frequent policy recommendation proposed by youth. This acknowledgment was described by youth as promoting an GSM-friendly atmosphere and giving them the space to be themselves. For example, one youth pointed out:

> A lot of people are intentionally ignoring it [GSM existence] because it's validated to intentionally ignore it. It's considered gross or inappropriate to even mention intersex people or transgender people. It's considered not a "dinner topic" … but it's not considered gross to talk about cisgender people.

Youth focused on the need for education institutions to reflect the lived experiences and histories of GSM people in their classes, course materials and curricula. One youth wrote:

> Growing up, I wish sex education in school included diverse sexualities and genders. I would love for future generations to learn health concerns and safety precautions for all sexualities and gender identities.

Youth participants expressed the need for young people to understand identity and self-expression outside of a normative, heterosexual, cisgender framework. For example, GSM families should be included in discussions about the make-up of families, and GSM sexual health topics should be included in sex education.

Other specific policy recommendations were for gender-neutral, safer washrooms to be the norm in all public places; for the police to build trust with marginalized youth; for service providers to use the correct pronouns; and for service providers and community agencies to acknowledge GSM people when providing services and to do so without resorting to stereotyping. (i.e., not assuming a client's sexuality based on their external appearance).

Fostering Survivance over Victim Narratives

Youth also recommended a positive, strengths-based approach within institutions toward GSM identity. Where a victim narrative constructs GSM youth as victims of circumstance unlikely to thrive because they fit into a minority group and experience discrimination, a strengths-based approach emphasizes the positives and recognizes the capacity of GSM people to affect change in their lives and the world. Some of the youth participants felt that health care professionals were not always open to their sexuality, gender fluidity or transgender status. One transgender youth talked about feeling stigmatized by the need to obtain a diagnosis of gender dysphoria from a psychologist to access trans-related health care needs. The youth indicated that requiring transgender people to "prove" that they experience gender dysphoria relies on preconceived understandings of gendered behaviour, as there is no clear way to quantify or judge a person's internal sense of self.

One participant described a doctor in Calgary being hostile to their trans partner and telling him, "You're not a man, I'll tell you when you're a man." This doctor was felt to see masculinity or the identity of "man" as something to be bestowed by medical professionals and not something an individual could claim for themselves. This youth said their partner never reported this doctor, fearing repercussions from the medical establishment that might affect his ability to transition.

Transphobia in a health care context coupled with long wait times for affirming care may place chronic stress on those who wait to access hormones and other trans-related health care needs. To improve access to gender-affirming medical care, youth repeatedly advocated for the bodily and medical autonomy of transgender people — this would mean respecting that youth know what medical care they need. More specifically, youth identified possible solutions, such as an increase in funding for transgender patients as well as more training about GSM issues for people working in medical contexts. One youth described how even when a transgender-competent physician tried to assist them, they oversimplified and made assumptions about trans experience when doing so:

> It's hard even when someone who's cisgender has the knowledge and education of learning about trans persons or trans experiences, they still don't know what it means to be trans because they're not trans themselves ... They have yet to know the experiences of an actual person who is living day to day as their true self. For them just to be like, "You have to do this based off the standards of care," they're depersonalizing the experience.

A key concern addressed among the GSM group was the proper use of gender pronouns and recognition of name changes upon gender transition. This topic came up weekly as different group members struggled with using the gender-neutral pronoun "they." While honest errors were endured with grace, the group noted that when such errors are made by service providers, especially during procedures related to transition or trans-related health care, they may trigger traumatic memories or simply be experienced as uncaring. When made by health practitioners even after being corrected or despite the patient's medical charts indicating their name and pronouns, what may begin as an honest mistake becomes visible as potential transphobia.

Another participant described being hit by a car while riding their bicycle. First responders kept referring to this youth as "she" and "her" despite their repeated requests to use gender-neutral pronouns as the other pronouns were incorrect and were exacerbating their anxiety. Not only did first responders ignore the request, the youth felt they did not even seem to understand it, as though no prior exposure to trans realities informed their service. One participant described how their fear of experiencing this discrimination or stigma caused them to avoid the health care system as much as possible.

Another trans youth described how a lack of education about the existence and lives of GSM people not only impacts the mental health of GSM youth through discrimination but may result in negative ramifications for their physical health as well:

> There's a lot of language that is used [in hospitals] that is so commonplace that no one ever questions it. There are a lot of concepts of biology that people think are a given, like "male" and "female," and they assume that someone with an "M" on their charts has XYZ hormones and XYZ body parts. They assume things about your life, about your health problems.

Here, a medical practitioner's lack of awareness regarding trans identity could negatively affect a trans person's medical treatment and lead to a misunderstanding and possible health ramifications. For this reason, among others, youth participants indicated that education and training around GSM issues for those working within medical contexts would not only help to combat discrimination but also directly impact the physical and mental health of GSM youth.

Future Directions

Health policy should take steps to improve care towards GSM youth in order to provide a fair and equitable health care system for all. The youth suggested several actions that could be undertaken to address structural violence. First, service providers and community agencies should create intake forms with a space to write in pronouns and, if relevant, preferred terms for body parts (i.e., a transgender person may prefer to hear doctors use the term *genitals* rather than the more specific terms *penis* or *vulva* to minimize gender dysphoria during medical appointments). Second, service providers, community agencies and systems of care should respect bodily and gender self-determination of GSM youth (i.e., affirming and supporting young people who express a desire to transition or validating young people who indicate they experience same-gender attraction). Finally, medical service providers must create a safe space to talk about GSM issues and work to build relationships with youth based on mutual understanding, respect and open-mindedness.

References

Baker, Emerance. 2007. "Loving Indians: Native Women's Storytelling as Survivance." *Resources for Feminist Research*, 32, 3–4: 193.

Bielski, Z. 2018. "Is Holding Hands Ok? How Same-Sex Couples Navigate Public Displays of Affection." *Globe and Mail*, 11 May.

Blair, K. 2019. "How Do You Feel Holding Hands with Your Partner In Public?" *Psychology Today*, 8 June.

Crenshaw, K. 1991. "Mapping the Margins: Intersectionality, Identity Politics, and Violence against Women of Color." *Stanford Law Review*, 43, 6: 1241–1299.

Denny, S., M.F.G. Lucassen, J. Stuart, T. Fleming et al. 2016. "The Association Between Supportive High School Environments and Depressive Symptoms and Suicidality Among Sexual Minority Students." *Journal of Clinical Child and Adolescent Psychology*, 45, 3: 248–261.

Holden, D. 2019. "Most LGBTQ People Are Super Fine with Bachelorette Parties at Gay Bars." *Buzzfeed News*, 25 June.

Meyer, I.H. 2003. "Prejudice, Social Stress, and Mental Health in Lesbian, Gay, and Bisexual Populations: Conceptual Issues and Research Evidence." *Psychological Bulletin,* 129: 674–697.

Plöderl, M, E-J, Wagenmakers, P. Tremblay, et al. 2013. "Suicide Risk and Sexual Orientation: A Critical Review." *Arch Sex Behav* 42, 5: 715–727.

Poteat, V.P., J.R. Scheer, and E.H. Mereish. 2014. "Factors Affecting Academic Achievement among Sexuality Minority and Gender-Variant Youth." *Advances in Child Development and Behavior,* 47: 262–294.

Richardson, C., and A. Wade. 2008. "Taking Resistance Seriously: A Response-Based Approach to Social Work in Cases of Violence against Indigenous Women." In J. Carriere and S. Strega (eds.), *Walking This Path Together: Anti-Racist and Anti-Oppressive Child Welfare Practice*. Winnipeg: Fernwood Publishing.

Taylor, C., and T. Peter. 2011. "'We Are Not Aliens, We're People, and We Have Rights.' Canadian Human Rights Discourse and High School Climate for LGBTQ Students." *Canadian Review of Sociology,* 48, 3: 275–312.

Veale, J., E. Saewyc, H. Frohard-Dourlent, S. Dobson et al. 2015. "Being Safe, Being Me: Results of the Canadian Trans Youth Health Survey." Vancouver, BC: Stigma and Resilience Among Vulnerable Youth Centre, School of Nursing, University of British Columbia. <http://www.saravyc.ubc.ca/2018/05/06/trans-youth-health-survey/>.

9

The Emotional Exhaustion Created by Systemic Violence

How We Respond through Social Movement, Action and Zines

Jenna Rose Sands

When I was around ten years old, I became aware of the looks I would get from people in stores. These were looks of suspicion and, at the time, I did not understand what these looks were rooted in. I felt like these employees thought I was up to trouble, which confused me because I was just following my mother. This feeling and experience has been echoed in the stories told by my now teenage nephews. The unveiling as to why we have been looked upon suspiciously by shop owners would eventually lead to the collapse of my childhood innocence and the subsequent beginning of a long journey of finding my own voice as an Indigenous woman, a journey I am still travelling and will be my entire life.

I was born and raised in London, Ontario, a city noted for having extremes in many areas; incredible wealth as well as high numbers of those living in poverty, many with strong conservative viewpoints living alongside communities that are progressive and inclusive at their core. I grew up in a neighbourhood that was once vying for the position of the best neighbourhood in Canada, so to say that I was privileged in where I grew up is an understatement. I attended a great elementary school and, while my memories there are largely positive, I can only recall one other Indigenous student, who attended for a year and was labelled a "problem child." There were not many students of colour. Our education about Indigenous issues was severely lacking and it was on the playground of this school where I was first called a "dirty Indian."

Being called a dirty Indian was something that confused me a lot. I knew I wasn't dirty, I took baths, cleaned up after myself, why was I dirty? The term Indian was still widely used in my youth and yes, I was an "Indian" to most, and I didn't see an issue with this. I saw zero problems in being an Indian and this was due to the other half of my life, the life away from London, and to the homogeneity of my non-diverse Euro-Canadian neighbourhood.

Every weekend for a large part of the year, I was away with family on the Pow Wow trail. As well, we spent large chunks of my summers on Walpole Island First Nation, where my mother is from. These weekends and summers hold some of the most cherished memories of my child-hood. Family, laughter and love surrounded me always. I spent my time on Walpole Island running in the bush and swimming in the river. Whether at Pow Wows or the Rez, I always had fun. My family has always loved to laugh, dance and be silly, and I have always loved this. To this day, my favourite times include sitting around a table with my family, giggling the night away over a cup of tea and a piece of pie. I have always described my childhood as being fairly idyllic. Sure, from time to time we had our struggles, but I was never in want of love.... love is always overflowing in Indigenous communities, it seems.

This living life in two very different spaces with radically different people continued well into my teen years. As a teenager, I began to find that I was having a harder and harder time joining these two halves together to find a cohesive voice. I transferred to a high school in downtown London to attend their celebrated art program, which was the home of London's creatively inclined youth or misfits. It was in the walls of these studios that I felt really truly heard for my own solo voice. You see, I am the child of a strong and well known Indigenous woman, and I met most of my role models through her and my older brothers. I was loved and doted on because my family was loved and dotted on. But in the arena of art, I felt I could begin to explore my sense of individuality and begin to find my voice, that voice that was mine and mine alone, at least I thought that is what it would be at the time.

It's a crummy fact of life that being a teenager is hard, and I've often contemplated on what it was that made my teenage years so difficult. Beyond dating, hormones and high-school cliques — what else was it that made finding my path so difficult? Did it all just stem from feeling like an awkward human? Why did I not feel whole and sturdy in my words and own story?

As a teen, I read the book *Demian* by Hermann Hesse, a book I highly recommend if you're searching for an existential crisis. I recall sitting on the bus and reading about a protagonist who had just realized that his father was capable of lying. When he realized this, cracks began to form in the foundation of how he perceived his childhood. This was profound for me, as it was echoing emotions and thoughts that I was currently experiencing in regards to my Indigeneity. I had these beautiful, gold coloured memories and feelings about Pow Wows, the Rez and my people. The love for this aspect of my childhood ran deep. So, when I experienced the first of many existential crises as a teenager, this love felt as if it was beginning to crumble.

There is a point in a person's life where their parents and role models realize that the child is "old enough." They are now "old enough" to watch scary movies, to stay out later, to walk home alone. And while I went through all these milestones, I also went through the "old enough" to have adults tell their stories in front of me. When you're young, adults tell each other information in hushed tones and at tables where children are not allowed to sit. One day, I just stayed sitting. I started to hear about what I now know are the effects of intergenerational trauma brought on by vicious colonialism and attempts to get the Indian out of us. I heard about violence, abuse, alcohol abuse, residential schools, children taken away, waterways polluted, language lost. In hindsight, I see that this was devastating to me. I began questioning everything, and suddenly all those looks and being called a dirty Indian made sense. I could not reconcile my blissful childhood with this awful reality, let alone reconcile all this with my life in the city, in my own neighbourhood. Learning of systematic racism, women missing and murdered, it was all too much. I wanted nothing of it. I couldn't comprehend it. I wanted far away from it.

During this traumatic unconscious revelation, I was also creating art, going to gallery openings, "schmoozing" and nurturing this creative voice. I wanted people to see and hear me for my voice and my art and absolutely not through the lens that creates those awful looks … you know those ones, the ones where you can tell someone is saying "that Indian" in their head. I also didn't want to recognize that these systems and communities that I grew up in, and in turn found safety in, could actually not be rooting for me. The idea that who I am as an Indigenous person could in any way affect my opportunities in this community was something I just could not admit to myself. I rebelled hard against my Indigenous self. I stopped dancing. I focused more on art and life in the city than on my Indigenous life at home, in my family and in the old ways. The cultural ways I grew up with were there still, but in a really muted way as I worked hard to convince myself and others that I was not just my skin colour, or simply just a savage that could read and write. Thank you John A. Macdonald, our founding father, for that quote.

It may be surprising to read that that this game plan did not work out very well. As with most issues people try to bury deep in themselves, it didn't go away. Instead, it grew larger, leaving me feeling hollow. I tried for a long time to brush off hurtful comments, wildly inaccurate information regarding Indigenous issues and ignorant people, because I wanted to feel that this stuff did not affect me. It didn't apply to me because I was Jenna Rose and my Indigeneity was not a prominent part of who I was. My unconscious and naive teenage logic was based on the notion that if I took the part of me that identified as Indigenous and forced it away then all of these awful issues relating to Indigenous people would not exist or affect me. I understand this thinking is wild because, logically, this sort of thinking never works for anyone. Pretending something doesn't exist doesn't mean it's not there. I was just choosing to not acknowledge this inner conflict in myself, and I was not ready to do the work to unpack it all.

Fast forward to me as an adult woman trying to figure out life and still looking for that voice. As mentioned, I tried to brush off being Indigenous and it did not work. In hindsight, it now seems funny as well as terribly sad. As time went on, that insecurity or the "effective assimilation" that was happening in my head slowly turned to anger. This anger was not an all-consuming vengeance rage. It was more of a "how is this still happening?" sort of rage. In the winter of 2017–18 we saw the heartbreaking failures of justice in the verdicts rendered in the murder cases of Tina Fontaine and Colten Boushie. Before this, there was a suicide crisis in Attawapiskat and youth being murdered in Thunder Bay. I could not turn my eyes any longer. I found myself in this state of helplessness and anger and with a feeling that I needed to do something, anything. My anger wanted me to move, to offer help, but I was for weeks paralyzed with a feeling of helplessness because … how can I as one single person create meaningful change? Everything felt bleak. I did not know what to do with this rage and emotional exhaustion. I was spinning out emotionally on heartbreaking information and I just avoided the news altogether.

I began to search my brain and heart for the ways that I might be able to create some change, no matter how small, in the community around me. I thought back to my strengths, my visual art and my naturally feisty nature with words. I was searching through the artistic Rolodex in my brain for mediums that would be both visually dynamic and carry the words I needed to get out of me. I began to seriously consider zines as a viable option for that change to occur when I thought back on how they've impacted me as an evolving being.

Zines were the social media of my teenage years: they are small, homemade publications that are a mixture of journals, magazines and the ever-private diary. Zines were used as a way to communicate emotions, politics, song lyrics and short stories and for the teaching of practical skills in the form of DIY how-tos. With social media in its infancy, youth created zines wherever photocopiers existed and traded them with one another wherever youth congregated. The zines I have read over the years were essential to my young self: they are quick and intense doses of intimacy all laid out in unique artistic formats.

When I started my zine project I knew a few things. Firstly, my aim was to educate those who knew nothing or very little of Indigenous history, all the information that was never taught in school. I found that every time I spoke with a person regarding Indigenous history and the horrors the Indigenous Peoples of Canada have endured, I was usually met with some variant of "Oh I had no idea!" Today, most Canadians should have a fundamental level of knowledge of what Indigenous Peoples have endured and continue to endure. It is critically important that those who seek to help Indigenous people and communities heal understand what has occurred and why, within these dark chapters in our collective history. Having insight as to where family and community intergenerational trauma begins is critical for finding successful methods and solutions. It is impossible to move forward without understanding the past; this seems to apply to anyone, Indigenous or not.

Secondly, I knew I was frustrated and that this zine project would have moments of sarcasm and dark humour. The title, *Atrocities against Indigenous Canadians for Dummies*, felt appropriate in its ability to convey both seriousness and my stern annoyance of having to get to this point to create such a project.

Thirdly, zines, while an older media form, are excellent vessels to share knowledge within communities. They're small in size and short in page length, and yet they are full of information and visual dynamics. The *Atrocities against Indigenous Canadians for Dummies* series pairs haunting words, experiences and discussion questions with visual art (mixed media) to create an informative read that is easily absorbed over a lunch hour, a commute on public transportation or during a coffee break. In an age when attention spans are short and news headlines bombard us nonstop, zines have found a resurgence in their ability to convey intimate and critical information straight from the source of the author. With zines being a small, physical booklet, they cannot be ignored as easily as closing an app or scrolling past on your phone. The zine has weight and presence and cannot be just closed and forgotten.

The final point I kept in my mind was that accessibility was an incredibly important element during every step of this project. I felt it important that experiences and facts not become lost in academic language. There are many incredibly important publications that discuss Indigenous history at great length, though many people will not read them either due to the length or the inaccessibility of the language. Words needed to be easily digestible as the content was the most critical aspect to drive home. Cost was also an important factor to consider, as money should never be a barrier to learning and growing, nor should it prohibit people from having their voice heard in dialogue and in the creation of solutions.

At present, there are three large zines in the *Atrocities against Indigenous Canadians for Dummies* series. Each one deals with a specific atrocity endured by Indigenous Peoples: the Canadian residential school system, missing and murdered Indigenous women and girls, and the Sixties Scoop. I also created two mini zines, one that deals with basic Pow Wow etiquette and another that presents the history of the Canadian residential school system in a manner appropriate for youth.

The process of creating these zines has been difficult yet cathartic. I spent many days on my couch crying while reading survivor experiences and reflecting on all those who did not come out of residential schools, who never made it home from a night out, who were shipped away and never saw their community again. I've found myself contemplating my own safety as an Indigenous woman after mulling over dozens of depressing statistics detailing how much more likely Indigenous women are to face physical violence. This project has not only helped to educate so many in my community, but it has also helped me join to parts of myself that I never thought could come together. I feel solid in my Indigeneity and also feel solid in seeing the path I can take to turn this anger, frustration and sadness into movement. I do not know what the future holds for Indigenous people, but that is the exciting part: we can sculpt a new narrative, one where truth and honesty about the past, present and future is paramount. This project of activism through art has opened a part of myself that felt so vulnerable for so long, and this feeling is absolutely freeing. It is time to hear the voices that past systems have failed; it is time to have real dialogue.

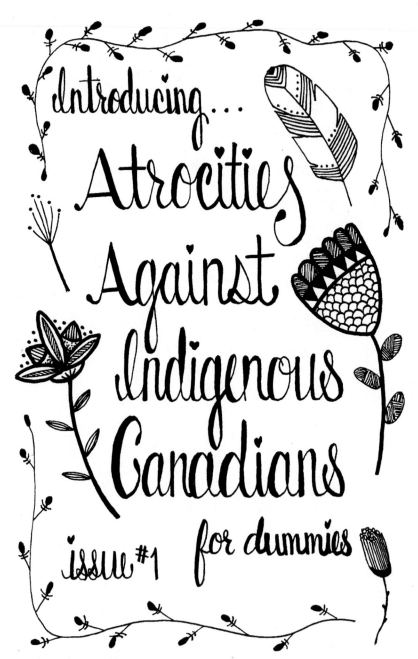

Issue #2 Front Cover, hand drawn by Jenna Rose Sands.

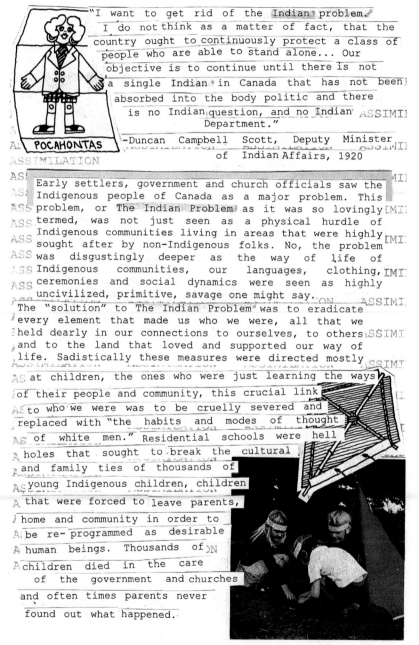

"I want to get rid of the Indian problem. I do not think as a matter of fact, that the country ought to continuously protect a class of people who are able to stand alone... Our objective is to continue until there is not a single Indian in Canada that has not been absorbed into the body politic and there is no Indian question, and no Indian Department."

—Duncan Campbell Scott, Deputy Minister of Indian Affairs, 1920

Early settlers, government and church officials saw the Indigenous people of Canada as a major problem. This problem, or The Indian Problem as it was so lovingly termed, was not just seen as a physical hurdle of Indigenous communities living in areas that were highly sought after by non-Indigenous folks. No, the problem was disgustingly deeper as the way of life of Indigenous communities, our languages, clothing, ceremonies and social dynamics were seen as highly uncivilized, primitive, savage one might say.
The "solution" to The Indian Problem was to eradicate every element that made us who we were, all that we held dearly in our connections to ourselves, to others and to the land that loved and supported our way of life. Sadistically these measures were directed mostly at children, the ones who were just learning the ways of their people and community, this crucial link to who we were was to be cruelly severed and replaced with "the habits and modes of thought of white men." Residential schools were hell holes that sought to break the cultural and family ties of thousands of young Indigenous children, children that were forced to leave parents, home and community in order to be re-programmed as desirable human beings. Thousands of children died in the care of the government and churches and often times parents never found out what happened.

Excerpt from Issue #1 – Residential Schools.

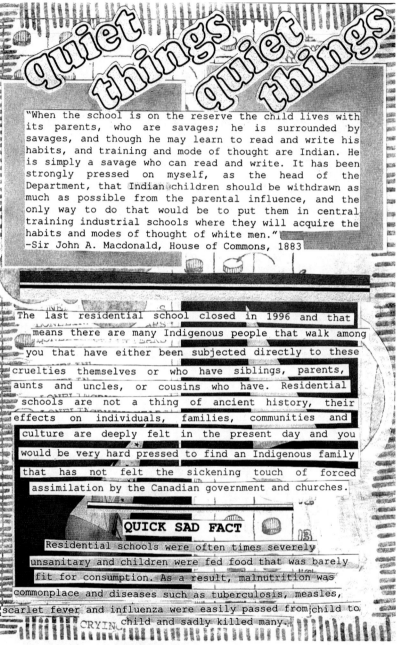

quiet things quiet things

"When the school is on the reserve the child lives with its parents, who are savages; he is surrounded by savages, and though he may learn to read and write his habits, and training and mode of thought are Indian. He is simply a savage who can read and write. It has been strongly pressed on myself, as the head of the Department, that Indian children should be withdrawn as much as possible from the parental influence, and the only way to do that would be to put them in central training industrial schools where they will acquire the habits and modes of thought of white men."
-Sir John A. Macdonald, House of Commons, 1883

The last residential school closed in 1996 and that means there are many Indigenous people that walk among you that have either been subjected directly to these cruelties themselves or who have siblings, parents, aunts and uncles, or cousins who have. Residential schools are not a thing of ancient history, their effects on individuals, families, communities and culture are deeply felt in the present day and you would be very hard pressed to find an Indigenous family that has not felt the sickening touch of forced assimilation by the Canadian government and churches.

QUICK SAD FACT

Residential schools were often times severely unsanitary and children were fed food that was barely fit for consumption. As a result, malnutrition was commonplace and diseases such as tuberculosis, measles, scarlet fever and influenza were easily passed from child to child and sadly killed many.

Excerpt from Issue #1 – Residential Schools.

HIGHWAY OF TEARS

In British Columbia, there is a 724km stretch of highway that joins the Northern BC hubs of Prince George and Prince Rupert. Highway 16 as it is technically known, is lined with dozens of small Indigenous communities that often hitchhike along the highway as a last resort option for transportation. Public transit along this stretch of highway is either inaccessible or non-existent. The vulnerable, mainly women, are often left with no other options to get home other than to risk their lives hitchhiking along the remote highway.

Highway 16 is also known by the communities that line this remote stretch of highway as the Highway of Tears. Since 1969, at least 18 women, mainly Indigenous, have gone missing and most determined to have been murdered along or near Highway 16. To local communities, the Highway of Tears has in reality claimed more than 18 lives, with most saying the true number is well over 30. As with most issues that involves violence against Indigenous women, the government, RCMP and local law enforcement were slow to act and it was not until the fall of 2005 that the RCMP started Project E-PANA to begin addressing and solving the disappearances and murders along the Highway of Tears. In the fall of 2007, the RCMP expanded the total number of missing women to 18 as well as

Excerpt from Issue #2 – Missing and Murdered Indigenous Women and Girls.

increased the number of kilometres investigated in the case to approximately 1,500km, this includes Highway 97 and Highway 5. The RCMP classifies a woman as missing along Highway 16 and thus a part of the investigation of Project E-PANA if they were either last seen or their remains found within a mile of the highway. This is a loose definition at best and one of the main reasons many believe the number of 18 women missing and murdered to be inaccurate. This definition relies on motorists recalling the women in and around the highways in question or perpetrators disposing remains near the highway, neither are reliable or predictable.

In 2006, a symposium was held in Prince George, British Columbia, that brought together representatives of the Indigenous communities along Highway 16, social workers, families of the missing women, RCMP officials and the Solicitor General. Many family members and Indigenous leaders criticized the government and law enforcement's failure to act and protect an obviously vulnerable population and many wondered if perhaps the crimes should be viewed as hate crimes as the target was specifically Indigenous women.

Out of the symposium came the *Highway of Tears Symposium Recommendations Report* which offered 33 recommendations for law enforcement and communities to enact in order to reduce the number of women reported missing and improve the safety for all. The 33 recommendations focused around four areas: victim prevention, emergency readiness, victim family support and community development.

Excerpt from Issue #2 – Missing and Murdered Indigenous Women and Girls.

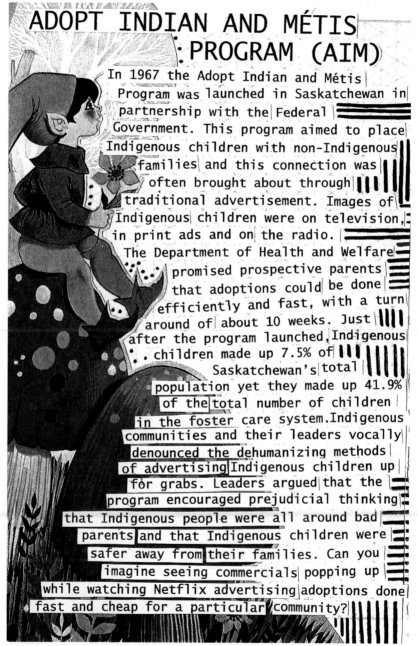

ADOPT INDIAN AND MÉTIS PROGRAM (AIM)

In 1967 the Adopt Indian and Métis Program was launched in Saskatchewan in partnership with the Federal Government. This program aimed to place Indigenous children with non-Indigenous families and this connection was often brought about through traditional advertisement. Images of Indigenous children were on television, in print ads and on the radio. The Department of Health and Welfare promised prospective parents that adoptions could be done efficiently and fast, with a turn around of about 10 weeks. Just after the program launched, Indigenous children made up 7.5% of Saskatchewan's total population yet they made up 41.9% of the total number of children in the foster care system. Indigenous communities and their leaders vocally denounced the dehumanizing methods of advertising Indigenous children up for grabs. Leaders argued that the program encouraged prejudicial thinking that Indigenous people were all around bad parents and that Indigenous children were safer away from their families. Can you imagine seeing commercials popping up while watching Netflix advertising adoptions done fast and cheap for a particular community?

Excerpt from Issue #3 – The Sixties Scoop.

Sad HISTORY TRUTH

-Residential schools were in operation across Canada from the 1870s to the 1990s

-The schools were operated predominately by the Anglican, Catholic, Methodist, and Presbyterian churches.

-In 1920, it became mandatory for every Indian child between the ages of 7-16 to attend an Indian residential school.

-In 1933, legal guardianship of children attending residential schools were assumed by the principals as parents were made to forcibly surrender legal custody of their own children.

-An estimated 150,000 Aboriginal children between the ages of 6-16 were forced to leave their parents, siblings, community and culture to live in schools where starvation and physical and sexual abuse were rampant

-It's estimated that approximately 6,000 children died while attending residential schools. It is an approximate number as the government stopped keeping track after 4,000 children died...

-The last residential school in operation was in Saskatchewan and closed down in 1996.

Excerpt from Issue #1 – Residential Schools.

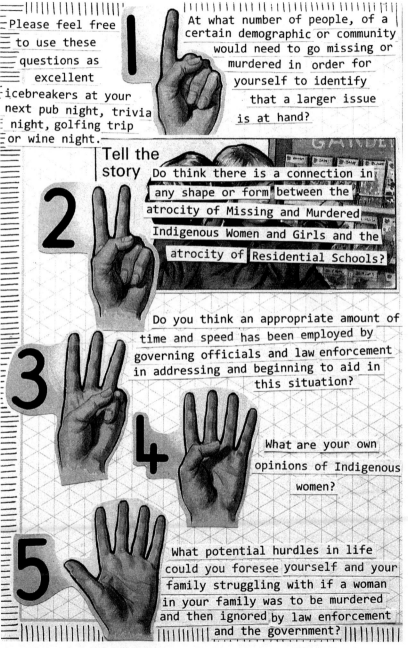

Please feel free to use these questions as excellent icebreakers at your next pub night, trivia night, golfing trip or wine night.

1. At what number of people, of a certain demographic or community would need to go missing or murdered in order for yourself to identify that a larger issue is at hand?

Tell the story

2. Do think there is a connection in any shape or form between the atrocity of Missing and Murdered Indigenous Women and Girls and the atrocity of Residential Schools?

3. Do you think an appropriate amount of time and speed has been employed by governing officials and law enforcement in addressing and beginning to aid in this situation?

4. What are your own opinions of Indigenous women?

5. What potential hurdles in life could you foresee yourself and your family struggling with if a woman in your family was to be murdered and then ignored by law enforcement and the government?

Discussion Questions from Issue #2 – Missing and Murdered Indigenous Women and Girls.

ostrich approach to child welfare problems—they just did not exist. The miracle is that there were not more children lost in this system run by so many well-intentioned people. The road to hell was paved with good intentions, and the child welfare system was the paving contractor"

Kimelman concluded his report with 109 policy recommendations for change within the Manitoba child welfare system. Some of those recommendations include:

• That policies and standards be implemented that would improve repatriation of Aboriginal children to their own communities and reunify Aboriginal children with their own families.

• That cultural awareness training be provided to all those working in Aboriginal communities or with Aboriginal people.

• That greater use be made of the extended family.

• That adoption in a non-Aboriginal home be used only as a last resort.

In the mid-80's, armed with reports from Johnston and Kimelman and protests from Indigenous communities and the public, the Canadian government amended policy to ensure that children removed from the family home were placed in homes in the following order:

1) In the home of an extended family member
2) In the home of another Indigenous family within the same community.
3) In the home of a non-Indigenous family

Excerpt from Issue #3 – The Sixties Scoop.

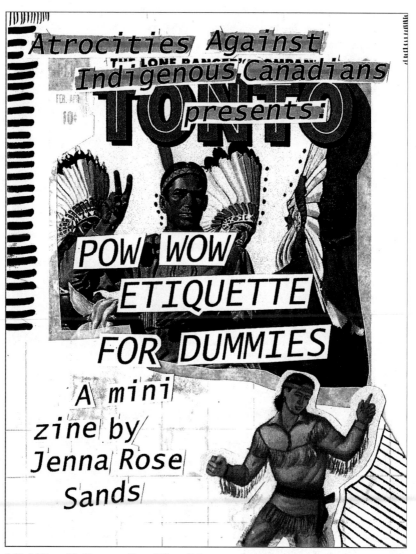

Mini Zine #1 Cover – Pow Wow Etiquette for Dummies.

What is a Pow Wow?

A Pow Wow is a social gathering that celebrates Indigenous culture and community through song, dance, arts, food and traditional crafts. While the term Pow Wow may have one time been used to describe a different gathering, it is now an umbrella term for various social gatherings of the Indigenous people of North America. Most Pow Wows still have elements that are sacred and have deep spiritual meaning therefore it is entirely inappropriate for a person to refer to their Monday morning meeting at work or their wine club as being a Pow Wow. Unless you are discussing an actual Pow Wow, don't use the name of this ceremonial event as an a description for anything else. Also, should an Indigenous person correct you on your usage, please don't roll your eyes and ask "what's the big deal?"

FREQUENTLY HEARD TERMS

REGALIA: is the proper term to refer to the clothing worn during a Pow Wow by dancers. Regalia is highly valued by its wearer and many elements have deep spiritual meaning. It is not an outfit, nor a uniform and it definitely is not a costume. *We are not Halloween costumes...*

DO NOT TOUCH REGALIA OR DANCERS WITHOUT EXPLICIT CONSENT.

It literally feels demeaning and icky when people do this.

"Me hope Tinker Tom and grandson Pete not try to cross river during storm," said Tonto. "Water rise heap fast."

Excerpt from Mini Zine #1 – Pow Wow Etiquette for Dummies.

Mini Zine #2 – What Is a Residential School?

PART 3

Speaking Out and Pushing Back: Learning from Youth

10

Can It Make a Difference?

Evaluating Y-PAR as a Health Promotion Strategy

Holly Johnson and Alyssa Louw

Research from a participatory action research (PAR) approach has emancipatory and transformational aims: it aims at freedom from oppressive conditions and individual and collective change (Lykes and Mallona 2008). PAR approaches democractize the means of knowledge production by involving exploited, oppressed or marginalized people fully and actively in the research process (Rahman 2008). According to John Gaventa and Andrea Cornwall (2008), "The role of participatory action research is to enable people to empower themselves through the construction of their own knowledge, in a process of action and reflection" (177). PAR thus can help research participants understand their experiences not as individual problems but as embedded in historical and macro structures.

PAR can be particularly empowering for young people since it recognizes their capacity to be agents of change rather than simply recipients of change made by adult "experts" on their behalf. PAR with youth (Y-PAR) considers young people to be not only "adults-in-training" but critical thinkers, experts on their own experiences and active agents (Mirra, Filipiak and Garcia 2015). Grounded in PAR methodology, the Voices against Violence (VAV) project engaged groups of young people in arts-based expression as a means of narrating their experiences of structural violence within intersections of multiple social identities, the meanings those experiences have for them and how these insights could help simulate community engagement and social action.

The engagement of youth in this research project took two tracks: participation of a large number of youth in arts-based discussion groups in multiple locations; and recruitment of a smaller number whose role it was to provide advice and input into all aspects of the larger project, in the form of the National Youth Advisory Board (NYAB). In the groups of young people across the country, youth engaged in arts-based methods of expression to critically reflect on the historical, political, cultural, economic and geographic contexts that shape their exposure to structural violence and how it affects their health. The young participants in each group were responsible for determining the form their expression would take and for interpreting the results and the policy implications. Members of the NYAB were recruited to "give this project and the team members advice, direction, and leadership on what they are doing and how they are doing it."

An important objective of the project was to evaluate the use of youth-centred participatory action approaches as strategies to promote health and empower young people to overcome, resist and prevent structural violence in their lives. This chapter presents an evaluation of the NYAB and selected arts-based groups to assess their adherence to PAR principles and to illustrate how a Y-PAR model looks in action.

Validity in Y-PAR Processes

Julie Ozanne and Bige Saatcioglu (2008) outline types of validity that are congruent with the assumptions and goals of PAR: outcome, democratic, process, catalytic and dialogical validity. Outcome validity is fundamental to the end goal of improving social life or at least generating useful knowledge and awareness for responding to, resolving or minimizing the conditions experienced by the participants. Democratic validity refers to "the extent to which relevant stakeholders in the problem participate deeply and fully in the research and the extent to which their perspectives and needs inform solutions" (426). Process validity is concerned with how problems are investigated and the extent to which this allows for ongoing reflection, learning and development of capacities. If research participants are not motivated to understand and change social conditions as a result of awareness and knowledge generated by participation in the study, catalytic validity is not present. Dialogical validity relates to critical debates with outsiders who challenge the explanations, assumptions, weaknesses and actions resulting from the study. In this chapter we outline the methods undertaken to assess the workings of the NYAB and the arts-based groups and present findings according to the various types of validity with one exception: the conditions to examine dialogical validity have yet to occur and it is thus beyond the scope of this evaluation.

Method for Evaluating the NYAB

Data for evaluating the NYAB consisted of semi-structured telephone interviews with nine members. Questions were framed around recruitment and the terms of reference developed collectively by the group. As they were recruited, the commitment NYAB members were undertaking was explained to them as: (1) collaboratively drafting terms of reference (ToR) for their work; (2) participating in conference calls once a month to discuss project activities and provide advice and direction to the project team; and (3) keeping up to date with how the project was progressing over email, phone or social media. The ToR for the group was drafted collaboratively with the two co-facilitators and youth members in the first year. The purpose of the NYAB was described as "offering ongoing expert advice in order to enhance the work of the project and allow the project to be conducted more effectively" and the role was to "identify issues concerning youth as they relate to inequality and structural violence and how these issues affect the health and well-being of youth." Two co-facilitators were selected by the executive of the larger project.

Outcome Validity

PAR strives to generate "practical knowledge for improving human welfare" (Ozanne and Saatcioglu 2008: 424). In the NYAB, the focus was on the extent to which the Y-PAR approach broadened knowledge about structural violence so that feedback and advice to the larger project would directly enhance the project goals. The interviews showed that participation on the NYAB introduced members to a new language for identifying and talking about structural violence in their own lives. Reflecting on how the project affected them, members stated:

> I'm a woman of colour, lower class. My parents had to use welfare so many times, and experience welfare and racism, but I didn't know how to articulate these experiences in terms of access and how, you know, how it actually related to my experiences ... [this project] helped me to articulate what I was experiencing too.

> Okay, I'm [a minority]. We have very, very overt racism as well as some of that kind of more structural stuff. But, I think learning from the other projects and how different things kind of intersect, and how

the role of being female comes in, as well as looking at the gender and realizing that lots of different groups experience it in similar but different ways, has been really valuable in my understanding.

[The project] helped me understand how I can also be an oppressor as well and how I can work as an ally to talk about these, you know, subjects and to engage in these discourses, so it has been very empowering.

These quotes reveal that NYAB members acquired new concepts and language to understand and discuss structural violence, and they reflected on the complex and overlapping ways that structural violence operated in their own lives and the lives of others. This knowledge was empowering to the youth in resisting individualistic explanations of social harm. Summarizing their learning, one participant stated:

I didn't know what structural violence was at first, or what structural violence is. Now I'm able to identify it when I see it around me, and now I'm aware of it. And you know, when I see something I'm able to say, no this is wrong, this is not the way it should be. This is structural violence.

Democratic Validity

The success of Y-PAR research depends largely on participants' meaningful and authentic involvement. One aspect of democratic validity relates to the extent to which participants engage in the research; another relates to the diversity of participants. One indicator of engagement is members' commitment to serving on the NYAB. Members were asked to commit for a minimum of two years, and the vast majority remained active members for at least that long. Throughout the five-year project, a total of twelve young people were recruited to serve on the NYAB and just two members were involved for less than a year, one due to unstable housing and the other felt overcommitted with studying and advocacy.

Overall, the nine NYAB members who were interviewed reported that they had been authentically engaged in the research process and felt their role was meaningful for the success of the project. Expressing this sentiment, members stated:

I think the work of the NYAB generally, like all of us, seems like it was really valued by the project, because we could see things happening as we suggested it. And it felt like a really authentic process, rather than just like, oh we're doing a project on youth, so I guess we have to involve some. You know, it felt really authentic and there was a real effort by everyone involved to really value the voices of youth all through, like, all through all stages of the project.

One of the things that I really liked was that I was able not only to give feedback and talk about the things that I care about, but I was able to participate … I was able to really talk about the things that matter to me and I was able to find the space for me to express myself.

This depth of participation did not occur by chance. Intentional steps were taken by the adult researchers to engage with the youth and to provide them with individualized opportunities for involvement. For example, one participant was offered a summer job through the NYAB that was based on her interest in communications and knowledge translation. The researchers also used youth-friendly social media tools to provide NYAB members with convenient opportunities to participate. Efforts were made to debrief youth after regional meetings and to integrate their feedback into future plans. These actions led the youth to feel their contributions were valued, as reflected in the following quotes:

It's different than any other project I've been part of because they valued our opinion so much, and as youth, that's very difficult to find. You know, people listen to you maybe, but really don't take you seriously, but in this project our opinion was taken very seriously and our input was valued.

Definitely people went above and beyond to kind of integrate what the NYAB were able to contribute, and asked for input, and we were included in meetings, and I appreciated the debriefs that happened before and after. Like you know, what went well in Toronto when we met and what could be better when we meet in Ottawa? And those changes were made.

While the large majority were pleased with their level of involvement, one member did not fully understand the long-term goals of the project and felt that there was sometimes a lack of focus in the conversations. She found it difficult to engage due to a sense of not feeling valued by the adult researchers.

> *Sometimes I was dealt with in that matter which didn't make me feel as supported in the group — as a person who can be vocal about things, and can be freely asked about things. So I felt supported, in terms of, you know, when I explained what I wanted to do, the researcher was like, let's do that. So, I thought that was great, but like, the thing about the whole condescending thing is that I see that everywhere, so it not just a personal thing of NYAB specifically.*

According to PAR principles, democratic validity is strengthened by the inclusion of a plurality of perspectives and interests (Ozanne and Saatcioglu 2008). In the interviews, participants described ways in which the NYAB was and was not diverse. One said:

> *It was done in such a great way and there was just so much diversity in our group. And yeah, it was just so diverse and that's always usually my thing, like maybe you need to make your groups a little bit more diverse? … But no, this project honestly has done it differently than I've ever experienced.*

NYAB members identified with a variety of racial, ethnic and religious backgrounds, and one-third were not born in Canada. Several had physical and/or mental health conditions. However, there was less diversity in gender identity with most identifying as female, and most had at least some post-secondary education. One member remarked that youth from western and northern Canada were under-represented. Under-representation of some groups poses a potential threat to the democratic validity of the research.

Process Validity

Process validity is the "extent to which problems are investigated in a way that allows for ongoing learning and improvement" (427). The establishment of a supportive and secure research environment and positive relationships early on can increase meaningful involvement in the research and facilitate the realization of broader goals.

NYAB members reported that overall, they felt supported by the facilitators and the adult researchers. They pointed to the early development of the ToR as helpful in fostering a culture of respect. The supportive and inclusive leadership style modelled by the co-facilitators also promoted a sense of security, and members perceived the facilitators as not only valuing the research, but also valuing their well-being: "I felt really supported. And it felt like the lines of communication were always open. In my experience it's not like I had to wait until we had a scheduled call. I could email or phone or whatever anytime ... there was just so much support and excitement for new ideas, and it felt like my opinions and my ideas were really valued by them both."

Another youth observed that "people were self-advocating for what they needed ... and seeing the leadership response to their needs was definitely a learning." The sense of security that developed allowed NYAB members to engage more meaningfully in the project. Furthermore, the modelling of a supportive and inclusive leadership style taught the youth leadership skills that were transferable to other contexts. For instance, one youth, who was pursuing an MBA that focused on managing high performance teams, began to ask questions about leadership and inclusion based on her experiences in the project. She questioned, "What do youth leadership and innovation really mean, and what are we defining that as? Does everyone belong?" This line of inquiry reflects a shift from more corporate values to those of inclusion and empowerment, which align with PAR principles. Another participant, who came from a small, "judgemental," culturally homogenous community, stated that her involvement taught her how to create a sense of security for others:

> Being part of this project, and through interacting with a lot of these youth and even the researchers, it does help me in my job today because I need to not be judgmental, you know? People feel safe around me in my space, so yeah, I've learned a lot from the NYAB members, especially about how to create a safe space with the people that you're working with, and yeah, really listening and having that no judgment zone.

Collectively, these findings indicate that the co-facilitators were able to create processes that enhanced trust and rapport among members of the group, and this facilitated their learning.

Catalytic Validity

Catalytic validity measures motivation to create "practical and workable approaches" to social problems that are more equitable than pre-existing social conditions (427). One way in which the youth demonstrated catalytic validity was through their aspirations for the project. They hoped that it would continue to contribute to community empowerment long after its completion, and suggested avenues by which the project could influence social change. Specifically, they hoped the art work produced by the groups across the country would be widely circulated. One NYAB member said:

> I think I would like to see the youths' artwork and what the youth did, live on. I would really like to see, at a conference, just having them come together and see the fruits of their labour. To see how they've impacted academia. The impact they had on research studies, on how we understand and research this topic.

Several youth hoped the VAV groups would continue on past the end of the research project. One hoped for the development of "easy, non-intense ways for young people to feel like they can access those conversations, whether through school or through outside groups" and noted that, after participating on the NYAB, members wanted to continue having conversations about structural violence.

> I definitely want more people to know about what structural violence is. I want this to have more dissemination towards the public, because there was a lot of stellar work being done ... It's important for people to know that a lot of oppressions are institutional, and once you know how to articulate what you're going through, you know knowledge is power, is a cliché but it's true. And that's what I want — more youth to know about this.

Reflecting on the broad goal of disseminating project results, one member stated: "I really hope that [the project] creates the opportunity for youth and community to be able to talk about structural violence more openly and recognize what it is and what it looks like and try to prevent it." Others hoped the research would result in broader policy changes.

Another way catalytic validity was demonstrated was through the project's influence on young people's choices in education and work. For some, the project motivated them to pursue education and careers relating to social justice causes or participatory research. One stated: "NYAB was something that promoted diversity and acknowledged intersectionality and it made me feel like I had a place, and it made me more interested in working with anti-oppression work."

These quotes reveal that youth left the VAV hoping it would continue to influence social change, and in some cases, changed their future plans to work toward social change. Thus their involvement in the project has increased their motivation to understand and act on structural violence and to engage meaningfully in their communities.

Method for Evaluating the Arts-Based Groups

Over the five years of the research project, thirty groups of diverse marginalized youth were convened by university researchers across the country to engage in arts-based methods to express their experiences with structural violence and its impacts. In the initial stages, evaluation of the work of these groups was envisioned to incorporate both quantitative and qualitative methods. Difficulties surfaced early on when group facilitators found that asking participants to complete an impersonal, highly structured survey interfered with efforts to build trust and create a cohesive group with marginalized young people. As one young person succinctly said: "This survey is structural violence."

The epistemological and ontological incoherence of forcing a quantitative survey into a Y-PAR process quickly became apparent, and the survey was dropped in favour of a flexible qualitative assessment. Group facilitators engaged with the youth in a discussion of what they had learned and what changed for them in terms of knowledge, awareness and social action, and whether and how Y-PAR principles were respected. A list of general questions was developed to guide the discussion but the format was up to each group to determine. Groups could decide to hold informal discussions or articulate their views via a collaborative arts-based activity. Examples below illustrate ways in which outcome, democratic, process and catalytic validity were demonstrated in the arts-based group work.

Outcome Validity

A group in rural Manitoba, designed to explore gender-based violence, provides evidence of outcome validity. Ten male and ten female participants, 16 or 17 years of age, participated in this group. Participants lived in a small, rural community and a nearby First Nation Territory. The group met once a week for twelve weeks at a community centre and was facilitated by a young woman who was completing a master's degree in conflict studies. During the sessions, the youth learned about structural and direct forms of gender-based violence and participated in activities and discussions about privilege and marginalization, social locations, stereotypes, gender roles, discrimination, objectification and media representation. After engaging in these discussions and activities, the facilitator noted that although the youth "had little prior experience exploring and discussing gender-based violence, they quickly developed strong opinions about ... victim blaming, objectification and stereotyping. Their disappointment was rooted in both the prevalence of gender-based violence as well as common responses to women once violence occurred."

This image illustrates an awareness of negative social influences on women, as well as structural barriers that women face as a group. As the young woman who created this image stated:

> *So for mine, the colours are the good and then there's always marginalization in between all the good. So it's not all good. And on the outsides is the good, I put things that are good for me. And in the body ... those are the marginalization which is like gender, age, ethnicity, and I put that in me.*

Excerpts from the group discussions demonstrate learnings about specific areas of structural and gender-based violence, how it harms women, and how it also affects men through placing unrealistic expectations on them or secondhand through violence against their female friends or family. The discussions were nuanced and personal. In one discussion the female participants expressed frustration with the way their male peers treated them, and how objectifying and demeaning it felt to them. The following are quotes are illustrative:

> *[They] show off for all the other guys but then when they're by*

Individual art activity representing one's marginalization/privilege visually.

themselves they'll be like oh I'm sorry I did that ... the guys will be complete jerks with all the other guys but then when they're like one-on-one they're fine.

I feel like if he was with another group of guys ... he would just turn you down or shut you down because they don't want to look *like that in front of all the other guys. And he wouldn't even take into consideration what you said. Like maybe afterwards he would think like, maybe I shouldn't have done that, but at the moment he would probably say something mean back to you because he wants to look good in front of all the other guys, you know?*

These frank discussions and uncovering of personal and collective experience is rooted in the feminist empowerment tradition, which is consistent with Y-PAR principles. Through discussing embodied experiences, the girls offered recognition and validation to one another and felt empowered through critically assessing and expressing their experiences. Participation in the group also appeared to positively affect boys' knowledge and beliefs about gender-based violence. In a discussion centring on the topic of victim-blaming, a young man who chose the pseudonym "Macho Man" for himself suggested: "It's like if a woman wears something 'too revealing' and they get raped, it's their fault because they wore that revealing thing ... but men should just learn to control themselves and not be like that ... teach the guys that girls aren't objects."

Democratic Validity

The make-up of the arts groups gave the youth direct experience with the forms of structural violence that they chose to explore. Illustrative of this is the work of a group in a small city in Ontario composed of three males and three females between the ages of 16 and 20, who had experienced homelessness or precarious housing, or had supported someone through such an experience.

The group demonstrated democratic validity through their positive contribution to the overall direction of the project. As reported by the group facilitator, the youth felt that "they had power to make choices in the group — alternatives were available and their input was definitely taken into consideration." The facilitators noted that "the majority of decisions were made based on collaboration between the facilitators and participants" and that "arts-based activities were tailored based on the participants' interests and numerous options were typically presented for the diversity of interests in the group." Of the options presented to them, the youth selected body mapping, mask-making, collages, painting and photovoice. Through these activities, they explored themes that they identified as reflective of their experiences with homelessness, such as visibility/invisibility in different spaces and places, the development of communities, addictions and mental health, and the importance of caring for one another.

A final way this group provided evidence of democratic validity was through the creation of a respectful and welcoming atmosphere. One young person commented that "it definitely helps when you don't have to worry about what you're saying." This statement expresses a sense of being

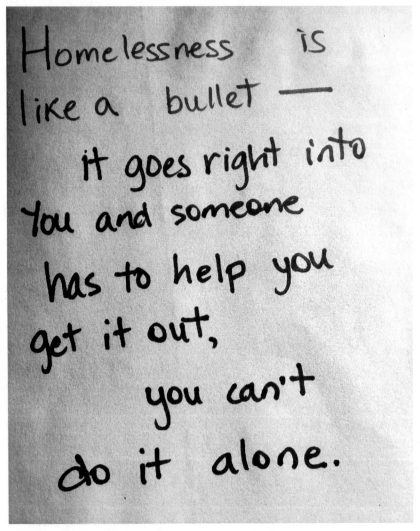

Youth-created poster: Homelessness is like a bullet.

welcomed into the learning environment, which contrasts with a more traditional top-down approach to education that can be disempowering to young learners, especially those who are marginalized. According to the group facilitator, perceptions that the group environment was welcoming increased the youths' sense of being respected and encouraged them to influence the overall shape of the project.

Photovoice activity: Everything in life doesn't come easy.

Process Validity

Examination of an arts-based group held in an urban centre in British Columbia illustrates process validity in action. This group was composed of Métis youth between 19 and 26 years of age who had moved to the city to pursue education or employment. Themes of cultural marginalization, racism, poverty, invisibility and lack of information about Métis people in the mainstream were explored by this group. Here, process validity was upheld by offering youth choices and encouraging them to participate in the ways they wanted to. The facilitator brought a variety of art supplies to each meeting to stimulate their sense of creativity and exploration. As well, the group activities were culturally relevant and included a Talking Circle with Elders, group theatre about colonialism and racism, painting and creating murals, sharing stories, crafts, and photovoice. During one activity, the youth created a mural of a canoe symbolizing a positive future for Métis youth in Canada. In another, the facilitator presented youth with small pieces of canvas on which they wrote messages or created drawings, and these were then woven together to represent the Métis flag. This image is presented below.

In this statement, the facilitator's supportive and respectful attitude towards the youth is evident and represents another dimension of practices by this group that enhance process validity.

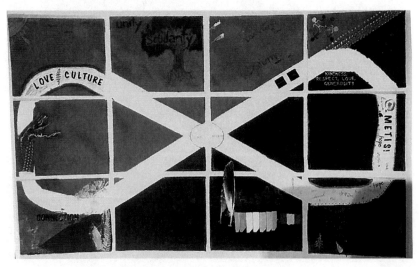

Métis collective project: Metis flag/I love culture.

The process and experience were amazing ... soulful, supportive, deep, profound, exploratory and meaningful. As a facilitator/ researcher, I felt moved to tears on multiple occasions. We structured safety by having the Elders present. As well, many of the youth participants shared really meaningful parts of their family experience, their cultural knowledge and their hopes/desires for Métis youth.

Catalytic Validity

An arts group in an Alberta city illustrates how catalytic validity was upheld in the context of a LGBTQ2S+ youth empowerment group, self-named the "Council of Awesome." It was a diverse group of six youth in their early 20s which included a transgender person, a transsexual person and a gay man born outside Canada.

The youth in this group were highly motivated to understand and change social conditions relating to forms of structural violence they had experienced. They engaged in consensus-based decision-making to select the topics they would focus on and the artistic methods they would use. The group decided to examine the ways in which LGBTQ2S+ people are marginalized according to their gender and sexual identities, as well as areas of resilience and resistance to systemic harm. In this project, the systems in which the youth identified the most urgent need for change were health care, education, culture (the need to address bullying and to create LGBTQ2S+-friendly social spaces) and religion.

After group discussions, the youth settled on the idea of painting a mural with "a graffiti inspiration of writing truth on the walls." The mural was intended to represent "a patch of wallpaper being torn back to reveal a better world possible beneath a surface of harm and distrust." Embedded in the mural are symbols relating to the youths' hopes for the project and for long-term social change. For instance, the theme of social inclusion is represented using the metaphor of the natural world as a complex and interconnected ecosystem; here it is inhabited by ladybugs, flowers, vines and a large tree. On the perimeter of this inclusive space is the word "it" crossed out to represent the need for society to use inclusive gender pronouns. The image of a prison represents the need to stop sending trans* people to cisgender facilities that are considered unsafe for them.

Following their involvement in the group, the youth proposed several

Graffiti inspiration of writing on the walls.

social changes they hoped would occur, such as increasing the availability of gender-neutral washrooms; providing LGBTQ2S+-positive training to police; and ending the practice of sending transgendered persons to prisons where they do not gender identify. The youth also spoke of the role of gay-straight/queer-straight alliances in Alberta schools in reducing bullying, and the need for curricula that accurately reflect their realities. The project concluded with two interactive public events: a collaging activity at a gender symposium and a dialogue with local United Church of Canada congregations. These actions illustrate the catalytic validity of the project.

Concluding Thoughts

This evaluation illustrates how the VAV project involved young people in Y-PAR processes. Youth were meaningfully involved in shaping the direction of the research through participation on the NYAB and engagement in arts-based groups where they expressed their personal experiences with structural violence. As well, the Y-PAR processes equipped young people with powerful tools for critically assessing and interrogating various forms of structural violence and ultimately motivated them to take steps to transform inequitable social conditions.

These findings are consistent with a social determinants of health framework, which goes beyond the traditional view of health as merely the absence of disease and instead sees health as possibility of developing fully, meeting one's potential and flourishing. Health depends on positive social conditions, such as peace, shelter, education, food, income, stable ecosystem, sustainable resources, social justice and equity, as well as the absence of racism, sexism, poverty, and other forms of structural violence. In this study, youth developed critical awareness of their social reality and a thoughtful resistance to structural violence, which, according to the social determinants of health framework, may help to protect and enhance health and well-being. It is our hope that this evaluation will offer encouragement and guidance to future community researchers who aspire to empower young people through participatory action research.

References

Gaventa, J., and A. Cornwall. 2008. "Power and Knowledge." In P. Reason and H. Bradbury (eds.), *Sage Handbook of Action Research*, 2nd edition. Thousand Oaks, CA: Sage.

Lykes, M.B., and A. Mallona. 2008. "Towards Transformational Liberation: Participatory and Action Research and Praxis." In P. Reason and H. Bradbury (eds.), *Sage Handbook of Action Research*, 2nd edition. Thousand Oaks, CA: Sage.

Mirra, N., D. Filipiak, and A. Garcia. 2015. "Revolutionizing Inquiry in Urban English Classrooms: Pursuing Voice and Justice Through Youth Participatory Action Research." *English Journal*, 105, 2: 49–57.

Ozanne, J., and B. Saatcioglu. 2008. "Participatory Action Research." *Journal of Consumer Research*, 35: 1–17.

Rahman, R.A. 2008. "Some Trends in the Praxis of Participatory Action Research." In P. Reason and H. Bradbury (eds.), *Sage Handbook of Action Research*, 2nd edition. Thousand Oaks, CA: Sage.

11

Speaking Truth to Power

Catherine Richardson/Kinewesquao, Helene Berman, Eugenia Canas

This study of structural violence experienced by young people in Canada draws attention to the ways in which everyday experiences of injustice, oppression, marginalization and exclusion influence and impede health and well-being. Our research experience has affirmed the reality that unlike other forms of violence, which are often accompanied by physical scars or other outward manifestations, structural violence and its perpetrators remain largely invisible and immune from accountability. Doubly damaging is its pervasiveness, infiltrating virtually every aspect of life for youth, and the fact that it is condoned in both subtle and explicit ways (Scheper-Hughes 2004).

This reality is more pervasive for marginalized youth, but even young people from well-to-do families have little influence over the body politic in Canada. When youth are involved in formal party politics, they are often tokenized and used to forward adult agendas. When youth are on important committees, they seldom have a vote. In the political arena, conservative and neoliberal politics deny many of the things that youth need — whether that be decriminalization of soft drugs, activism and homelessness; the provision of particular services to marginalized groups; or radical and progressive health interventions without judgement.

Neither has Canada seriously reconsidered the system of student loans, which keeps many students in debt well into their adult years. Recently in Canada, NDP leader Jagmeet Singh proposed lowering the voting age, but this kind of initiative is not the norm in Canada. Despite the neglect of many youth issues, Canada will send young people into combat at age 18, even if they joined the military for reasons of poverty or as a means to achieving an education. Although we do not attend to their particular needs very well, Canada is not hesitant to ask a lot from young people while offering relatively little support for their life aspirations. In this final chapter, we reiterate some of our key findings and offer some reflections for others interested in youth-centeed research.

Doing Y-PAR

With respect to engaging in participatory research, it is important to join with and work alongside the group being studied. This imperative is particularly paramount when the research involves youth. If insufficient attention is paid to the ethical and power-balanced collaboration, youth-centred PAR risks becoming "a trendy method for co-opting urban youth into social research" (Fine 2009: 1). As many of the researchers, adults and youth affiliated with this project were philosophically aligned with the principles of social justice, we shared a commitment to Y-PAR's origins and fundamental purpose:

> To seek to resurrect and reflect on the radical beginnings, delicate practices and strong commitments of youth participatory action research as a form of theoretically grounded research, designed in social struggle, with youth and families, for radical, ethnic, gendered sexual and economic justice. (Fine 2009: 1)

We can be what Vikki Reynolds calls "imperfect allies" (2013), acknowledging power differentials and trying to mitigate them with awareness (Dulay et al. 2018). As such, it was important for us to move fluidly, to make space for new and unexpected outcomes, possibilities and maximum diversity.

Since there are multiple youth identities, it was valuable to engage with youth, and adults, from various social locations and landscapes, including focusing on the youth who are likely to experience the most severe forms of structural violence in Canada. We also realize that despite the existence of a safety net in some locations, structural violence can transcend all boundaries. For example, abuse, loneliness and hate towards LGBTQ2S+ can be directed at youth who have access to wealth as well as to those who do not. As Michelle Fine reminds us, "youth grow up in profoundly uneven developmental contexts" (2009: 1). The youth involved in our research groups stated at a team meeting in Toronto that an intersectional analysis is important as it prompts consideration of various key aspects of life and location, such as gender, race, level of ability, economics and privilege. However, considering the context of the youth does not preclude an analysis of the violence of the state and the structures, and how they carry out and represent their violence (Coates and Wade 2007).

The diverse processes of the thirty research groups in this project showed that, for the youth and adult facilitators, getting to a point of naming the violence took creative and concerted work. The youth participants acknowledged that the state and perpetrators of structural violence were committed to not naming the violence. They confirmed the theoretical awareness of researchers such as Linda Coates and Allan Wade (2007), who discussed "the four operations of language" and how violence is typically hidden or minimized by the state and media, including making the perpetrator invisible and hiding the deliberate nature of violence. Resistance is also concealed in descriptions of events, because the presence of resistance points to the perpetrator's abuse of power. Where there is no perpetrator to hold accountable, the victims, in this case the youth, are blamed for the social problems (Berman and Jiwani 2014). While structural violence is often presented, particularly by conservative, neoliberal governments, as "just the way things are," the youth spoke of the importance of naming the violence, of speaking truth to power.

Through social policy, or perhaps more accurately, through the implementation of particular economic policies which benefit the wealthy, barriers are put in place which make it difficult or impossible for youth to access what they need, whether it's money, housing, food, identification, drugs, their pet or anything else. Older conservative bias is echoed through time-worn ideas, such as the youth should "just get a job" or "buckle down and work hard" or "pull themselves up by the bootstraps." Yet, these platitudes ignore the realities of violence and abuse which often prompt youth to leave home, to become unhoused, to exist on the margins of established communities. This type of analysis tends to individualize the human being and their responsibility, to ascribe blame to youth for the circumstances they face in everyday life, neglecting the fact that many impediments are structural, deliberately and ideologically embedded into the political system. Perhaps in relation to the many stressors, due to economic insecurity and fears that they will not thrive, many youth today experience anxiety and depression. These are manifestations of isolation, loneliness and alienation. We believe that these emotional challenges relate to a feeling that they don't really matter, that they are not valued in their communities. Vikki Reynolds notes that "where there is depression, there is oppression" (2013).

A number of philosophers, including Karl Marx, spoke of capitalism's alienating effect. Today's youth have inherited a world plagued by environmental destruction, the threat of devastation through climate change and the isolation and loneliness in modern society. In this context, youth seek meaning and purpose. These forces, coupled with high rates of violence against particular youth, create the conditions where anxiety and depression appear to be flourishing. Thus, it is not surprising that many of the youth who participated in our research spoke about feelings of anxiety and depression, showing us that it is difficult to feel well in a social world that can be isolating, alienating, lonely and unjust. One group in our research which focused on the immigrant and newcomer experience discussed the idea of "emotional death," how that exists on a spectrum and is a reality for many immigrant youth. Emotional death means they are living, but they feel dead inside. They do not feel hope or joy, and they are just sustaining day-to-day.

One youth commented that "they seem to deny us everything that we need." When we study the youth experience of domestic violence historically and contextually, we can see how things like the Indian Act and child welfare policies have robbed and denied youth and their families of their cultural wealth and access to land. Research by Michael Chandler and Christoper Lalonde (1998) in BC showed that the more Indigenous communities have land and sovereignty over their community programs, the less frequent is the incidence of youth suicide. Twenty years later, across Canada and across populations, young people who witness others dying around them due to an opioid crisis wonder why the government will not intervene to create more safety for these highly marginalized people who are suffering. They realize that substance use is most often indicative of pain and suffering, often due to violence, grief and loss. For youth who are street involved, the precarity of their life on the street often keeps them without any official form of identification, making access to medical care and various social programs impossible. In some respects, the alienation associated with the constant struggle to survive parallels a loss of land and sovereignty: it is a loss of citizenship and the rights that come with it.

A Diversity of Experience, a Diversity of Resistance Tactics

We understand that certain capacities and knowledges emerge as a result of hardship and oppression. The fact that oppression breeds multi-generational wisdom, desire and tactics of subversion has been well-documented by radical scholars (Coates and Wade 2007; Fine 2009; Freire 1970; Richardson and Wade 2008). But resistance is not merely "bred": it is a response on the part of individuals who are carefully considering their environment and applying whatever response makes sense in that moment, logically, contextually and in terms of historical knowledge and experience. Resistance defies generalization. It cannot be generalized, advised or assessed by mental health professions. Typically, resistance is context and situation dependent. The acts of resistance observed in this research were as diverse as the youth themselves and rooted in their individual experiences and lives.

The theme of diversity permeated our research and the analysis. Our focus was on a diverse group of youth in Canada who encounter a diversity of social experiences in the particular context of their own lives and who respond to those experiences in a diversity of ways. However, while there is great diversity in people, there are a great deal of similarities in the strategies and policies of structural violence. This includes some of the familiar colonializing mechanisms, such as marginalization, separation, isolation, social exclusion, removal from land and housing, and external control over and monitoring of access to money, resources and social programs. We see a similarity here to the structures behind the residential school system, which was run by the government, articulated and supported by the Indian Act, and carried out by sub-contractees often guided by dogmatic tenets of Christianity. A key upshot of these mechanisms is the structural control over group and individual senses of identity — whereby all these mechanisms serve to define and limit what it means to *be*. The chapter by Yasmin Jiwani gave examples of how Indigenous youth were sometimes cast as "beyond help" or "savage," with the implication that resources would be wasted on them. This is what stigmatization does. It creates an "other," who is seen as embodying less humanity. Under these conditions, youth have to fight for their dignity, for their analysis and for their own definition of who they are, to find some ground upon which to grow.

In resistance to oppression and dehumanization, the youth employed a diversity of tactics (de Certeau 1984; Reynolds 2013) for enhancing their safety and dignity. Stories captured ways in which the youth had to "manage" their service providers, in order to get what they needed. They had to present as "depressed" when they showed up in the office but could not really be too depressed to get out of bed or they would be denied resources. Sometimes, "performing" on the outside what others expected from them preserved a privacy of mind or inner integrity where they could exist. Going deeper inside oneself is a tactic for dignity preservation, to make oneself oblivious to what others are saying about one, to preserve one's sense of self. Examples are African-descended people having to be "cool" when the police show up, or Métis people acting with "aplomb" to avoid being blamed for crimes they did not commit (Richardson 2004). During the course of our research, both in small groups and when we came together for team meetings, the youth fought their oppression by naming the unnamed violence, by articulating their social analysis and by fighting stigma both directly and through playfulness and laughter. The youth reinforced the notion that coming together in a safe space can offer support and an opportunity for collective conscientization (Berman and Jiwani 2014; Freire 1970; Richardson 2016).

Being Unhoused

The youth in this research consistently spoke about the need for a safe, nurturing home. One youth described being unhoused, wanting others to know that loneliness and isolation are some of the most hurtful and alienating aspects of being unhoused:

> *While an adult worker in an office may blame the youth for their own homelessness, they did not always try to deconstruct the systemic reasons for being unhoused, they did not always try to assist in helping the youth address some of the bi-products of homelessness, such as the spiritual condition of loneliness.*

Another youth echoed this sentiment: "Being on the street is a weird thing that most people don't get unless you've been there.... You're surrounded by people, they're actually everywhere, but you feel completely and utterly alone."

Living on, or close to, the street brings its own set of dangers and risks for exploitation. Among these risks are the possibility of being arrested for petty crime, being recruited into prostitution and drug sales, and experiencing the health risks that go along with this life. Currently, one of these risks is the insertion of fentanyl into street drugs such as cannabis, crystal meth and heroine. There has been a loud call to address the opiate crisis, with the need for safe injection centres and safe heroin (Reynolds n.d.; CBC Radio 2017; Fischer, Vojtila and Rehm 2018). The realities youth co-researchers shared highlight the insufficient supports available to them and their families in the realms of education, employment and/or social services such as housing/shelters. The absence of such supports is a manifestation of structural violence, the unfair distribution of societal resources lived in the flesh by these youth. Conservative agendas that enact cuts to social services in the name of fiscal restraint, and thus promote social negligence for the sake of capitalist or business gain, perpetrate this violence.

Fending for Ourselves

Despite the multiple mechanisms through which structural violence is expressed in everyday life, our research found that most youth who participated in our groups believed they had to "fend for ourselves." The reality and complexity of structural violence were not even on the radar of many health professionals, social service professionals, educators or parents. Or, if structural violence and its obstacles were acknowledged, the situation was often decontextualized and reduced to concepts such as "poverty" or "vulnerability," as if these factors were inevitable. Most professionals did not use language that responsibilized violent perpetrators and structures, with terms such as "impoverization" or "vulnerabilization." Often, victim-blaming accompanied these inaccurate and misleading formulations of social issues. For example, if a youth had sore gums and other dental problems related to a lack of nutrition, vitamins and minerals, they may be accused of not taking care of their dental health. Other examples are the lack of access to healthy and affordable food, particularly in northern and Indigenous communities, and the boil-water advisories currently in effect in 161 Indigenous communities. These facts have not been called out as part of ongoing colonization with demands to the federal government to remedy the problem. Indigenous youth were well aware that many of the problems they face would not be tolerated in white, middle-class Canadian communities. Yet, Indigenous resistance is not discussed and seen as evidence that social change is needed; rather, it is seen as misguided and a threat to the social order in Canada. After the Oka crisis, where the Mohawks of Kanesetake protested the encroachment of a golf course on their ancestral burial ground, national newspapers stated that "the Mohawks are the terrorists of Canada." When resistance is decontextualized, the victims are made out to be the perpetrators.

Resistance Gets Pathologized

Similarly, for the youth, the ways in which young people in Canada respond to and resist structural violence are pathologized and seen as signs of illness, deficit or vulnerability. Decontextualization creates a problem in the representation of events and tends to work in favour of the system and power structures, deflecting responsibility onto the individual. The reality that a deliberate systemic force is behind these conditions is obfuscated. In vague and misrepresented terms, we hear political statements from politicians and through media that issue platitudes about Canadian values. For example, many districts don't want to provide clean heroin and safe injection sites to prevent opioid overdoses (Wiart 2016; Reynolds 2013). Some public discourses say that policies that help people with "special needs" (e.g., affirmative action) discriminate against rich and able-bodied people. Ableist thinking makes life extremely difficult for minorities, for people who are "different" or "differently-abled" and for victims of state-sanctioned interpersonal violence. Addressing poverty is seen as an affront to the rich, partially because capitalism has always flourished on the backs of an exploitable, servant class.

Violence Is Minimized

Our research indicates that even when structural violence is acknowlededged, it tends to be dismissed, trivialized and normalized. It is presented as an inevitable part of everyday life, as "just the way things are." Acts of resistance are often recast as symptoms of illness or mere "coping" rather than forms of intelligence, survival and even thrivance. As the young people who shared deeply personal aspects of their lives with us have observed, structural violence tries to invade all aspects of our lives as an oppressive force: "It's like the system expects us to always be on about how bad things are." "One act of resistance is to think however we like and to be ourselves." "There is no norm, and people of all kinds have always existed." Rethinking and self-depathologizing is one way these youth refuse to let structural violence win, each and every day. Sometimes, when youth use particular language to describe themselves or their situation, they are merely using the discourse needed to access services. Saying "I have depression and anxiety" is more likely to get them help than saying "I am experiencing an existential crisis related to neoliberalism and capitalism and how they attack one's humanity." In this way, the youth who were in a group related to homelessness managed their mental health needs.

Re-thinking Research, Re-thinking Violence and Re-thinking Health

This project was, in many respects, an effort to *re-think* what it means to conduct research, to *re-think* what we mean when we speak about violence and to *re-think* prevailing notions of health and what health looks like when violence is a part of everyday life. Through our enactment of youth-centred participatory action research, we challenged ourselves to work across divides that are rarely crossed and to transcend barriers that are firmly entrenched. The youth, many of whom came from communities that have been marginalized and silenced, were asked to commit themselves to a research initiative, despite the fact that research hasn't always been kind to their communities and to "vulnerable" populations more broadly. The history of exploitation in research is well-documented, and we anticipated that we would encounter suspicion and mistrust. The notion of "collaborative engagement" required a critical reflection and a re-thinking about what it means to conduct research — to examine the role of power amid inherent power differentials and to pay careful attention to whose voices were heard and whose were not heard.

Academic researchers, who typically are accustomed to maintaining control over all aspects of the research process, were now being asked share that control. Participation in this research necessitated collaboration with youth throughout every stage of the research — on decisions about the questions to ask and how to ask them and what to do with the knowledge we generated. Not only did this approach require researchers to move out of their usual zone of comfort and familiarity, but it entailed the use of methods, methodologies and partnerships that are time-consuming, difficult to implement, occasionally messy and often non-linear, and not always valued within the academic world. The decision to use arts as the medium through which to address structural violence was new to some of us, and there were lengthy discussions as to what, precisely, constitutes data. As noted elsewhere in this book, the youth raised concerns about the survey questionnaire that had been developed. They found some of the questions demeaning and offensive. In response, a decision was made to collect the necessary information through qualitative methods that were more acceptable to the youth and that seemed more congruent with the overall project. While most of our team were fully supportive of this decision, a few expressed concerns, and one individual ultimately chose to disengage from the research.

Our implementation of y-par methodology required the creation of honest, meaningful and authentic spaces for youth and knowledge users to participate fully in the research, spaces in which youth voices were heard, listened to and acted upon. We rejected tokenistic processes that involve seeking "input" from youth or that give an illusion of consultation and collaboration, while ultimately advancing the interests and priorities of those in dominant positions of power. Undertaking this type of research necessitated a re-thinking of relationships and of power, and a deep contemplation about what it means to conduct research that is participatory, engaged and activist. Any suggestion of equality within the team would have been, in effect, a negation of inherent power differentials; deeply ingrained inequities can't be eliminated by wishing them away or being "nice people." Instead, our process was one that acknowledged these differentials and dynamics and continually considered how they shaped our work together. In a most fundamental sense, our process required us to collectively take risks, venture into a process that was complex and messy and do a fair degree of decision-making as the research unfolded.

Bridging the Divides in Youth-Adult Collaboration

In contrast to the angst that the research evoked for some of the academic members of the team, the youth consistently spoke positively about their participation in this research. We had initially requested a two-year commitment, but many remained involved well beyond this length of time. As Holly Johnson and Alyssa Louw reported in their evaluation, presented earlier in this book, participation in this research offered the youth new understandings about the research process and insights into the ways that structural violence affected their own lives and those of others. The process was described as empowering, health-promoting and, as their stories revealed, transformative. They perceived the project leaders as supportive and inclusive and felt that there was a valuing, not only of the research process, but of themselves as well. The youth acknowledged the many opportunities afforded through involvement in the research. For example, some were able to transition into new roles as research assistants, complete work on our website or develop social media tools. Others spoke of more indirect benefits, including the opportunity to participate in national and international conference presentations. Through the research, the youth acquired skills that enabled them to articulate strategies for social change, within their own communities and beyond. Because our funds to support conference travel were limited, and consistent with our assumption that academic researchers often have access to other sources of funding for research activities, we developed a process that prioritized financial support for the youth. These experiences were invaluable, enabling youth to develop a new set of skills, while meeting with others engaged in similar types of work. Some noted that participation in this project motivated them to pursue higher education and careers related to social justice causes, medicine and participatory research.

Recognizing that research itself cannot be separated from the structures that marginalize the experiences of youth, our research methodology included the continual enactment of anti-oppressive practices in the development and application of knowledge. Reflecting contemporary conceptualizations of youth, including young people as partners in research, was an effort on our part to acknowledge them as active "agents of change," rather than as the recipients of change made by adults on their behalf.

Recommendations

Our attention to structural violence reflects a re-thinking about violence. It was a deliberate decision to shift the conversation away from prevailing discourses that focus almost exclusively on interpersonal violence and instead pay attention to the underlying social and structural inequalities that are the root causes of that interpersonal violence. When we turn our attention away from root causes, we limit our ability to develop comprehensive and lasting solutions. In effect, we limit our ability to resist and overcome the problem.

Collaborative Engagement

A central premise of this initiative was that collaborative engagement with youth was, and is, in itself a health promotion strategy. Historically, the study of health and health-related issues in youth has mainly focused on "lifestyle behaviours" and has been approached as an individual behavioural attribute, largely estranged from context. Attention is commonly directed to poor choices made in the heat of adolescent turmoil, a developmental stage that will soon be outgrown. The net result is victim-blaming and shaming and the delivery of derogatory messages, either implicit or direct. When young people come together in the act of sharing stories through art, bearing witness to and validating their experiences individually and collectively, they are engaging in a *conscientization* process (Freire 1970), which can lead to empowerment, connection with others and even social change. Around the world, youth — and other marginalized peoples — have long initiated wide-scale social change. As youth critically reflect on the circumstances of their lives and gain insights into the structural inequities that are so pervasive and profound, they become able to name their realities and consciously consider strategies to change, overcome and resist those realities.

In the context of our work, the groups we facilitated across the country afforded youth the opportunity to collectivize their struggles. Rather than viewing the challenges they faced in their everyday lives as individual problems that they alone experienced, the groups fostered a sense of shared struggle and helped participants to acquire a new language for understanding and naming structural violence. While we were able to provide opportunities for youth to engage in this process during the course of our research, our activities were short-term and time-limited. The duration of the groups varied in our project, with each group deciding how long the group would last, typically from one to three months. Regardless of the length of time, strong bonds were formed and the youth described a unique sense of solidarity and support. Endings often seemed abrupt, and we didn't have clear opportunities to offer beyond the project. In some communities, there were organizations or programs with which they could become involved, but few of these explicitly addressed structural violence. While the youth consistently spoke about the new insights and understandings they had gained, they generally felt disconnected from opportunities and initiatives for broader, long-lasting social and structural change.

From a programmatic perspective, the tendency is for social forces to privilege particular interventions at particular times and with particular populations. When these fall out of favour for a multitude of possible reasons, they are discontinued. In the absence of a strong political commitment and a social movement that can challenge the structural inequalities and hierarchies of exclusion that allow structural forms of violence in the lives of youth to flourish, programs will continue to be short-lived and short-sighted. More importantly, the experiences of young people who live with structural violence will continue to be trivialized, silenced and ignored. A counter-hegemonic discourse is critically needed, one that is validated and reproduced within the margins and that over time could become the dominant discourse. The youth have great insights into what this new discourse could look like, but we need to develop programs more systemically that are grounded in real and meaningful ways in the lives of young people and in the politics of liberation in order to begin to take this new discourse seriously. While opportunities are needed for youth to develop strategies that enable them to individually resist and overcome the violence in their lives, these alone are insufficient.

More Dialogue

There is a pressing and urgent need for Canadian-based research related to structural violence in the lives of youth, and more specifically, for research that examines the interrelations between and among interpersonal and systemic forms of violence and how these are produced and reproduced through the culture of power. Further, research is needed that examines the effects of subtle and explicit forms of violence on the health and well-being of young people. While there is a great deal of research regarding "problems" commonly found among youth, few of these studies attempt to examine these within the context of structural violence.

The current polarization of community and academic research continues to be problematic, and efforts are needed that lessen this divide. Academic research findings that remain within the academic terrain, and community findings that remain within the community, have far less persuasive power than those which are developed through a process of dialogue between these respective realms. Within academia, the ability to publish research is often hampered by the relatively narrow prescriptions as to what constitutes legitimate forms of knowledge generation and dissemination. As most critical and feminist researchers know, publishing work using methodologies that transcend the traditional scientific methods is often a challenge.

Much of the research that has been conducted regarding youth has been based upon models that are deeply entrenched in the discipline of psychology and to a lesser degree, medicine, both of which tend to individualize and pathologize the realities faced by young people today. Typically, such approaches focus on coping mechanisms and "at risk" populations, on resilience and "protective" factors. Missing from these approaches and models is consideration of systemic and institutional racism, cultural corrosion and uprooting or displacement from family and community as well as youth responses and resistance to these situations. While talking about resiliency can offer a form of compliment, analyzing resistance helps reflect back to the youth what they actually do … their intelligence, acumen and ability to assess difficult, multi-faceted situations. This goes way beyond merely coping.

Finally, research is needed on the kinds of opportunities that are available for youth to mobilize and engage in strategies of liberation. In the Voices against Violence project, we mentored young people in the conduct of research, teaching them a repertoire of narrative and arts-based research approaches. But the learning was neither linear nor uni-directional. The adult researchers learned alongside the youth as we forged new paths to knowledge development. An assumption underlying this approach was that creating this type of "space" where the youth would become active participants in the research process would constitute one of those avenues. But we struggled with what happens when the research ends. When we create "empowering" spaces for youth, in the absence of societal structural change, how do they negotiate the multiple contours of the structures of power that they encounter upon the completion of our research? Creating a place within our work where their voices count, but still existing within a larger society where this is not necessarily the case, creates a "disconnect" that may, in fact, inadvertently do youth a disservice.

Ultimately, we need to carefully contemplate the implications, both positive and negative, of our research initiatives with young people in Canada and elsewhere. As long as we continue to exist in a world where certain groups of youth are silenced and marginalized, the extent to which it is possible to create isolated pockets of liberation is limited. While these are difficult issues for which there are no simple solutions, it is imperative that we continue to work on multiple levels to simultaneously challenge all forms of structural violence — racism, sexism, classism and other oppressive ideologies — as they manifest themselves at the individual, social and structural levels.

Take on the Challenges of Participation

Throughout the course of this project, we have learned a great deal about what works and what doesn't work. Although arts-informed methods proved valuable as a means to create safe spaces for youth perspectives to be heard, Y-PAR proved to be a complex methodology to implement across a large, national project with multiple sites and diverse partners who, at times, faced differing priorities and agendas. If true to the tenets of participation, Y-PAR researchers are likely to encounter situations that challenge the process outlined in the funding and ethics protocols. We've described here a change in data collection methods that was required midway through our project. This flexibility allowed us to both be responsive to, and respectful of, our co-researchers while simultaneously meeting the requirements for rigorous research evaluation. This type of flexibility and receptivity to emerging ideas is critical in the context of participatory action research approaches, in keeping with the tenets that call for the creation of a self-critical community, ongoing self-reflection and the active commitment to create spaces for youth empowerment (Flicker et al. 2008; Ozanne and Saatcioglu 2008). This negotiation represents a fine balance that researchers designing participatory projects face, and it resonates with Caitlin Cahill's characterization of project ownership rooted in true participation, claimed by the youth themselves (2007). While researchers need to articulate methods with sufficient detail to satisfy potential concerns among funders, we also have an obligation to listen authentically and respond to issues and concerns raised by participants. From our perspective, an ethic of doing no harm means that the youth-centredness of Y-PAR ultimately trumps an inflexible adherence to methods initially set out by the research protocol. If youth perceive the research process to be disempowering or oppressive, the priority must be to change the process.

According to Julie Ozanne and Bige Saatcioglu (2008), democratic validity refers to the depth of participation of those involved in the work and the extent to which they are informing the outcomes. At face value this assertion is obvious; participation needs to be authentic, not tokenistic. In this research, representation was integrated throughout in multiple, diverse and creative ways. Our process, however, was not without tensions and challenges which arose regarding who speaks for whom. Although the National Youth Advisory Board had approved the survey tool, as noted above, other youth found it uncomfortable. It is particularly noteworthy that members of the NYAB typically occupied different social locations from many of the youth who participated in our groups. The NYAB members tended to have access to more social capital, were less likely to be in immediate crisis and were generally more attuned to research processes. These differences speak to the problem of the generic category of "youth" or the presumption that any youth can speak for all youth. Through this type of essentializing, we conceal and silence the diverse voices and experiences within this highly heterogeneous population. How then can we balance the pragmatics of participation across diverse populations with effective representation? Likely, it is through the establishment of safe spaces whereby the voices of all participants can be heard and there is the flexibility to be guided by these voices, while never presuming that representation sufficiently addresses diversity.

Many forces inherently challenge the process of participation: funding guidelines, time limitations, existing relationships and competing priorities, to name a few. These realities will strain participatory processes that are intentional, that move at the speed of the community, that make space for multiple voices, and that strive for a shift from tokenism to authenticity. Therefore, it is crucial that a team focused on enacting the tenets of Y-PAR imbed the required participatory principles into explicit aspects of their project. In our work, we facilitated approximately thirty youth groups across the country led by multiple co-researchers. Achieving the tenets of participation involved the development of clear protocols to follow in creating and facilitating these groups. At the same time, the process could not be too restrictive as there was a need to allow for local decision-making, even if at times it meant that data from a local group could not be as easily "rolled up" into the larger study for analysis. Again, authentic participation involves accepting that data may take a variety of forms and that this variety can add complexity to data analysis. To make the best use of project time and resources, much effort was put into supporting local team members to run effective groups. Each group had to complete a clear proposal to be reviewed by the project's steering committee, which ensured the quality of the participatory process. Similarly, each group had a clear process in terms of effectively reporting group outcomes and tracking local knowledge translation. These protocols ensured consistency with the Y-PAR methodology across the team and over time.

Enact Y-PAR Values in Future Research

As Cahill (2007) warns, quality participatory methods do not inherently lead to change-making. Authentic participation is important, but critical PAR also includes knowledge-in-action. Although considerable work exists on how to enhance the quality of participatory processes, there is much less to guide researchers in how these processes can be used to confront oppressive structural components. In particular, how can youth who are often pushed to the margins be fully engaged in knowledge-in-action processes that alter the fundamental structures that perpetuate this marginalization? Future efforts should focus on the change mandate of participatory work, including how to move from critical reflection on policy, to policy-making, social change and the elimination of systemic inequities.

Youth-centred participatory action research is a promising methodology to simultaneously generate new knowledge while confronting structures and systems that risk marginalizing youth. However, Y-PAR requires both flexibility and rigour, which can be an unfamiliar way to approach research proposals, involving tough decisions about who speaks for whom. By building in flexibility, being critical about voice and having clear protocols to guide implementation, some of these challenges can be addressed. Through participatory approaches that entailed fulsome engagement with young people in research, it became possible to create more vibrant research agendas and new theoretical possibilities and push scholarship in new directions. This realized commitment draws attention to the ways in which research discourses may empower or disempower youth and play a role in structural violence (Denzin and Giardina 2009). Our goal was for youth to share in the creation of safe spaces where they could critically evaluate the circumstances of their lives and collectively engage in the identification of strategies to overcome, resist and prevent structural violence.

Yet the warnings of Fine (2009) must be heeded: participatory research can often be a far stretch from participatory action research. Engaging youth to foster growth and understanding is often co-opted into neoliberal and adult-centric goals and desires of educational attainment, deeper understanding and skill development. This type of engagement reifies rather than confronts power inequities. As a new methodology, there is much space for researchers to engage in work that best meets the full tenets of Y-PAR. As future research demonstrates policy application, Y-PAR will continue to be refined as an effective methodology through which the vision of youth can be articulated and brought into the world.

The Last Word

While it was impossible to share so many of the things expressed by the youth in this project, it is important to note that the view from their vantage point is somewhat different than that of some of the more "seasoned" researchers. Some popular cultural theorists may attribute that to the differences that come with being "children of the sixties," Baby Boomers and those from the so-called Generation X. While not all youth march in the streets holding placards, they all experience the forms of resistance described by Wade (1997) or in Richardson's medicine wheel of responses (2016). These can be acts of self or collective care, tears, anger-driven expression or the heart's longing. Spiritual responses included holding the faith that life is worth living and that perseverance is desirable, despite all evidence. Moreover, within many marginalized communities, the mere act of surviving, of continuing to exist may in itself be considered an act of resistance.

We have chosen to end this book with a poem that demonstrates one form of poetic aspiration, a spoken word piece shared by Dobijoki Emanuela Bringi, a member of our National Youth Advisory Board. For Dobijoki Emanuela, this poem speaks to the intersectional experiences that she carries as a diasporic young woman in Canada, raised African from a country with a strong history of war, South Sudan. It expresses her feelings about identity as a young African woman who wants to experience home, yet knows it is not that easy because the violence perpetrated onto her people through civil conflict holds layers of structural violence. Her message captures the spirit shared by many of the remarkable young people who participated in our research: she wants to experience peace, which is home.

> I am an African
> from Bilad Al-Sudan
> now South Sudan
> born in Egypt
> raised in Canada
> working hard
> so I can one day
> make assida (fufu)
> in the village
>   with no shoes on
> wearing a kitenge
> and feeling so good
>   to be home.
> —Dobijoki Emanuela Bringi

References

Berman, H., and Y. Jiwani (eds.). 2014. *Faces of Violence in the Lives of Girls in Canada*. London, ON: Althouse Press.

Cahill, C. 2007. "Doing Research with Young People: Participatory Research and the Rituals of Collective Work." *Children's Geographies*, 5, 3: 297–311.

CBC radio. 2017. "Is it Time for a National Strategy on the Opioid Crisis?" *Cross Country Checkup*, 2 June. <https://www.cbc.ca/radio/checkup/is-it-time-for-a-national-strategy-on-the-opioid-crisis-1.4145776>.

Chandler, M.J., and C.E. Lalonde. 2009. "Cultural Continuity as a Moderator of Suicide Risk among Canada's First Nations." In L.J. Kirmayer and G.G. Valaskakis (eds.), *Healing Traditions: The Mental Health of Aboriginal peoples of Canada*. Vancouver: UBC Press.

Coates, L., and A. Wade. 2007. "Language and Violence: Analysis of Four Discursive Operations." *Journal of Family Violence*, 22, 7: 511–522. DOI: 10.1007/s10896-007-9082-2.

de Certeau, M. 1984. *The Practice of Everyday Life*, trans. S. Rendall. Berkeley, CA: University of California Press.

Denzin, N. and M. Giardina, 2009. *Qualitative Inquiry and Social Justice: Towards a Politics of Hope*. New York: Routledge.

Dulay, B., S. Krasnow, V. Reynolds, and G. Sampson. 2018. "Talk-Listen: Centering Youth Wisdom in Group Work at Peak House." *Relational Child and Youth Care Practice*, 31, 3: 6–23.

Fine, M. 2009. "Postcards Metro America: Reflections on Youth Participatory Action

Research for Urban Justice." *The Urban Review*, 41, 1: 1–6.

Fischer, B., L. Vojtila, and J. Rehm. 2018. "The 'Fentanyl Epidemic' in Canada: Some Cautionary Observations Focusing on Opioid-Related Mortality." *Preventive Medicine*, 107: 109–113.

Flicker, S., O. Maley, A. Ridgley, S. Biscope, C. Lombardo, and H. Skinner. 2008. "Using Technology and Participatory Action Research to Engage Youth in Health Promotion." *Action Research*, 6, 3: 285–303.

Freire, P. 1970. *Pedagogy of the Oppressed*. New York: Bloomsbury Academic.

Ozanne, J., and B. Saatcioglu. 2008. "Participatory Action Research." *Journal of Consumer Research*, 35: 1–17.

Reynolds, V. 2013. "'Leaning in' as Imperfect Allies in Community Work." *Narrative and Conflict: Explorations in Theory and Practice*, 1, 1: 53–75.

____. n.d. <https://vikkireynolds.ca/opioid-epidemic-responses/>.

Richardson, Catherine. 2016. *Belonging Métis*. Vernon, BC. John Charlton Publications.

____. 2004. "Becoming Métis: The Relationship Between the Sense of Métis Self and Cultural Stories." Unpublished dissertation, University of Victoria.

Richardson, C., and A. Wade. 2008. "Taking Resistance Seriously: A Response-Based Approach to Social Work in Cases of Violence Against Indigenous Women." In S. Strega and J. Carriere (eds.), *Walking this Path Together: Anti-Racist and Anti-Oppressive Child Welfare Practice*. Winnipeg, MB: Fernwood Publishing.

Scheper-Hughes, Nancy. 2004. "Dangerous and Endangered Youth Social Structures and Determinants of Violence." *Annals New York Academy of Science*, 1036: 13–46

Wade, Allan. 1997. "Small Acts of Living: Everyday Resistance to Violence and Other Forms of Oppression." *Contemporary Family Therapy*, 19, 1: 23–39.

Wiart, N. 2016. "Why Canada Has So Few Supervised Injection Sites: Critics Say an Onerous Application Process Means Waiting Years." *Maclean's*, 17 Aug. <https://www.macleans.ca/society/health/why-there-are-so-few-supervised-injection-sites/>.

Index